The Handbook of French Science Fiction

OTHER RELEVANT TITLES FROM BLACK COAT PRESS

by Jean-Marc & Randy Lofficier
The French Fantasy Treasury 1: The World's Edge (ISBN 978-1-61227-544-4)
The French Fantasy Treasury 2: Myths & Legends (ISBN 978-1-61227-545-1)
The French Fantasy Treasury 3: Far Realms (ISBN 978-1-61227-546-8)
Shadowmen: Heroes and Villains of French Pulp Fiction (ISBN 978-0-9740711-3-8)
Shadowmen 2: Heroes and Villains of French Comics (ISBN 978-0-9740711-8-3)
The Handbook of French Fantasy & Supernatural Fiction (ISBN 978-1-64932-165-7)
The Handbook of French Fantastic Cinema & Television (ISBN 978-1-64932-166-4)

by Brian Stableford
The Plurality of Imaginary Worlds: The Evolution of French Roman Scientifique (ISBN 978-1-61227-503-1)
Tales of Enchantment and Disenchantment: A History of Faerie, with an Exemplary Anthology of Tales (ISBN 978-1-61227-838-4)

The Handbook of French Science Fiction

by

Jean-Marc & Randy Lofficier

A Black Coat Press Book

Acknowledgements: Portions of this book have previously appeared in *French Science Fiction, Fantasy, Horror & Pulp Fiction* published in 2000 by McFarland.

CONSULTING EDITORS:
Henri ROSSI
Jean-Luc RIVERA
Brian STABLEFORD

Copyright © 2022 by Jean-Marc & Randy Lofficier.
Cover illustration Copyright © 2022 by Vincent Laik.

Visit our website at www.blackcoatpress.com

ISBN 978-1-64932-161-9. First Printing. October 2022. Published by Black Coat Press, an imprint of Hollywood Comics.com, LLC, P.O. Box 17270, Encino, CA 91416. All rights reserved. Except for review purposes, no part of this book may be reproduced or transmitted in any form or by any means, electronic or mechanical, including photocopying, recording, or by any information storage and retrieval system, without permission in writing from the publisher. The stories and characters depicted in this novel are entirely fictional. Printed in the United States of America.

TABLE OF CONTENTS

Foreword 7
The Utopias 13
The Imaginary Journeys 19
    Journeys to Other Worlds *20*
    Journeys to Other Lands *25*
    Journeys to Other Times *30*
The Voyages Extraordinaires 35
    Journeys to Other Worlds *36*
    Journeys to Other Lands *41*
    Journeys to Other Times *42*
Jules Verne 51
The Golden Age 61
  Major Authors 62
  Other Notable Authors 79
    Journeys to Other Worlds *79*
    Journey to Other Lands *82*
    Jouneys to Other Times *94*
  Mainstream Authors 105
The End of the Golden Age 115
  The Publishers 117
  Major Authors 119
  Other Notable Authors 126
    Journeys to Other Worlds *126*
    Journeys to Other Lands *132*
    Journeys to Other Times *150*
  Mainstream Authors 155
A Period of Transition 165
  Major Authors 166
  Other Notable Authors 173
    Journeys to Other Worlds *173*
    Journeys to Other Lands *175*
    Journeys to Other Times *180*
  Mainstream Authors 183
The Silver Age 187

The Publishers	188
Major Authors	192
Other Notable Authors	206
Mainstream Authors	220
The YAs	229
The 1970s	239
The Publishers	239
Major Authors	243
Other Notable Authors	260
Mainstream Authors	267
The YAs	270
The 1980s	277
The Publishers	278
Major Authors	279
Other Notable Authors	287
Mainstream Authors	293
The YAs	294
The 1990s	297
The Publishers	297
Major Authors	298
Other Notable Authors	304
Mainstream Authors	307
The YAs	308
Afterword: 2022	311
Index	317

Foreword

When embarking on any study about science fiction in literature, it is often customary to start with an attempt to define these genres.

In French, the word "*fantastique*" carries with it a much larger definition, or "semantic field", than its approximate English equivalent, which would be "fantasy". Because it is easy to lose oneself in complex arguments about definitions, about what belongs to the genre and what does not, we subscribe to Pierre Gripari's simple definition: "The *fantastique* is everything that is not rational".

Within this definition, science fiction can be viewed, as Belgian writer Jacques Sternberg once did, as nothing more than a *succursale* [a branch] of the *fantastique*. However, while recognizing that Sternberg has a point, we shall nevertheless treat science fiction as a wholly separate genre from the *fantastique*, and not as a mere subset.

We do this because we believe that, from their very inceptions, the two genres, *fantastique* and science fiction, reflected two sharply different literary objectives on the part of their writers, as well as filled two sharply different literary needs from the standpoint of their readers. Which is why literary works belonging to fantasy, horror, the supernatural, and the *fantastique* in general, will be chronicled and reviewed in our companion volume, *The Handbook of French Fantasy & Supernatural Fiction*.

For the purpose of these handbooks, science fiction, unlike the *fantastique*, is defined as works appealing to the head, the intellect and the mind, and not the heart. Its true roots lie with humanism, the Renaissance, and the 18th century *Esprit des Lumières*, or Age of Enlightenment. It is, ultimately, based on logic, on science and on testing hypotheses.

Science fiction, even when used as a social allegory, which it often is, always relies on a shared pretense of verisimilitude between the writer and his reader.

Science fiction in France can be said to have started with the Utopias of the 16th century, which eventually turned into Imaginary Journeys, then *Voyages Extraordinaires* [Extraordinary Voyages], a subset of literature eventually popularized by the great master himself, Jules Verne.

Verne single-handedly launched modern science fiction by combining his Extraordinary Voyages with scientific anticipation and was soon widely imitated. The formula he devised, rather than the more sophisticated one used by H. G. Wells, was the template borrowed by Hugo Gernsback, the Luxembourg-born father of American science fiction.

But Verne's impact on science fiction was not entirely positive. Scholars have observed that, because he was published and characterized as a writer of juvenile novels, the genre itself became tarred with that brush in the eye of the critics and the literary establishment. Because of the dominance of realism imposed by 19th century values, and the French literary establishment's overall rejection of science and progress, the growth of French science fiction, unlike that of its American counterpart, became somewhat stunted, often relegated to the province of juvenile entertainment.

Yet, despite this, the genre flourished in the 1920s and 1930s, which are, in the eyes of many, the true golden age of French science fiction. In the United States, *Amazing Stories* was created in 1928 and *Astounding Science Fiction* in 1930. Yet, in France, between the wars, magazines like *Sciences & Voyages*, *Je Sais Tout*, *Lectures pour Tous* and others published such celebrated authors as J.-H. Rosny Aîné, Maurice Renard, etc., who easily surpassed their English-speaking colleagues in imagination, maturity and sophistication.

After World War II, the year 1950 represented an important divide in the history of science fiction in French literature.

In 1950, American science fiction began to be translated and published in France on a regular basis. Publishing imprints such as *Le Rayon Fantastique* (est. 1951) and *Présence du Futur* (est. 1954), and magazines like *Fiction* (the French edition of *F & SF*, est. 1953), changed the nature of the genre virtually overnight,

Until then, French science fiction had been slowly developing a specific and unique voice. However, the publication in the early 1950s, in one fell swoop, of American masterpieces by writers such as Isaac Asimov, A. E. Van Vogt and Ray Bradbury delivered French science fiction a blow from which it took almost twenty years to recover.

By the start of the 21st century, however, one can firmly state that science fiction and fantasy are healthier in France than in any other western country outside of the United States.

It is often too common to hear American and even British pundits deplore the state of science fiction outside the English-speaking world. It must be said that such statements arise out of ignorance, fostered in the most part by the inability to process information written in another language, and perhaps by a lack of curiosity from the part of Americans and a lack of proselytism from the part of the French.

If quantity alone is a yardstick of health, French science fiction can be said to be very healthy, with no less than several imprints putting out half-a-dozen novels by native French writers every month and several magazines as well. (And this does not include juvenile novels and genre works published in more mainstream imprints.) This represents an output of well over a hundred new works each year, certainly unmatched in Italy, Spain, Germany (excluding the *Perry Rhodan* series), Scandinavia, etc.

Quality is, of course, a more subjective argument. Yet, contemporary French science fiction, and fantasy, whether from the 1960s, 1970s, 1980s or 1990s, boasts many talented voices, fully equal to those of their American counterparts.

These, then, are our terms of reference, the literary canvas against which we propose to paint the history of French science fiction.

It will not escape the knowledgeable reader's attention that large sections of this book (and its three companion volumes, *The Handbook of French Fantasy & Supernatural Fiction* and *The Handbook of French Fantastic Cinema & Television*) first appeared in our 800-page bibliographical work, *French Science Fiction, Fantasy, Horror and Pulp Fiction: A Guide to Cinema, Television, Radio, Animation, Comic Books and Literature from the Middle Ages to the Present*, published 2000 by McFarland. According to *The Encyclopedia of Science Fiction*, "the Lofficier text covers the French fantastic with a comprehensiveness and intensity equaled only by the central texts of English-language bibliography and reference".

A natural offshoot of this project was the founding in 2003 of our small press publishing company, Black Coat Press, which over the last twenty years has released more than 600 English translations of French-language works, all annotated in this volume, including a staggering number of novels and collections in competent translations by the great British author Brian Stableford, each volume normally accompanied by an informative introduction.

Due primarily to this outpouring of significant texts, it has become clear to English-language critics and readers that French science fiction is not a counter-tradition conditional upon the central flow of the genre in the UK and the United States, but an extremely formidable tradition in its own right.

It is our hoped that this contextualized overview of the genre history in France will inspire readers to seek some of the works now available in English from our publishing house.

It should also be understood that, throughout this book, we have used the word "French" in the sense of French-language, that is to say, including Belgian, Swiss and French-Canadian works and/or authors whenever appropriate We have, however, strived to identify such non-French-national works and/or authors.

Finally, no project of this type is ever perfect, or complete. We have tried to be as comprehensive as possible and correct all mistakes that appeared in the McFarland tome. Nevertheless, in a book of this scope, no matter how careful one is, omissions are still bound to creep in, as well as the occasional mistake. We will be grateful to anyone pointing out such errors or omissions to us, for future reference and inclusion in subsequent reprints. One thing we have not tried to do, however, is update the McFarland tome beyond its original end point, which was the year 2000. We have left the description of French science fiction in the 21st century to future genre historians.

Jean-Marc & Randy Lofficier

Gargantua.

M. D. XXXVII.

The Utopias
(1500-1650)

The Renaissance of the 16th century was marked by the emergence of new ideas and literary trends, often as a reaction against what was perceived as the "obscurantism" of the Middle Ages.

Among the factors which contributed to the Renaissance were: the discoveries of new continents by Christopher Columbus, Vasco da Gama, Fernand Magellan, Giovanni da Verrazano and Jacques Cartier, which offered new imaginary vistas in which to locate stories; the scientific and technical discoveries of scientists such as Copernicus and Ambroise Paré; and, finally, Johannes Gutenberg's discovery of the printing press c. 1450, which made the greater circulation of literary works possible.

After the fall of Constantinople in 1453, Greek intellectuals moved to Italy, which quickly became the cultural center of the Renaissance, drawing talent from all over Europe. From the Latin word *humanitas* [culture] then came the humanists, who taught humanism, a school of thought based on the ancient Greco-Roman ideals of wisdom, tolerance and rational thought. One of foremost humanists of the times was the philosopher Erasmus who, although born in Holland, spent a considerable amount of time in France.

The Renaissance bloomed in France during the reign of King Francis I (reigned 1515-1547). As Charlemagne had done before, François 1st created a favorable environment for the development of letters, arts and sciences. He founded several scientific colleges, attracted foreign artists, such as Leonardo da Vinci, to the French Court and, more generally, gave a seal of official tolerance towards the publication of the new philosophy.

It was during the French Renaissance that proto-science fiction first split from the *fantastique*. The thirst for learning combined with a natural sense of optimism in science and progress to produce the Utopias.

The invention of the first Utopia was to be credited to British writer Sir Thomas More who, inspired by Erasmus, wrote *The Utopia* in 1516 in Latin. In it, a Portuguese sailor returned from his journeys and described the perfect, humanistic society he discovered on the Island of Utopia. Even though More's *Utopia* was translated into French in 1550 (but in English only in 1551!), it clearly inspired French writer François Rabelais who, in a unique literary cross-over, chose to locate several of his stories in the same island.

Rabelais was a scholar, a humanist, a physician and a writer. His works constituted an extraordinary blend of political and sociological satire, extraordinary voyages, pre-*Utopia* utopias, and heroic-fantasy quests. His literally larger-than-life, colorful characters with "gargantuan" appetites were also literary archetypes that spawned many imitations. Rabelais, a former monk who had studied medicine, strongly believed that Man's body and spirit should be freed from medieval restrictions. He trusted nature and progress and saw unlimited horizons ahead for mankind. This, combined with his vivid imagination and prodigious sense of satire, led him to create an array of imaginary lands and societies which remains, today, among the most complex ever devised in imaginary literature.

Furthermore, Rabelais' fantastic worlds were not places serving only satirical or comparative purposes, i.e.: designed to be contrasted by the reader with the real society of the time. They also contained clearly drawn speculative statements about the future, making him the first proto-science fiction author in French literature.

For example, Rabelais' masterpieces, *Pantagruel* (1532) and *Gargantua* (1534), about the adventures of two giant kings—Gargantua was King of the Dipsodes and Pantagruel's father—mentioned a trip to the Moon, advanced surgical techniques (such as organ grafts), advanced military tactics (such as fortifications and deep-sea diving), as well as more fantastic concepts, such as that of miniaturization *à la Fantastic Voyage*. On another level, the gigantism of Gargantua and Pantagruel was not only literal, but allegorical. For Rabelais, mankind itself was the giant ready to awaken. In this, he anticipated Jonathan Swift, Olaf Stapledon, and, closer to modern times, Frank Herbert.

With the Reformation and its ensuing series of civil wars, including the infamous massacre of St. Bartholomew's Day in 1572, the political climate changed during the second half of the 16th century; religious and political intolerance gained new ground, and Rabelais' works were forbidden. Even though his *Third* (1546), *Fourth* (1548-52) and *Fifth* (published posthumously in 1564 and of dubious authenticity) *Books* were much safer politically, they nevertheless caused their author many problems, even forcing him into internal exile for a while. From a science fiction standpoint, however, these later works remained interesting because, in them, Rabelais developed the literary device of the *Voyage Imaginaire* [Imaginary Journey] to a heretofore unprecedented extent.

Borrowing from a tradition going back to Homer's *Odyssey*, and inspired by the real-life journey of explorer Jacques Cartier, Rabelais described how French travelers to India, who used the legendary North-West passage, came across and explored twenty-one islands, each one with a strange society of its own: an island where people fed on wind, one where sound could be frozen and unfrozen at will, one where the local king used magnetic force to stop cannonballs, etc. In these books, Rabelais gave form to a genre which was later exploited by such luminaries as Cyrano de Bergerac, Jonathan Swift, Jules Verne and, in modern times, Jack Vance.

The other great writer of the French Renaissance was Michel Eyquem, a.k.a. Michel de Montaigne, a formidable essayist and philosopher, whose lifework, the introspective three-volume *Essais* [Essays] (1580-88), still carries a deep influence on French philosophy today.

Even though less inclined towards the Imaginary than Rabelais, Montaigne's profound hatred for dogmatism of any kind led him to take an occasional journey to Utopia himself. In Chapter XXXI of Book 1 of the *Essays*, entitled "*Des Cannibales*" [Of Cannibals], Montaigne described a mythical land peopled by "good savages." We shall note in passing that Montaigne was aware of the existence of Plato's fabled Atlantis, since he took pains to rule it out as the location of his own imaginary island.

Rabelais was not alone in breaking new literary grounds. Other writers worthy of being mentioned here include:

Bonaventure des Périers, with his *Cymbalum Mundi* (1537), a book comprised of four dialogues, allegedly told by the author/translator to a man named Pierre Tryocam, in which the god Hermes made fun of philosophers and then discovered that someone stole the Book of Destinies that Zeus had entrusted to him.

Raoul Spifame, with his *Dicacarchia Henrici, Regis Christianissimi, Progymnasmata* (1556).

Béroalde de Verville , with *L'Idée de la République* [The Idea of the Republic] (1584) and *Discours de Jacophile à Limne* (1605).

Finally, one should also note a remarkable work by the noted physician and medical pioneer Ambroise Paré, *Les Monstres, Tant Terrestres que Marins, avec leurs Portraits* [Monsters, Terrestrials as well as Seafaring, with their Portraits] (1579), in which the "scientific" evidence of the existence of dragons, hermaphrodites and unicorns was taken for granted.

Cymbalū mūdi

EN FRANCOYS,

Contenant quatre Dialogues Poetiques, sort antiques, ioyeux, & facetieux.

Probitas laudatur, & alget.

M.D.XXXVII

The Imaginary Journeys
(1650-1800)

The 18th century was known to French historians as the *Siècle des Lumières* [Century of Lights], or the Age of Enlightenment. Starting with the accession to the throne in 1643 of the Sun King Louis XIV, France entered a period of political, artistic and scientific *grandeur*, before settling into the decadent reigns of Louis XV (1710-1774) and Louis XVI (1754-1793).

The Age of Enlightenment could be arguably said to have started with René Descartes in 1637 with his *Le Discours de la Méthode*, or in 1687 when Isaac Newton published his *Mathematical Principles of Natural Philosophy*, the basis for a comprehensive, mathematical description of the Universe, which demonstrated the power of science over the material world.

The prevailing modes of Enlightenment thinking were rational thought and skepticism. Throughout the use of reason, Man would master nature and himself. Nothing exemplified this better than Denis Diderot's massive, seventeen-volume *Encyclopedia* (1751-72), a sum of knowledge whose advocated purpose was to disseminate information, reduce superstition and improve the human condition.

In literature, the *baroque* was replaced by classicism during the reign of the Sun King, with its roster of great playwrights. The so-called "Quarrel of the Ancients and the Moderns" (c. 1690) then freed French authors from the need to imitate the literature of antiquity. Finally, the passion for new philosophical ideas, incarnated by Voltaire, and the spread of cosmopolitan influences, such as those of Spinoza, Newton and Goethe, fostered a climate of debate that would eventually produce the blueprints for a new, modern society. The cereation of that "new society" would become the project—and ultimately the failure—of the French Revolution, which could therefore be said to be the brainchild of the proto-science fiction writers of the 17th and 18th centuries.

It was during the late 17th century that a growing distinction began to appear between the pure utopias, the purpose of which remained social satire and philosophical discourse, and the first *Voyages Imaginaires*, which aimed to entertain. It was also during the 18th century that many of the now-classic themes, such as journeys through the cosmos, to the center of the Earth, and even to the future, were first defined in literary terms.

Journeys to Other Worlds

Following in the footsteps of Rabelais, and a contemporary of Roger Bacon (whose *New Atlantis* had been published in 1629), Tommaso Campanella (whose *City of the Sun* had been published in 1637), and Francis Godwin (whose *The Man in the Moone* had been published in 1638), was Charles Sorel, the author of the three-volume *Le Berger Extravagant* [The Extravagant Shepherd] (1627) and *La Maison des Jeux* [The House of Games], which included the "*Récit du Voyage de Brisevent*" [Tale of Brisevent's Journey] (1642), which both contained utopias inhabited by fantastic beings.

In the latter, Sorel wrote, "some men have affirmed that there are many worlds, which some have placed in the planets, and others in the fixed stars; for my part, I believe there is a world on the Moon." In describing a trip there, Sorel imagined a "Prince as ambitious as Alexander, who shall come to conquer this world," doing so by using "great engines, to descend or ascend."

The most famous French author undoubtedly influenced by Sorel was Savinien de Cyrano de Bergerac, whose *Histoire Comique des Etats et Empires de la Lune* [Comical History of the States and Empires of the Moon] was published posthumously in 1657, soon followed by *Histoire Comique des Etats et Empires du Soleil* [Comical History of the States and Empires of the Sun] in 1662, eventually collected as *L'Autre Monde* [Other Worlds].

Cyrano de Bergerac is mostly famous today famous as the hero of a superb 1898 play by Edmond Rostand, which made his swordsmanship and the size of his nose illustrious. But he was also a poet, a soldier of fortune and a distinguished man of letters, whose writings were published after his death to avoid persecution and prosecution for the crime of heresy. He wrote two remarkable utopias-cum-social satires which were also noteworthy because of their author's attempts at devising various methods of space travel, some of them clearly fanciful (even at the time they were written), but others more scientific (rockets, parachutes, use of magnetism). Cyrano de Bergerac certainly influenced the later works of Voltaire and Jonathan Swift.

Well versed in esoteric matters—the Rosicrucians are mentioned in passing in *L'Autre Monde*—Cyrano de Bergerac described magical rituals and alchemical process in various of his letters, collected in *Pour et Contre les Sorciers* [For and Against Sorcerers] (published in 1663), even making use of the real-life alchemist Agrippa de Nettesheim as his fictional character. In the same fashion, he had the ghosts of Campanella and Descartes appear in *L'Autre Monde*.

But what made *L'Autre Monde* remarkable as a work of proto-science fiction, perhaps the first of its kind, and different from all the utopias which preceded it, was that Cyrano de Bergerac added to the usual satirical and philosophical discourse elements based on his knowledge of physics and astronomy. The book featured the concepts of rocket power, hot air balloon, and the phonograph. Another remarkable innovation was the creation of pseudo-alien societies, such as that of the bird-men who live on the "dark side" of the Sun and hate all men. In Cyrano de Bergerac's colorful universe, Man was not only no longer the sole sentient species in the universe, but he was not even the most important one.

In 1686, Corneille's nephew, Bernard Le Bovier de Fontenelle took the theme of cosmic exploration one step further and published his *Entretiens sur la Pluralité des Mondes* [Conversations on the Plurality of Worlds], a pseudo-documentary work about the possibilities of life on other planets. This was one of the earliest works popularizing the concepts of astronomy and possible life on other planets. It proved enormously influential on all subsequent proto-science fiction works. The book was written as a series of exchanges between the author and the fictional Marquise de G***, and did much to popularize scientific astronomical concepts. In his foreword, De Fontenelle stated that he "did not want to imagine anything about the inhabitants of these other worlds that could be either entirely impossible or chimerical; [he] tried to describe everything that could reasonably be formulated, and even the visions [he] added had to have some foundations in reality". This was, clearly, an approach that was characteristic of a work of science fiction, not of fantasy.

The success of Cyrano de Bergerac's works popularized the concept of journeys into outer space and to other worlds, and spawned many imitators, such as Anne Mauduit de Fatouville (who signed her works Nolant de Fatouville)—a woman, no less, sadly forgotten today!—with her *Arlequin, Empereur de la Lune* [Harlequin, Emperor of the Moon] (1684).

The next thematic leap was accomplished by the distinguished satirist François-Marie Arouet, a.k.a. Voltaire, in his novella *Micromegas* published in 1752. The title character was a giant alien from Sirius who, accompanied by an equally gigantic Saturnian, had come to visit Earth. Even though Voltaire's primary purpose was satire, he nevertheless relied on well-researched scientific foundations, as shown in this excerpt: "Our space traveler was well acquainted with the laws of gravity, and all of its attractive and repulsive nature." Voltaire went on to state how comets and solar rays could be used to travel between planets.

Once created, the concept of cosmic voyages grew and developed, usually as the pretext for some thinly disguised utopias, but more often than not including some startling proto-science fiction contents. For example, in 1750, the Chevalier de Béthune published a *Relation du Monde de Mercure* [The World of Mercury],[1] a colorful utopia about the immortal, winged beings inhabiting the planet Mercury. In developing his world, the author shaped one of the few "Creationist fantasies" entirely unaffected by religious dogma. His Mercury shines with originality, adventurousness and, especially, bizarrerie. The description of the aerial conflict between the defenders of Mercury's Great Mountain and the monstrous invaders from the "crust" expelled from the Sun is triumphantly eccentric, a match in its colorful extravagance for any space battle featured in the great tradition of 20th century space opera.

In 1753, in *Amilec, ou La Graine d'Hommes qui Sert à Peupler les Planètes* [Amilec, or The Seed of Man Which Is Used to Seed the Planets],[2] Charles-François Tiphaigne de la Roche conceived the concept of journeys through both the macro-cosmos and the micro-cosmos. His extrapolation of the manner in which human seeds are used to populate other planets may seem primitive, but it is a fascinating prediction of what will eventually become cosmology and embryology.

In 1757, Swiss writer Emmerich de Vattel penned probably the first novel ever written about a journey to the world of insects. In *Les Fourmis* [The Ants],[3] a man transfers his mind into that of an ant and discovers the new perspectives of a microscopic world.

In 1761, Daniel de Villeneuve, a.k.a. Listonai, wrote *Le Voyageur Philosophe dans un Pays Inconnu aux Habitants de la Terre* [The Philosophical Voyager in a Land Unknown to

---

[1] Black Coat Press, ISBN 978-1-61227-410-2.

[2] Black Coat Press, ISBN 978-1-61227-033-3.

[3] In *Nemoville*, Black Coat Press, ISBN 978-1-61227-070-8.

the Inhabitants of the Earth],[4] an elaborate utopia featuring a flying space galley, complete with pilot, astronavigator and crew. On the Moon, the protagonist meets the Selenite Arzame who takes him to the fortified city of Selenopolis, a perfect square built according to symmetry and universal philosophical principles, whose citizens always behave with intelligent discernment and view the universe in ways that are radically different than those expressed by the people of Earth. *The Philosophical Voyager* is the most spectacular early attempt to put narrative flesh on the idea of progress as it was understood in the Enlightenment Era, and it remained the boldest and most wide-reaching work of its kind for at least half a century.

In 1765, Marie-Anne de Roumier-Robert wrote *Le Voyage de Milord Céton dans les Sept Planètes* [The Voyages of Lord Seaton in the Seven Planets][5] in which the hero and his sister travel to seven different planets on the wings of the angel Zachiel. In this space travel story, the inhabitants of each planet were chosen to represent a human character trait— Martians were bellicose, Venusians lovers, etc.

In 1775, industrial chemist Louis-Guillaume de La Follie, a scientist and industrial chemist, penned *Le Philosophe sans Prétention* [The Unpretentious Philosopher],[6] a utopia which featured an electric-powered starship remarkably ahead of its times. In it, a scientist from Mercury, Scintilla, undertakes a voyage of exploration to Earth, and becomes stranded on our planet when his ship crashes. This forces him to embark on a long search for the exotic materials required to repair it, giving him an opportunity to communicate his advanced understanding of science to an inquisitive Earthling. The author was the first writer of *contes philosophiques* to put the "hard" sciences of physics and chemistry at the heart of his endeavor. His ambitious purpose is to communicate new scientific ideas by using entertaining fictional devices. *The Un-*

---

[4] Black Coat Press, ISBN 978-1-61227-367-9.

[5] Black Coat Press, ISBN 978-1-61227-446-1.

[6] Black Coat Press, ISBN 978-1-61227-136-1.

pretentious Philosopher is truly a plea in favor of "science fiction," a concept that would not be invented for generations to come.

Finally, in the 1790s, the noted utopist, playwright and journalist Louis-Abel Beffroy de Reigny, better known as Cousin Jacques, wrote a number of satirical plays taking place on other planets: *Nicodème dans la Lune, ou La Révolution Pacifique* [Nicodeme on the Moon, or The Peaceful Revolution] (1791), *Les Deux Nicodèmes, ou les Français dans la Planète Jupiter* [The Two Nicodemes, or Two Frenchmen on the Planet Jupiter] (1791), and a novella, *La Constitution de la Lune* [The Moon's Constitution] (1793). Cousin Jacques also self-published *Les Lunes du Cousin Jacques, ou le Courrier des Planètes* [The Moons of Cousin Jacques, or The Planetary Mail] (1785-1791), the first fanzine in the history of science fiction.

After the French Revolution, the theme of cosmic journeys eventually became trivialized. In 1875, one of Jacques Offenbach's operettas was even entitled *Le Voyage dans la Lune* [The Journey to the Moon]. It would take the prodigious talent of Jules Verne to restore luster and scientific credibility to the concept of space travel.

Journeys to Other Lands

To differentiate himself from those writers sending their heroes on cosmic journeys, Gabriel de Foigny wrote *La Terre Australe Connue* [The Known Austral Continent] (1676), later reissued as *Les Aventures de Jacques Sadeur dans la Découverte et le Voyage de la Terre Australe* [The Adventures of Jacques Sadeur in the Discovery and Exploration of the Austral Continent] (1693), an elaborate utopia about an enlightened Antipodean race.

Denis Veiras penned a four-volume *Histoire des Sévarambes* [The History of the Sevarambi] (1677-79), another utopian description of the mores of the fictional people inhabiting the so-called Austral Continent. Interestingly, Veiras' work was first published anonymously in English in 1675.

In 1683, Abbot Maillot published *Relation du Voyage Mystérieux de l'Île de la Vertu* [Tale of a Mysterious Voyage to the Island of Virtue]. And in 1690, Gabriel Daniel penned *Voyage du Monde de Descartes* [A Voyage to the World of Descartes**Error! Bookmark not defined.**] (1690), a utopia centered around the ideas of philosopher René Descartes.

Simon Tyssot de Patot dispatched his heroes to an imaginary land located near South Africa in *Voyages et Aventures de Jacques Massé* [Voyages and Adventures of Jacques Massé], published in 1710.[7] In it, the author dispatches his protagonist to an imaginary land in an heretofore unknown austral continent, where he comes across so-called "living fossils," giant birds and strange flora that survived from prehistoric times, arguably making it the first modern Lost World novel. The text also includes an early appearance by the Wandering Jew with a visionary narrative attributed to the folklore of the polar continent, in which a character discovers a subterranean portal to the "abode of the blessed."

The concept of a journey to the center of the Earth was also first introduced by Tyssot de Patot in his 1720 novel, *La Vie, les Aventures et le Voyage de Groenland du Révérend Père Cordelier Pierre de Mésange* [The Life, Adventures & Trip to Greenland of the Rev. Father Pierre de Mesange].[8] This was the first time that the notion of a journey to the center of the Earth was introduced in a realistic, pseudo-scientific fashion, as opposed to the various mythological journeys to Hell, such as *The Divine Comedy* of the early 14th century. The author's eponymous hero discovers a secret underground kingdom inhabited by the descendants of African colonists who left their homeland four thousand years earlier and spends

---

[7] In *The Strange Voyages of Jacques Massé and Pierre de Mésange*, Black Coat Press, ISBN 978-1-61227-370-9.

[8] In *The Strange Voyages of Jacques Massé and Pierre de Mésange*, q.v.

several years recording their stories and fables. This proto-*Pellucidar* is lit by a mysterious fire ball and was also inhabited by small man-bat creatures.

These two novels constitute is a truly remarkable achievement, marking a highly significant watershed in the evolution of literary accounts of imaginary voyages, predating Jonathan Swift's satirical account of the travels of Lemuel Gulliver, published in 1726, and Jules Verne's classic *Journey to the Center of the Earth* by 140 years! The only other seminal work on this theme is Danish writer Ludvig Holberg's *Voyage of Nikolas Klimius*, but it is dated from 1741.)

More conventional utopias continued to rely on fictional lands. Even a renowned literary figure such as famous writer and essayist Montesquieu devoted Letters XI to XIV of his *Lettres Persanes* [Persian Letters] (1721) to the fictional *Histoire des Troglodytes* [History of the Troglodytes]. This essay used a fictional lost race to depict a utopian society.

In 1759, in *Candide*, Voltaire described the mythical country of Eldorado, the ancient land of the Incas.

In 1760, Tiphaigne de la Roche sent his heroes to the secret land of *Giphantie* in Africa, where a race of secret supermen lived in royal isolation. The novel also featured a concept remarkably similar to that of television. The following year, in *L'Empire des Zaziris sur les Humains ou la Zazirocratie* [The Empire of the Zaziris Over Mankind, or The Zazirocracy] Tiphaigne anticipated many future tales of secret alien invasions by postulating that mysterious beings, the eponymous Zaziris, descendants of the mythical sylphs and djinns, lived hidden among us and secretly controlled the destinies of Mankind.[9]

Of even greater interest is Nicolas-Edmé Restif de la Bretonne, a prolific author of semi-autobiographic and somewhat pornographic novels. His proto-science fictional works were rediscovered by well-known sf scholar Pierre Versins, who devoted a full eight pages to them in his prodigious 1972

---

[9] Both in *Amilec*, q.v.

Encyclopédie de l'Utopie, des Voyages Extraordinaires et de la Science Fiction, calling Restif the "master of conjecture, utopia, and science fiction."

Restif produced over 180 books, totaling some 57,000 pages, many of them printed by his own hand, on almost every conceivable subject. Praised in Germany, he was mostly forgotten in France until being rediscovered by the Surrealists in the early 20th century. Two of his most important seminal works are being presented here for the first time in English in a four-volume edition.

In *La Découverte Australe par <u>un Homme Volant</u>* [Discovery of the Austral Continent by a Flying Man],[10] published in 1781, a young scientist, Victorin, devises a set of artificial wings and parachute, which enable him to reach speeds of over a hundred miles per hour, in order to abduct his beloved Christine, before setting her up on top of a mountain as queen of her own utopia. At that point, Victorin considers using air power to become master of the world, but eventually, embarks on the exploration of the Southern Hemisphere, where like Rabelais before him, Restif has him visit several fantastic islands inhabited by giants and other variant human species, including beast-men combining the features of humans and animals. His voyage ends in the great City of Sirap, another utopia located in Megapatagonia.

The book is unique, not only within Restif's *oeuvre*, but within the context of French imaginative fiction. By virtue of the deft combination of its technological element with the theoretical element, it is undoubtedly the most significant work of science-based speculative fiction produced before the French Revolution.

In 1721, an anonymous author published *Relation d'un Voyage du Pôle Arctique au Pôle Antarctique par le Centre du Monde avec la Description de ce Périlleux Passage et les Choses Merveilleuses et Étonnantes qu'on a découvertes sous*

---

[10] Black Coat Press, ISBN 978-1-61227-512-3.

le Pôle Antarctique [A Journey from the Arctic Pole to the Antarctic Pole via the Center of the World].[11]

Finally, in 1737-38, long before George MacDonald and William Morris, Charles de Fieux, Chevalier de Mouhy, a one-time friend of Voltaire, prolific author of popular and mildly scandalous potboilers (including the first sensational novel about the Man in the Iron Mask) and polemicist, penned one of the first and most extravagant "Extraordinary Voyages," ever, the eight-volume *Lamékis, ou Les Voyages Extraordinaires d'un Égyptien dans la Terre Intérieure avec la Découverte de l'Île des Sylphides* [Lamekis, or The Extraordinary Voyages of an Egyptian in the Inner Earth with the Discovery of Sylphides' Island].[12] This metafictional novel is an unparalleled work of kaleidoscopic imagination and multiple, exuberant narratives focusing on the life and times of Lamekis, the son of a High Priest of Ancient Egypt. In it, the hero rescues a blue-skinned man who came from an underground land called Trifolday. The fugitive tells the boy how he fought there against races of snake-men, toad-men and worm-men. Edgar Rice Burroughs' fans would feel quite comfortable in the Chevalier de Mouhy's colorful descriptions of the fantastic kingdoms existing under and above the Earth.

Lamekis deals with themes of friendship, unrequited love, murderous jealousy, violent power struggles, the quest for immortality and the cosmogonic vision of the universe with competing gods and levels of reality. Its extravagant settings include the subterranean world mentioned above and the celestial Island of the Sylphs, where beings can ascend to the Heavens, all depicted with their strange cultures and alien languages. The author himself is, at one point, dragged into the narrative where he is rebuked for his poetic license, given secret messages, witnesses his unfinished novel as a series of bas-reliefs, is shown the inside of his mind, is invited to be

---

[11] In *The New Moon*, Black Coat Press, ISBN 978-1-61227-443-0.

[12] Black Coat Press, ISBN 978-1-61227-003-6.

initiated into the mysteries of the Sylphs, has the final part of his novel written for him by an invisible force, and falls foul of the royal censor.

Journeys to Other Times

For those who preferred not to travel to outer or inner space, there was always the future.

In 1659, Jacques Guttin wrote *Epigone, Histoire du Siècle Futur* [History of the Future Century]. In it, the author did not resort to the well-known literary trick of dreams or imaginary journeys, but merely told a story that took place in the future. Guttin described the future history of France, ruled by the "Clodovist" kings, and the peregrinations of the young heir to the French throne.

In *Telliamed*, a visionary book published in 1748 and sub-titled "Conversations of an Indian Philosopher with a French Missionary on the Decrease of the Seas, the Origins of Earth and of Man", Benoît de Maillet anticipated Olaf Stapledon by telling the story of the evolution of man, from his origins in the sea—a startling breakthrough concept if there ever was one—to his future among the stars.

Louis-Sébastien Mercier's *L'An 2440, Rêve s'il en fut jamais* [The Year 2440, A Dream If There Ever Was One], published in 1771, depicted a future France governed according to the principles of Enlightenment. It was one of the first literary works to make the transition from utopia to scientific anticipation, featuring intercontinental dirigible flights. Its importance had less to do with its literary value -- in it, the author just wakes up seven hundred years later -- than its historical consequences. *L'An 2440* not only helped shape the philosophies that led to the French Revolution, but it was also the first utopia of its kind to be translated in America, in 1772.

Mercier was not the only thinker whose works of fiction paved the way for the French Revolution. Others included the pseudonymous Morelly with his *Naufrage des Isles Flottantes*

[Wreck of the Floating Islands] (1753), Listonai, Voltaire, La Follie, etc.

Mercier's *Voyages Imaginaires, Songes, Visions et Romans Cabalistiques* [Imaginary Journeys, Dreams, Visions & Cabalistic Novels] (1788) also featured a scientific device anticipating communications between the Earth and the Moon, achieved through the equivalent of a modern-day laser.

In 1791, with *Ma République* [My Republic], Jean-Baptiste-Claude Delisle de Sales penned one of the first parallel history, or "what if" novellas, in the history of science fiction by describing what the French Revolution might have been had King Louis XVI been a better politician.

Restif de la Bretonne's *L'An 2000* [*The Year 2000*] (1789), in spite of its prophetic title—perhaps the first time that a now such common title was used in the history of science fiction—was only a comedy of manners. But in one, prodigious novel, a four-volume work entitled *Les Posthumes* [Posthumous Correspondence] (published only in 1802), [13] which combined in a dazzling display of imagination all of the proto-science fiction themes, and more.

In the beginning, the protagonist, Fontlhète, makes contact with Yfflasie and Clarendon, two discorporated souls and learns of their adventures in the afterlife, using a process which the author took pains to qualify as "physical and not supernatural."; Later, he acquires artificial wings, uses his new-found power to oppose evil and fight crime, taking on tyrants and warmongers, then gains the ability of exchanging identities by taking over other people's bodies with his own soul.

Then, the author introduces another hero, the Duke Multipliandre, whose adventures include not only the acquisition of several superpowers, including invisibility, but a vast series of erotic exploits, some involving the ability of exchanging identities by taking over other people's bodies. After visiting

---

[13] Available in three volumes, Black Coat Press, ISBNs 978-1-61227-513-0, 978-1-61227-514-7 and 978-1-61227-515-4.

many exotic lands, Multipliandre boldly crosses the boundaries of the known world, in order to explore the hypothetical world of Restif's cosmogonic and evolutionary theories, traveling to the Moon and Mars, like the hero of Stapledon's *Star Maker*, occupying the bodies of various alien races.

Multipliandre visits the other known planets of the solar system and numerous other worlds then unknown to science, including trans-Uranian planets, a comet and three planets within the orbit of Mercury, and interacts with their peculiar inhabitants. After that, he sets off to visit several other solar systems, including those of Sirius and Vega, and several nebulae, before concluding his journey in the "astral center," into which the entire universe will one day be dissolved, before being regenerated as an entirely new universe.

Multipliandre then returns to Earth, where, immortal by virtue of his super-powers, he settles down to witness the entire future of our world, initially coping with a new form of life born from a close encounter between the planet and a comet, which produces, among other plant and animal species, a race of winged humans, whom Multipliandre calls "angels". Finally, Multipliandre watches Earth as it plummets towards the Sun some three million years in the future.

Pierre Versins dubbed *Les Posthumes* a brilliant, visionary, but scattered work. Nevertheless, it was intended to be the most ambitious, fantastic and all-encompassing of all the exotic literary endeavors that Restif had originally planned to write, the ultimate version of his speculative cosmogony.

This chapter would not be complete without a mention of editor-publisher Charles-Georges-Thomas Garnier, who in 1787 launched a 36-volume specialized collection—the first science fiction imprint ever—entitled *Voyages Imaginaires, Songes, Visions et Romans Cabalistiques* [Imaginary Journeys, Dreams, Visions and Occult Novels]. During the two years of its existence, *Voyages Imaginaires* reprinted and popularized works by French authors such as Cyrano de Bergerac, Montesquieu, Mouhy, Foigny, Veiras, Voltaire, Mercier, Cazotte, etc.

L'EMPIRE
DES
ZAZIRIS
SUR LES HUMAINS,
OU LA
ZAZIROCRATIE.

A PEKIN,
Chez D s M G T L F P Q X Z.

M. DCC. LXI.

The *Voyages Extraordinaires*
(1800-1860)

Despite all its excesses, the French Revolution succeeded in imposing the values of scientific progress and so-called Cartesian thinking on French society, thus setting the stage for the Industrial Revolution, which itself gave rise to the socialist ideas of Pierre Proudhon in France, and Karl Marx in England.

The 19th century also became a period of colonial expansion, with fierce competition between France and the other European powers for most of Africa, a good part of Asia and many Pacific Islands.

Literature being the mirror of society, some of these notions were bound to be reflected in the novels of the times, and indeed they were among the powerful social forces that shaped modern science fiction. During the early part of the 19th century, proto-science fiction, such as utopias and imaginary journeys, evolved into the *voyages extraordinaires* and, from 1864 onward, thanks to the incomparable Jules Verne, the first, true works of modern science fiction.

Science fiction became a literature of ideas rather than style, of concepts rather than characters. This dichotomy was a direct result of the conflict in French society between the past and the future, conservative and radical ideas, literature and science, classicism and progress. The concerns of science fiction, such as "what if" scenarios, considerations on the impact of technology and scientific anticipation of the future, were, by their very nature, deemed to be inferior by the guardians of French culture to the nobler concerns of true literature.

This perception, which to some extent still exists today, was reinforced by the fact that the works of Verne were arbitrarily, and somewhat unjustly, catalogued as being aimed at young adults.

Even worse, science fiction proved to be a fertile field for all kinds of pulp-like, popular adventure serials, where thrills were more important than a well-turned sentence. As a result, French science fiction was firmly categorized as second-rate literature, at best juvenile, at worst obscene, no matter how talented some of its authors or enlightened some of its novels.

There was, sadly, very little science fiction that was published in the 19th century that belonged to what scholars called "real" literature, and when it happened, it certainly was never labeled as such. A good novel, by a startling example of circular logic, could never be a science fiction novel. In England and America, Edgar Allan Poe and H. G. Wells were universally regarded today as major literary figures. Sadly, in France, Verne and J.-H. Rosny Aîné were treated as marginal and/or juvenile authors.

Prior to Verne's grand entrance onto the science fiction stage in 1864, the earlier part of the century showed no clean break with the literary tradition inherited from before the French Revolution. In fact, the Napoleonic regime which followed the Revolution even encouraged a return to a certain literary classicism. Despite this, however, a deliberate and growing scientific spirit was applied to even the most old-fashioned utopias of the pre-Revolutionary period. Some works emerged from this period as true, conceptual breakthroughs which established and defined new boundaries for the growing new genre.

As we did in the previous chapter, we have somewhat arbitrarily grouped the pre-Vernian science fiction of the times according to three themes: Other Worlds (i.e., Outer Space), Other Lands and Other Times (i.e., the Future).

Journeys to Other Worlds

Cosmic journeys were a tradition firmly established by Cyrano de Bergerac. They continued to thrive during the first half of the 19th century, remaining more often than not a pretext for thinly veiled social satire. However, as we mentioned, these stories increasingly incorporated scientific elements and began to aim for believability, an essential ingredient of modern science fiction.

In 1832, in his collection of short stories simply entitled *Nouvelles* [Short Stories], Jacques Boucher de Crèvecoeur included "*Mazular*", the tale of a journey to the Moon.

Victor Considerant's *Publication complete des nouvelles découvertes de Sir John Herschel dans le ciel austral et dans la lune* [The Complete News from the Moon] (1836)[14] is a utopia in which the society described is only related to existing societies in satirical terms, and very subtly.

French botanist and geologist Pierre Boitard published *Voyage au Soleil* [Journey to the Sun] (1838),[15] the first story of adventure and scientific popularization for young people, depicting a voyage through the solar system, with the beings of each of the planets representing a different stage of Man's evolution. Two years earlier, the author had penned *Paris Avant l'Homme* [Paris Before Humankind],[16] well before the emergence of paleontology; it was the first Darwinian narrative, including pre-historical ape-men.

In chapters 14 and 16 to 18 of *Les Aventures Amphibies de Robert-Robert et de son fidèle compagnon Toussaint Lavenette* [The Amphibian Adventures of Robert-Robert and his Faithful Companion Toussaint Lavenette] (1853), a sprawling juvenile saga serialized in the *Journal des Enfants* [*The Children's Journal*], Louis Desnoyers described the travels of Cousin Laroutine on the Moon. In a typical pre-Revolutionary style, however, our satellite was reached via a hot air balloon, and the tone was definitely one of social satire.

---

[14] In *The Humanisphere*, Black Coat Press, ISBN 978-1-61227-511-6.

[15] Black Coat Press, ISBN 978-1-61227-517-8.

[16] In *Journey to the Sun*, Black Coat Press, q.v.

The same means of travel was employed in *Les Aventures d'un Aéronaute Parisien dans les Mondes Inconnus* [The Adventures of Parisian Aeronaut in Unknown Worlds] (1856),[17] a far more visionary work by Alfred Driou which described an advanced society of Selenites living on the Moon.

The most remarkable novel of the period, and perhaps the first modern space opera ever written, certainly the first interstellar epic in history, was without a doubt *Star, ou Psi de Cassiopée* (1854) by Charles-Ischir Defontenay.[18] This astonishing novel described in amazing details the long history of an alien civilization based on a far-off planet with three stars and five satellites. Not much was known about Defontenay, a French doctor who, a full forty years before H. G. Wells, wrote this remarkable science fiction novel, distinguished not only by its contents but by its mature, poetic, literary style, a far cry from the latter works of Verne and his followers.

Star opens with a poem, anticipating the "free verse" of the surrealists, describing the discovery in the Himalayas of a hollow meteor, which is revealed to be a cosmic cache of alien books and manuscripts. Once translated, these documents turn out to be a correspondence between two wise men from the far-off world of Star. Through them, we learn of the existence of a planetary system with four suns (including a red dwarf), one planet and five satellites. Defontenay's amazing powers of imagination provided us with wonderfully realistic descriptions of the alien seasons, flora and fauna of Star, including its *bramiles* and *psarginos*, and describe the slow progress of its inhabitants on the road to planetary civilization. Star is peopled by various races: the Savelces, the Treliors, the Ponarbates, etc. We witness their histories, their wars, their natural disasters and are offered a glimpse into their alien cultures. The Nemsedes" for example, are asexual beings who live for a thousand years, and use their wisdom for the benefit of other races. The Eras, on the other hand, are evil and use

---

[17] Black Coat Press, ISBN 978-1-61227-067-8.
[18] Black Coat Press, ISBN 978-1-932983-99-9.

devolution to enslave others. Finally, Defontenay tell us of the end of the Starrian civilization, brought about by a plague. But the novel does not end there. Some Starrians escape the plague and, using a starship powered by anti-gravity, flee to Tassul, the planet's inner satellite. (This device was very similar to Wells' "cavorite".) Eventually, overpopulation drive more Starrians to emigrate to Lessur, the second satellite, which turn out to be a living planetary organism. Two centuries later, other Starrians move to Rudar, the third satellite. Finally, the Starrians travel to the fourth moon, Elier, which is transparent and, therefore, uninhabitable. They eventually return to their homeworld, reconquer it, and establish a new interplanetary civilization, one that gather all the races and cultures they met during their cosmic travels.

The history of the Starrian race, as presented by Defontenay, is comprised of a collection of poems, plays and sagas culled from its various centuries. Their quality is such that they could be real poems from a real culture. In *Star*, Defontenay single-handedly anticipated many of the now-classic themes of space opera. His "Farewell to the Reader" shows that he was conscious of the originality, if not sheer uniqueness, of his novel. The expression "ahead of its times" barely began to describe *Star*. Unlike most of the novels of the period, it is still readable today, and was warmly greeted by the public when it was reprinted in 1972. One is tempted to speculate about the future of science fiction had *Star* been emulated instead of ignored... *Star Maker* in 1860, *Foundation* in 1900, *Dune* in 1920?

Famous astronomer, author and publisher Camille Flammarion popularized astronomy and cosmology, and was fascinated by the possibility of alien life. In *La Pluralité des Mondes Habités* [The Plurality of Inhabited Worlds] (1862), *Les Habitants de l'Autre Monde* [The Inhabitants of Another World] (1862) and *Les Mondes Imaginaires et les Mondes Réels* [Imaginary and Real Worlds] (1864), Flammarion speculated on the physiological properties of extraterrestrial life.

He was also one of the first writers to seriously study science fiction as a separate genre.

In 1865, the very year when Verne published his notorious *De la Terre à la Lune* [From the Earth to the Moon], two other writers also penned similar cosmic journeys.

Alexandre Dumas, the renowned author of *Les Trois Mousquetaires* [The Three Musketeers] and *Le Comte de Monte-Cristo* [The Count of Monte-Cristo] wrote a novella entitled "*Voyage à la Lune*" [Trip to the Moon], in which our satellite is reached by a spacecraft powered by a substance that is said to be "repelled" by the Earth.

The second notable writer to engage in interplanetary exploration was Achille Eyraud, with *Voyage à Vénus* [Voyage to Venus],[19] in which space travel was achieved through the use of "reaction engines" which some have construed as rockets. In fact, Eyraud used the recoil effect to propel his spacecraft; however, since the water expelled was recovered in a container towed behind the craft, it would not have been scientifically workable. On the planet Venus, his heroes discover a utopian society, in which the sexes are equal and solar-powered robots toil in the fields.

Two other "interplanetary" works of note were also published in 1865:

Henri de Parville published *Un Habitant de la Planète Mars* [An Inhabitant of the Planet Mars],[20] in which the calcified body of a Martian, taken away from the red planet by a comet a long time ago, is dug up and recovered in Colorado. Initially written as a hoax by the science correspondent of the French newspaper *Le Pays*, the story immediately caught the attention of Verne's publisher who released it in an expanded book version that included the minutes of the scientific commission summoned to investigate the phenomenon. Parville, a renowned 19th century scientific journalist, broke new ground regarding the possibilities of extraterrestrial life. By keeping

---

[19] Black Coat Press, ISBN 978-1-61227-005-0.
[20] Black Coat Press, ISBN 978-1-934543-45-0.

his straightforward narrative to a minimum, he achieved a striking combination of quasi-non-fiction and speculative ambition, developing a theory of life and the universe that was remarkably ahead of his time.

Baron Alfred d'Espiard de Colonge wrote *La Chute du Ciel ou Les Antiques Météores Planétaires* [They Fell from the Sky or Ancient Planetary Meteors] (1865), a pseudo-scientific treatise in which he hypothesized that life on Earth had originated on another planet and had traveled to our world as a result of a planetary collision.

Journeys to Other Lands

Ancient Atlantis was the subject of Belgian author Charles-Joseph de Grave's three-volume *République des Champs-Elysées ou Monde Ancien* [The Republic of the Elysean Fields, or The Ancient World] (1806), a pseudo-erudite treatise on the existence of an antediluvian world that preceded recorded history.

In the same vein, but a little later, Népomucène-Louis Lemercier wrote *L'Atlantiade, ou La Théogonie Newtonienne*, an epic poem published in 1812. And Godefroy de Roisel penned *Les Atlantes* [The Atlanteans] in 1874.

Swiss writer-artist Rodolphe Toepffer was not only a pioneer of comic books but was also one of the first modern writers to have introduced the concept of a "Lost World" in his prose novel *Voyages et Aventures du Docteur Festus* [Voyages & Adventures of Dr. Festus] (1833) (not to be confused with the eponymous graphic novel). In it, his hero flew above Antarctica where he spotted a mysterious land inhabited by prehistoric creatures.

Other notable works in this vein included:

Étienne Cabet's *Voyage et Aventures de Lord W. Carisdall en Icarie* [Voyage and Adventures of Lord W. Carisdall in Icaria] (1840), a communist utopia.

Isidore Grandville's *Un Autre Monde* [Another World] (1844), illustrated by "Taxile Delord" (a pseudonym of the author), revealed the existence of two intelligent subaquatic races, the Tritons and the Nereids, but was mostly remarkable for its illustrations. It probably was the first, fully illustrated science fiction novel.

In 1864, Henry de Kock's *Les Hommes Volants* [The Flying Men] was, to a large extent, a retread of Restif's *La Découverte Australe*.

Finally, in 1865, renowned author Amantine Lucile Aurore Dupin, a.k.a. George Sand, wrote *Laura ou le Voyage dans le Cristal* [Laura or The Voyage Inside the Crystal], in which Alexis, a young geologist, first mind-travels to a crystalline universe located inside a gem. Then, the hero embarks on a physical journey to reach the Center of the Earth—Verne's notorious novel had been published the preceding year—and, at the North Pole, discovers a warm-climate sea and a Lost World island inhabited by "living fossils", i.e.: long extinct creatures still alive. At the center of that island is a tall mountain where he eventually finds the passage leading to the Earth's Core.

Journeys to Other Times

The earliest and most notable work in this bold and fertile sub-genre was *Le Dernier Homme* [The Last Man] (1805) by Jean-Baptiste Cousin de Grainville, the first novel ever written on this now-popular theme. In it, the narrator meets an Incarnation of Time who tells him the saga of Omegare, the Last Man on Earth. A bleak vision of the future emerges, of a time when a dying Earth has become totally sterile. Omegare travels to Brazil where the last men have found refuge. Ormus, the God of the Earth, tries to manipulate Omegare to make him father a new race of monstrous cannibals, doomed to live in eternal darkness, but the vision of this awful future terrifies Omegare, who instead chooses death.

A number of startingly accurate predictions about the future were made in Pierre-Marc-Gaston de Levis' two-volume *Les Voyages de Kang-Hi, ou Nouvelles Lettres Chinoises* [Kang-Hi's Journeys, or New Chinese Letters] (1810), a proto-scientific anticipation which mentions the concepts of the Suez Canal, air conditioning, air pollution, and electric railways.

Strangely enough, the saga of Omegare, the Last Man on Earth, was not over, and gave rise to one of the first unauthorized sequels in literary history. In 1831, Auguste-François Creuzé de Lesser published an expanded version of Cousin de Grainville's work, including a description of aerial cities and a failed attempt by Mankind at leaving Earth to go and colonize another planet.

The character of Omegar (this time, spelled without an "e") returned again in *L'Unitéide ou la Femme Messie* [The Uniteide or The Messianic Woman] (1858), a complex philosophico-poetic saga, self-published by Paulin Gagne. *L'Unitéide* takes place in the year 2000, when, according to the author, there are only twelve countries. In it, God has sent the eponymous female messiah to save the world. The following year, Gagne's own wife, Élise Gagne, wrote *Omégar ou Le Dernier Homme* [*Omegar, or The Last Man*] (1859), yet another poetic epic about the final days of the Earth.

The future doom forecasted by Antoine-François Rey-Dussueil in *La Fin du Monde* [The End of the World] (1830) and *Le Monde Nouveau* [The New World] (1831) was a far more immediate prediction. In the first volume, Biela's 1832 comet pushes Earth off its axis, causing the ice to melt and the world to be flooded. A man and three women survive at the top of the Mont-Blanc. The building of massive Noah's Arks was a pretext for the author to criticize the politics of his time. The second novel was mostly political satire. While Rey-Dussueil failed to fully exploit the theme of a cosmic catastrophe bringing about the end of the world as we know it, he nevertheless earned the right to be considered the first serious "cataclysmic" author of the 19th century.

The future of Man was also a concern of Charles Nodier who, in 1833, penned *Hurlubleu*,[21] in which the hero, who already lives a hundred years in the future (i.e.: in 1933), is placed in suspended animation and is awakened 10,000 years later. What Nodier did was to tell the story of two different worlds: that of 1933, and that of the future kingdom of Hurlubière, located on a top-shaped Earth, made bigger by the inclusion of the Moon. In that far future, the hero embarks on a ten-year picaresque search for the perfect android, manufactured four thousand years before by the great scientist Zeretochthro-Schah.

More realistic was Félix Bodin's *Le Roman de l'Avenir* [The Novel of the Future] (1834).[22] A historian himself, Bodin wrote an amazing novel, for which he coined the term "futuristic literature." In it, he tried to predict the events of the late 20th century, allegedly revealed to him by an Italian magus. Some of his predictions included the devaluation of the currency, the growth in power of Northern Africa, the creation of the Panama Canal, the reform of Islam, flying fortresses and parachutes, the breakup of the Russian Empire, the creation of a new Babylonian Empire, and he creation of a Jewish State in Palestine.

The same year, Louis Desnoyers, in the last chapters of his four-volume *Paris Révolutionnaire* [The Paris Revolution] (1833-34), also attempted to predict what the future of the French capital would be, up to the end of the 19th century.

In 1841, Alexandre-Jean-Joseph de La Ville de Mirmont staged a futuristic play merely entitled *L'An 1928* [The Year 1928].

In 1846, Émile Souvestre published the ambitious *Le Monde Tel Qu'il Sera* [The World As It Will Be], a full-blown dystopia and scientific anticipation which featured some remarkable predictions. In it, Maurice and Marthe are taken to

---

[21] In *The Germans on Venus*, Black Coat Press, ISBN 978-1-934543-56-6.
[22] Black Coat Press, ISBN 978-1-934543-44-3.

the year 3000 by a man named "John Progress" on a flying, steam-powered, time-traveling locomotive. There, they find steam-powered metros, sub-marines, synthetic materials imitating real wood and marble, telephones, air conditioning, giant fruits and vegetables obtained through what we would call today genetic engineering, and more. The world is one, single state, the capital of which is Tahiti. As in Aldous Huxley's *Brave New World*, eugenics and genetic manipulation are used to manufacture new races of men tailored to specific tasks.

Other visions of the future published at that time included:

Joseph Déjacque's *L'Humanisphère* (1859),[23] an anarchist utopia.

Hippolyte Mettais' *L'An 5865* [The Year 5865] (1865),[24] a remarkable novel, consisting of a first-person narrative related by a character living 4000 years hence, after various disasters have obliterated almost all the documents relating to the world with which we are familiar. In consequence, the narrator's knowledge of the reader's world is severely limited and densely clouded by myth. His *Paris Avant le Déluge* [Paris Before the Deluge] (1866),[25] is a novel that incorporates the lost city of Atlantis, the biblical story of the Flood, and the founding of Paris. Set more than four thousand years in the past, it is a lesson about the rise and fall of civilizations with its credible mixture of exotic locales, spurned lovers, power grabs, lost dynasties and the constant quest for the favor of ancient gods. Within this mythological antediluvian world, the author unfolds a tale of religious and revolutionary sentiments that remains an important document in the history of French speculative fiction as well as the modern development of the Atlantis legend.

---

[23] Black Coat Press, ISBN 978-1-61227-511-6.
[24] Black Coat Press, ISBN 978-1-61227-100-2.
[25] Black Coat Press, ISBN 978-1-61227-328-0.

Samuel-Henry Berthoud's *L'Homme depuis Cinq Mille Ans* [Man for Five Thousand Years] (1865)[26] is a scientific novel about the History of Man which begins with a prehistoric prologue and ends with a grand finale taking place in the year 2865.

Fernand Giraudeau's prophetic *La Cité Nouvelle* [The New City] (1868),[27] a visionary dystopia describing the ultra-capitalistic world of 1998, and a society enslaved by the use of small steam or wind-powered motorcars.

Ernest Jonchère's *Clovis Bourbon: Excursion dans le 20ème Siècle* [Clovis Bourbon: Travel to the 20th Century] (1868).

Dr. Tony Moilin's *Paris en l'An 2000* [Paris in the Year 2000] (1869).[28] A year later, Moilin was charged with involvement in a plot to assassinate Napoleon III and sentenced to prison for five years. He was liberated during the Prussians' siege of Paris and enlisted in the National Guard as a surgeon. When the Commune took control of Paris, Moilin agreed to accept the position of Mayor of the 6th arrondissement. He was taken prisoner when the Commune fell, court-martialed, ostensibly for having accepted the administrative post, and summarily executed by firing-squad at age 39. The publication of *Paris en l'An 2000* was likely a factor in prompting the French authorities to trump up a charge and then execute him, for this scrupulous account of an ideal socialist society likely terrified his judges.

Alfred-Louis Franklin's *Les Ruines de Paris* [The Ruins of Paris] (1875),[29] in which archeologists from a future New Caledonian civilization from the year 4875 unearthed the ruins of Paris.

---

[26] In *Martyrs of Science*, Black Coat Press, ISBN 978-1-61227-229-0.

[27] In *The Humanisphere*, q.v.

[28] Black Coat Press, ISBN 978-1-61227-160-6.

[29] In *Investigations of the Future*, Black Coat Press, ISBN 978-1-61227-106-4.

Even the renowned writer Victor Hugo, in his poetic epic *La Légende des Siècles* [The Legend of the Centuries] (1859), felt obliged to write a section anticipating the 20th century.

It was a short leap from visions of the future to visions of alternate Earths, parallel histories and worlds that might have been. The first tale of a totally fictional, and yet real-sounding alternate universe, one in which Napoleon subdued Russia in 1812, invaded England in 1814 and went on to become the enlightened ruler of the world, was written by Louis Geoffroy in 1836. Entitled *Napoléon et la Conquête du Monde* [Napoleon and The Conquest of the World] (1812-32; then revised in 1841 as *Napoléon Apocryphe*),[30] it detailed with great and methodical precision the conquest of the world by the Emperor, and the technical and scientific achievements made by a united planet under Napoleon's wise leadership: electric-powered zeppelins, weather control, flying cars, typewriters (dubbed "writing pianos"), miracle cures, making sea water drinkable, the discovery of a new planet named Vulcan (!) and more.

In 1848, renowned author Théophile Gautier penned the novella "*Les Deux Étoiles*" [The Twin Stars] about a plan to rescue Napoleon from Saint Helena by sub-marine, and in 1851, "*Paris Futur*" [Future Paris].[31]

More elaborate was *Hurrah!!! Ou La Révolution par les Cosaques* [Hurrah!!! Or The Revolution of the Cossacks], published in French in London in 1854 by Ernest Coeurderoy. In it, the decadence of Western Europe was followed by an invasion of Barbarians from the North, the death of civilization as we know it and, finally, the glorious rebirth of a new socialist era led by the Cossacks and, behind them, the Asians. *Hurrah!!!* may well have the dubious honor of being the first "yellow peril" novel in genre history, followed closely by Belgian writer Iwan Gilkin's *Jonas* (1900).

---

[30] *The Apocryphal Napoleon*, Black Coat Press, ISBN 978-1-61227-579-6.

[31] In *Investigations of the Future*, q.v.

Also in 1854, Joseph Méry, the nearest French equivalent to Edgar Allan Poe as a ground-breaking pioneer of speculative fiction. imagined that Napoleon's life had taken a different turn in Egypt in 1799. *Histoire de ce qui n'est pas arrivé* [The Story of What Did Not Happen][32] reminds us that, in 1799, Napoleon Bonaparte launched sixty attacks on Saint-Jean-d'Acre and did not capture it. There was a tower there, nicknamed the "Infernal Tower," that resisted every assault. Bonaparte eventually lifted the siege, uttering these words, which no one understood: "The fate of the world resides in that tower." But what if Saint-Jean-d'Acre had fallen? Bonaparte could have become Emperor of India, and History would not have recorded neither Austerlitz, nor Waterloo. The "Infernal Tower" was the Tower of Destiny, *Turris fatidica*.

Other notable genre stories by Méry include "*La Verité sur la Creation*" [The Truth About Creation] (1836), which argues in a mock-serious manner that there is nothing supernatural about God; s creation of the world; "*Les Lunariens*" [The Lunarians] (1836), inspired by the *New York Sun*'s famous Moon hoax of 1835, which offers a colorful picture of a Selenite civilization; "*Les Explorations de Victor Hummer*" [The Explorations of Victor Hummer] (1836), which describes the rediscovery of a mythical city in Egypt; "*Ce qu'on verra*" [What We Shall See] (18236), which outlines the Utopian prospects of future human progress, and "*Les Ruines de Paris*" [The Ruins of Paris] (1836), which includes some striking imagery of a future Paris.[33]

---

[32] Published as *The Tower of Destiny*, Black Coat Press, ISBN 978-1-61227-101-9.
[33] All in *The Tower of Destiny*, q.v.

Jules Verne

And then came Jules Verne and everything changed forever.

Verne made his genre beginnings with two novellas entitled "*Un Voyage en Ballon*" [A Voyage in a Balloon], an adventure tale published in 1851, and "*Maître Zacharius*", a fantasy featuring a clockmaker and the Devil, published in 1854. Verne's literary influences were Edgar Allan Poe, from whom he drew his sense of wonder and the ability to project the cold light of scientific logic upon the wildest of notions, Victor Hugo for his romantic spirit, and Alexandre Dumas, for his sense of melodrama and adventure.

In 1850, Verne had a non-genre play, *Les Pailles Rompues* [The Broken Straws], produced at Dumas' own *Theâtre Historique* in Paris. And in 1897, he penned his own sequel to Poe's *Narrative of Arthur Gordon Pym* entitled *Le Sphinx des Glaces* [The Sphinx of the Ice]. It is also worth noting that Verne, who was born in the Atlantic port city of Nantes, had tried to embark on a ship when he was young.

Verne burst onto the literary scene with the serialized version of *Cinq Semaines en Ballon* [Five Weeks in a Balloon], the tale of a Trans-African balloon journey, published in 1863 in a magazine founded by visionary publisher Pierre-Jules Hetzel, who immediately realized Verne's enormous potential.

Strangely, Verne and Hetzel's relationship began with a rejection. The second novel—or more appropriately novella—submitted by Verne to Hetzel in 1863 was entitled *Paris au 20ème Siècle* [Paris in the 20th Century]. It was a grim, Orwellian story about a young poet, Michel, who desperately tries to fit into a soulless, technological society dominated by huge corporations, and who, having failed in his efforts, eventually dies from the cold, homeless.

The handwritten manuscript of *Paris in the 20th Century* was found by accident in 1994 by Verne's great grandson, Jean, in a forgotten safe that had belonged to Verne's son, Michel. The safe's key had been lost, but this had been deemed unimportant, since the strong box was believed to be empty. The manuscript was thoroughly checked by experts who unanimously pronounced it authentic. A further proof of its veracity comes from the fact that its margins bore numerous, handwritten annotations by Hetzel, who had rejected it, telling the 35 years-old author to return to writing adventure stories.

One can better understand Hetzel's rejection because, even though *Paris in the 20th Century* was a stunning display of forecasting, probably unique and towering in the annals of science-fiction, it nevertheless was a meandering, mawkish, sentimental novel, even by the standards of the times. Yet, in it, Verne foresaw a world suffering from overpopulation, illiteracy, pollution and deforestation, a world where wars were no longer waged by vast armies but by powerful machines, a world of political apathy, unemployment and homeless people dying from the cold. Uncannily, these predictions even included accurate descriptions of music made with synthesizers, staged sitcoms produced by teams of writers, male fashion (long hair) and single-parent families.

The technology prophesied by Verne was as incredibly accurate as that of his society. He depicted a fully electrified Paris where streets were jammed with automobiles (proudly and accurately detailing their principles and operation!) and where commuters piled themselves into elevated trains. Some of today's metro stations are exactly as foreseen. The offices contained elevators, computers (giant calculating machines), photocopiers, faxes (!) and even automated alarm systems, which could trap would-be burglars, and the electric chair was the preferred means of capital punishment. Verne even mentioned a 500-foot-tall lighthouse dominating Paris' skyline and built on the very same spot where the Eiffel Tower was erected 26 years later!

In order to fully appreciate all these staggering predictions, one must recall that, at the time the book was written, America was in the throes of the Civil War. Gasoline-powered engines were developed in 1864 (even though the principles were known since 1859), typewriters were introduced in 1867, telephones in 1876, phonographs in 1877, filament lightbulbs in 1879, the electric chair in 1888, and the Paris Metro in 1898.

Paris in the 20th Century goes against the traditional view of Jules Verne, which often contrast him with H. G. Wells, as the provider of thrilling but somewhat superficial adventure stories heralding the wonder of future science. Instead, as early as 1863, Verne saw the 20th century as a foreboding time, when technology and money would eradicate literature and poetry. In a satirical scene from the book, a librarian cannot fulfill the hero's request for a novel by Victor Hugo, having never heard of him!

As mentioned above, this was not the type of novel Hetzel expected! As he put it in his rejection letter: "You undertook an impossible task, and you did not pull it off. Nobody will ever believe your prophecies." Meekly, the author followed his publisher's advice, buried the manuscript in a drawer and never returned to it, only cannibalizing an occasional idea or quote for his later works.

Verne's first, full-blown genre novel was therefore the enormously successful *Voyage au Centre de la Terre* [Journey to the Center of the Earth] (1864), which introduced all the elements which became characteristic of his style, and indeed of much of later science fiction: An initial fantastic concept, a thrilling adventure, a sense of wonder, some wonderful vistas, a few momentary views into even more fantastic elements, but always careful to not go too far in order to never become unbelievable.

For example, in this novel, the heroes cross a vast, inner sea and glimpse the occasional living, prehistoric monster, but nothing more. In a startling break with the past, and in a fashion that has since become a hallmark of science fiction writers, Verne was always careful to strive for believability before all. Another of his archetypal contributions to the genre was the character of the daring, often eccentric, even renegade, scientist-hero, whose genius is doubted by his peers, but whose will and boundless curiosity drives the plot forward. Professor Liddenbrock from *Journey to the Center of the Earth* was but the first in a very long line of similar characters, who are still being used today.

De la Terre à la Lune [From the Earth to the Moon] (1865) and its sequel, *Autour de la Lune* [Around the Moon] (1870), became the seminal works on spaceflight in the 19th century, inspiring Tsiolkovsky, Goddard, Oberth, Von Braun and Gagarin. In it, a group of American industrialists devise a scheme to fire a cannon shell to the Moon from the fictional Stony Hill, located near Tampa, Florida, less than a hundred miles from Cape Canaveral. The shell eventually carries three passengers, including the French adventurer, Michel Ardan. The spacecraft orbit the Moon, upon which the remains of an ancient civilization can be glimpsed, then return safely to Earth.

In *From the Earth to the Moon*, Verne did his scientific homework. No less an authority than Professor Von Braun stated that his calculations were "nearly as accurate as the knowledge at the time permitted." While it was true that the passengers would have been crushed by the acceleration, Verne was well aware of this and even voiced these objections himself in the novel. But he was striving for believability, in effect deliberately sacrificing scientific accuracy for the sake of fictional verisimilitude. Again, his was a process that became characteristic of science fiction writers. Had he chosen to use rockets, by the standards of the times, he would have had to make his craft either a huge powder keg, or combine tens of thousands of small rockets, both of which would have been deemed ludicrous by his audiences. In any event, his accurate foretelling of space travel far outweighed any purposeful liberties that he took.

The success of *From the Earth to the Moon* was enormous and proved that Verne's approach was right. The story was further popularized in an 1875 Offenbach opera whose libretto, and the classic 1902 film by Georges Méliès, *Le Voyage dans la Lune* [A Trip to the Moon].

In 1867, Hetzel granted Verne his own imprint dubbed "*Voyages Extraordinaires*" [Extraordinary Voyages], a first in publishing history. For almost forty years thereafter, Verne continued to produce a regular, steady flow of novels.

His next seminal work was *Vingt Mille Lieues sous les Mers* [Twenty Thousand Leagues Under the Sea] (1870) which, with its sequel, *L'Île Mystérieuse* [Mysterious Island] (1875), introduced the character of Captain Nemo. Nemo has since joined the ranks of Sherlock Holmes, Tarzan, and Superman, as one of the most famous modern fictional characters. He is a Byronesque figure: a brilliant scientist, an adventurer, a loner beyond the reaches of man's society, a law unto himself, like Dumas' Count of Monte-Cristo, a man so wronged that he is willing to commit unspeakable deeds in the name of revenge. Nemo is an avenger who stands for freedom and justice, almost an anarchist, virtually a modern anti-hero.

The prodigious odyssey of Professor Arronax and harpooner Ned Land aboard Nemo's nuclear-powered submarine, the *Nautilus*—a name as well known today as *Star Trek*'s *Enterprise*, and which was given by the US Navy in homage to Verne to the world's first nuclear submarine in 1954—is too well known to need retelling. In addition to the various technological wonders described therein, from deep sea diving suits to navigating under the North Pole, one should mention the glimpses of sunken Atlantis seen by its heroes.

Other significant Verne novels included *Les Indes Noires* [The Child of the Cavern] (1877), a story about an underground civilization; *Hector Servadac* (1877), in which an inhabited piece of Earth (located near Algeria) is carried away after a collision with a small asteroid, christened Gallia by its unwilling passengers. During its eccentric orbit, which takes them as far as Saturn, one of the travelers, an astronomer, calculate the precise moment when Gallia will swing by Earth again. Then, using a makeshift hot air balloon, they return to our world. *Hector Servadac* accurately described the physical conditions of life on a planetoid, the problems of survival in deep space, and the beautiful, cosmic vistas of Jupiter and Saturn. *Sans Dessus Dessous* [Topsy Turvy] (1889) saw the return of the gun-loving protagonists of *From the Earth to the Moon*, and features a crazy scheme to move the Earth off its axis.

Robur le Conquérant [Robur the Conqueror] (1886), and its sequel, *Maître du Monde* [Master of the World] (1904), were variations on a theme already explored with Nemo, except that, in this case, it was a flying machine, the *Albatros*, not a submarine, that terrorized the world. Its creator was quite unlike the romantic Nemo: the steely, grim, megalomaniacal Engineer Robur, who becomes a dangerous madman in the second volume, represents the dangers of unfettered science. Robur was one of the first mad scientists in science fiction, and his plan to make himself "Master of the World" was to become one of the most notorious genre clichés of all times.

In *Face au Drapeau* [*Facing the Flag*] (1896), Verne's fictional inventor Thomas Roch designs a rocket-powered missile intended to be launched from a submarine, the first time this military device was created. Amusingly, the real-life French chemist Eugene Turpin, a pioneer of rocket engineering, enraged by what he saw as unpleasant similarities between him and the fictional Roch, sued the writer for libel, and lost.

The pessimism that had originally been present in *Paris in the 20th Century* and suppressed during most of Verne's prolific career, resurfaced in tales like the short story "*L'Éternel Adam*" [The Eternal Adam], written in 1905, but published only in the collection *Hier et Demain* [Yesterday & Tomorrow] in 1910. In it, a far future historian discovers that our civilization was destroyed by a cataclysm, and that Adam and Eve are cyclical reoccurrences.

In *L'Étonnante Aventure de la Mission Barsac* [The Amazing Adventure of the Barsac Mission], written in 1903, but published only in 1910, a scientist was shown to be unwittingly working on various nefarious projects in a hidden scientific city.

On the other hand, *La Chasse au Météore* [The Chase of the Golden Meteor], written in 1902, published in 1908, was a lighthearted romp in which the delightful eccentric scientist Zephyrin Xirdal finds a way to cause a meteor made of gold to crash to Earth. And *Le Secret de Wilhelm Storitz* [The Secret of Wilhelm Storitz], written in 1902, published in 1910, was a beautiful, romantic novel on the theme of invisibility, in which the invisible heroine is finally able to become visible again after giving birth to her child.

It is impossible to underestimate the impact of Jules Verne on modern science fiction. As we have seen, many of the classic themes had already appeared sporadically in before him, and he did not so much *create* as *reshape*. Defontenay and a few others may have been more brilliant, more visionary, and better writers, but it was Verne who reached the masses, who popularized the concepts of science fiction, and gave them their modern form.

Like Robert Heinlein much later, Verne made scientific anticipation popular with both younger and older readers. He came to exert such a powerful influence on the genre that it can safely be claimed that, without him, there would be no science fiction at all. The Luxembourg-born father of modern American science fiction, Hugo Gernsback, was a fan of Verne and published translations of his stories in his magazine *Modern Electrics* starting in 1908, which eventually led to the creation of *Amazing Stories* in 1926.

In France, Verne cast an enormous shadow on the entire genre, until World War II. His undeniably huge commercial success also created an industry virtually overnight. It can be claimed that, by tying science fiction to the juvenile market,

Verne contributed to the fostering of a typical French cultural prejudice towards the genre, claiming that it could not be a mature form of literature. Yet, before him, science fiction novels were few and far between, usually the result of some writer's lonely attempt at breaking new ground. After Verne, however, we see the emergence of a true literary phenomenon, where one can no longer pick a few isolated titles along thematic lines, but is forced to look at an entire industry, the output of which numbers in the hundreds. With Jules Verne, the Golden Age of French science fiction had begun.

The Golden Age
(1860-1914)

The imprint devoted to Verne, *Voyages Extraordinaires* (1867-1910) was but the first of a series of imprints that contributed to create the Golden Age of French science fiction. Other similar pre-World War I imprints which followed included:

Romans d'Aventures [Adventure Novels] (1884-1905), also published by Hetzel, devoted mostly to Verne's occasional collaborator, André Laurie.

Voyages Scientifiques Extraordinaires [Extraordinary Scientific Voyages] (1892-94), published by Arthème Fayard and featuring works by Georges Le Faure.

Les Grandes Aventures [Great Adventures] (1888-1900), published by Ernest Flammarion and featuring works by Louis Boussenard.

Le Roman d'Aventures [Adventure Novels] (1908-11), later retitled *Les Récits Mystérieux* [Mysterious Tales] (1912-14), published by Albert Méricant and featuring works by Gustave Le Rouge and Paul d'Ivoi.

In a more popular vein, we find publisher Jules Tallandier's *Romans d'Aventures et d'Explorations* [Novels of Adventure & Exploration] (1900-1920) and *Romans Populaires* [Popular Novels] (1900-1935), which featured numerous genre works by Boussenard and Jean de La Hire.

Finally, the Golden Age of French science fiction also included numerous illustrated pulp magazines such as the monumental weekly *Le Journal des Voyages* [The Journal of Voyages] which started in 1875 as *Sur Terre & Mer* [On Land & On Sea], then adopted its definitive title in 1877. Its publishing history lasted more than seventy years: 1st series (1877-1896), 1012 issues published; 2nd series (1896-1915):

941 issues published; 3rd series (1924-25): 29 issues published; 4th series (1925-29): 159 issues published; and finally, 5th series (1946-1949): 149 issues published. This chauvinistic, sometimes xenophobic, yet visionary magazine, serialized novels by Boussenard, d'Ivoi, René Thévenin, Albert Bonneau (writing as "Maurice Champagne"), Gaston and the notorious , Capitaine Danrit.

Other pre-World War I magazines of note included:

La Science Illustrée [Illustrated Science] (1887-1905), edited by Adolphe Bitard then the influential Louis Figuier, that featured works by Boussenard, Flammarion, Albert Robida and H. G. Wells.

The monthly *Lectures Pour Tous* [Reading for All] (1898-1940), 581 issues in all, published by Louis Hachette featured works by J.-H. Rosny Aîné, Octave Béliard, Raoul Bigot and Albert Bailly.

Its direct competitor, the monthly *Je Sais Tout*"[I Know Everything] (1905-39), published by Pierre Lafitte featured works by J.-H. Rosny Aîné, Gaston Leroux and Maurice Renard.

Finally, *L'Épatant* [Amazing] (1908-37) and *L'Intrépide* [Fearless] (1910-37), subtitled "Adventures, Voyages & Explorations," both published by the Offenstadt brothers, and aimed at young adults, published a successful mix of comics and adventure novels, including works by José Moselli, Pierre Adam, André Falcoz (writing as Élie Montfort) and Guy d'Armen. The company eventually became the Société Parisienne d'Édition and *L'Épatant* returned as a full-blown comic book from 1951-69; *L'Intrépide* was sold to Cino Del Duca and also returned as a comic book from 1948-62.

Major Authors

Of all the authors who followed in the footsteps of Jules Verne, perhaps the most important was Albert Robida, a writer/artist who also deserves a place in genre history as the founding father of science fiction illustration, with the possible exception of Isidore Grandville, mentioned above) Robida not only illustrated genre stories by Rabelais, Cyrano de Bergerac and Flammarion, but he also wrote and illustrated his own scientific anticipations, starting with a deliberate homage to Verne entitled *Voyages Très Extraordinaires de Saturnin Farandoul dans les 5 ou 6 Parties du Monde et dans tous les Pays Connus et même Inconnus de M. Jules Verne* [The Very Extraordinary Voyages of Saturnin Farandoul in the 5 or 6 Continents of the World and in all the Lands Known or Even Unknown to M. Jules Verne], a *Voyage Extraordinaire*-like novel serialized over a hundred issues in 1879 and later collected in a single volume in 1883.[34]

Robida's masterpiece of scientific anticipation was *Le Vingtième Siècle* [The 20th Century], a *Dinotopia*-type of book, serialized in 50-plus issues in 1882-83, and entirely devoted to the visual description of scenes of daily life of the mid-to-late 1950s. The author proved constantly inventive in the imagining of futuristic devices, such as videophones, flying taxis, etc. The book also included the idea of the Moon being drawn closer to the Earth by a battery of giant magnets, which may have later influenced André Laurie's *Les Exilés de la Terre* [Exiled from Earth]. So popular was *Le Vingtième Siècle* that Robida continued in this same vein with *La Guerre au Vingtième Siècle* [War in the 20th Century] (1883),[35] set in 1975, and *La Vie Électrique* [Electric Life] (1890),[36] set in 1955, which offered more of his satirical, pessimistic view of the future, and often contained frighteningly accurate predictions, such as the possibility of germ warfare.

But Robida was not only a gifted artist and the author of remarkable scientific anticipations. In a startlingly different vein, he also wrote a classic novel, *L'Horloge des Siècles* [The

---

[34] Black Coat Press, ISBN 978-1-934543-61-0.
[35] In *Engineer Von Satanas*, Black Coat Press, ISBN 978-1-61227-425-6.
[36] Black Coat Press, ISBN 978-1-61227-182-8.

Clock of the Centuries] (1902),[37] in which time started running backwards, the dead came back to life and the entire human society was thrown into utter chaos. The novel stopped when time had regressed to the battle of Waterloo and remained one of the most striking novels ever written on this classic theme, later explored in Philip K. Dick's *Counterclock World* (1967), among others.

Other notable works by Robida included was *L'Ingénieur von Satanas* [Engineer Von Satanas] (1919)[38] written four years after World War I, which is still relevant today because the threats it describes still exist and still serve as a significant motor of anxiety in contemporary science fiction, and *Un Chalet dans les Airs* [Chalet in the Sky] (1925),[39] his last novel and literary swan song, in which he boldly steps into the far future when Man has emigrated to other worlds and depicts the travels of a colorful cast of characters aboard their aerial villa above a bleak and exhausted Earth.

André Laurie was another of publisher Hetzel's discoveries, and had collaborated with Verne on *Les Cinq Cent Millions de la Begum* [The 500 Millions of the Begum] (1879), *L'Étoile du Sud* [The Southern Star] (1884) and *L'Épave du Cynthia* [Salvage from the Cynthia] (1885). Prior to this, Laurie's political activities on behalf of the Commune had caused him to temporarily exile himself to England. One of his most interesting genre novels was *Les Exilés de la Terre, Séléné Company Ltd.* [Exiled from Earth] (1887), probably one of the most fanciful cosmic tales of all times. In it, a consortium which intended to exploit the Moon's mineral resources decides that, since our satellite is too far to be reached, it must be brought closer to the Earth. A Sudanese mountain composed of pure iron ore becomes the headquarters of the newly established Selene Company. Solar reflectors are used to provide the energy required to convert the mountain into a huge elec-

---

[37] Black Coat Press, ISBN 978-1-934543-13-9.
[38] Black Coat Press, q.v.
[39] Black Coat Press, ISBN 978-1-93555887-3.

tro-magnet, with miles of cables wrapped around it. A spaceship-cum-observatory is built on top of that mountain. When the experiment begins, the mountain is ripped away from the Earth and catapulted to the Moon. There, the protagonists have various adventures and eventually return to Earth by re-energizing the mountain.

Other notable works by Laurie include *De New York à Brest en Sept Heures* [New York to Brest in Seven Hours] (1888), which predicted a transatlantic tunnel; *Le Secret du Mage* [The Secret of the Magician] (1890), in which evidence of an advanced antediluvian civilization was discovered; *Le Rubis du Grand Lama* [The Ruby of the Great Lama] (1894), which featured a steam-powered flying island; *Atlantis* (1895), which described how the mythical kingdom survived under a glass dome at the bottom of the sea near the Azores; *Le Maître de l'Abîme* [The Master of the Abyss] (1905), featuring a revolutionary sub-marine; and finally *Spiridon le Muet* [Spiridon The Mute] (1907), a remarkable novel about a human-sized, intelligent ant.[40]

In it, a young surgeon, Dr. Cordat, discovers an island off the coast of Corsica inhabited by intelligent ants. Their king, Spiridon, is remarkably brilliant and converses with Cordat through telepathy. Curious about human society, Spiridon travels to Paris with Cordat. There, using his advanced knowledge, he becomes a famous doctor effecting seemingly miraculous cure. However, jealous competitors unmask him. Forced to protect himself, Spiridon reveals his alien nature and is forced to kill. Eventually wounded, Spiridon loses his intelligence on the operating table. The character of Spiridon, depicted as a non-human alien, gifted with great knowledge, an insatiable scientific curiosity, but no human feelings or emotions, the victim of mankind's petty jealousies and racial fears, was a striking departure from the Vernian influence that permeated the rest of Laurie's works.

---

[40] Black Coat Press, ISBN 978-1-934543-61-3.

Another thriving successor to Jules Verne was Louis Boussenard whose popular adventure novels were serialized in the *Journal des Voyages*. His most memorable novels were *Les Secrets de Monsieur Synthèse* [The Secrets of Mr. Synthesis] (1888) and its sequel, *Dix Mille Ans dans un Bloc de Glace* [Ten Thousand Years in an Ice Block] (1889).[41] In the former, we are introduced to Mr. Synthesis, a mad scientist who seeks to control the evolution of Man and then modify the orbit of the Earth. In the latter, Mr. Synthesis wakes up from ten thousand years of hibernation in a future where Earth is now inhabited by the Cerebrals, little men gifted with huge mental powers, descended from Chinese and Africans.

Other notable Boussenard novels included *Les Français au Pole Nord* [The Frenchmen at the North Pole] (1893); *L'Île en Feu* [Island on Fire] (1898), which featured a liquid hydrogen-propelled dirigible, and *Les Gratteurs de Ciel* [The Sky Scrapers] (1908), an aerial saga in which super-powered dirigibles fight with nuclear grenades that anticipate tactical nuclear devices.

The four-volume *Les Aventures Extraordinaires d'un Savant Russe* [The Extraordinary Adventures of a Russian Scientist] (1888-96) by Georges Le Faure and Henry de Graffigny was a much more ambitious cosmic saga.[42] Introduced by Camille Flammarion, it told the story of the exploration of the solar system and beyond. Both authors were familiar with rocket science; in 1904, De Graffigny had actually designed a rocket-powered model airplane and, in 1915, he had proposed catapulting a capsule into orbit using centrifugal force. Their scientific speculations were therefore more advanced than Verne's. In the first volume, a spaceship is launched from a canon built inside a volcano, the explosive being the suddenly released lava. The heroes protect themselves against the accel-

---

[41] Both in *Mr. Synthesis*, Black Coat Press, ISBN 978-1-61227-161-3.
[42] Two volumes, Black Coat Press, ISBNs 978-1-934543-81-8 and 978-1-934543-82-5.

eration with mattresses. The ship is made of a nickel-magnesium alloy. Oxygen is stored in tablet form and carbon dioxide is removed with potassium hydroxide. Electricity provides light and heat.

Once on the Moon, the travelers switch to a jet-propelled craft. Their subsequent flight takes them to Venus, and then to Mercury, this time using the pressure of solar winds onto a hollow craft. The heroes then continue their journey on a fragment of Mercury torn away by a comet. As it passes near Phobos, which is atmospherically connected to Mars, they travel in a balloon down to the Red Planet, wearing pressure suits. The protagonists then go from Mars to Jupiter in a barrel-shaped, reaction-powered starship, which sucks in cosmic debris at one end and expels it at the other. Another remarkable prediction was a means of communication between planets through beams of light picked up and modulated through selenium photocells.

Le Faure was also singly responsible for a number of Vernian adventure novels such as *Quinze Mille Lieues dans l'Espace* [Fifteen Thousand Leagues in Space] (1893) and *Les Robinsons Lunaires* [Robinsons of the Moon] (1893), in which a propellor-driven airship crashes on the Moon, as well as a number of militaristic anticipations. De Graffigny, still inspired by cosmic journeys, penned *De La Terre aux Etoiles* [From the Earth to the Stars] (1887), in which Earthmen travel to the Moon, then to Venus, and then aboard a comet throughout the Solar System; and *La Ville Aérienne* [The Aerial City] (1910), about a flying city.

By far the most commercially prosperous and influential successor of Verne was Paul d'Ivoi, whose 21-volume series, "*Les Voyages Excentriques*" [Eccentric Voyages] was published by Charles Furne between 1894 and 1914, often after being first serialized in *Le Journal des Voyages*. His best-known book is an *Around the World in 80 Days* variant entitled *Les Cinq Sous de Lavarède* [Lavarède's Five Sous]

(1894),[43] the first in the series, in which the young and daring Armand Lavarède embarks on a Phileas Fogg-like journey around the world with only five pennies in his pocket.

Lavarède returned in more genre-oriented stories such as *Cousin de Lavarède* [Lavarede's Cousin] (1897), which featured a super-powered flying speedster. D'Ivoi's novels were more adventure-oriented, pulpish, and faster-paced than Verne's, but they did include a number of futuristic vehicles, weapons and gadgets. Their heroes circumnavigated the globe, in the air or under the oceans, fought a variety of mad scientists, international conspiracies and megalomaniacal tyrants, and even discovered evidence of advanced, ancient civilizations.

Among the most notable volumes of the series were *Corsaire Triplex* [Corsair Triplex] (1898), a variation on *Twenty Thousand Leagues Under The Sea*; *Docteur Mystère* [Doctor Mystery] (1900),[44] with its plethora of deadly gadgets; *Miss Mousqueterr* [Miss Musketeer] (1907),[45] in which light is used as an all-purpose weapon by Violet Mousqueterr and her companions to defeat a secret Hindu cult; *L'Aéroplane Fantôme* [The Phantom Airplane] (1910); and *Les Dompteurs de l'Or* [The Gold Tamers] (1913),[46] featuring a mind-control device. D'Ivoi also collaborated with Colonel Royet on several other serials.

Clearly, not all genre writers of the times felt compelled to imitate Jules Verne. The prolific Jules Lermina, the author of several Poe-inspired collections of fantastic tales, was one of them. In his short story "*À Brûler (Conte Astral)*" [To Be Burned (An Astral Tale)] (1888), he introduced a secret society of Hindu sorcerers who have inherited the scientific secrets

---

[43] *Around the World on Five Sous*, Black Coat Press, ISBN 978-1-61227-369-3.

[44] Black Coat Press, ISBN 978-1-64932-128-2.

[45] Coat Press, ISBN 978-1-64932-108-4.

[46] To be published by Black Coat Press in 2023 under the title *The Knight of Illusions*.

of Atlantis, a theme later developed by Talbot Mundy. *Le Secret des Zippelius* [The Secret of Zippelius] (1893)[47] featured the controlled disintegration of water. The two-volume *La Bataille de Strasbourg* [The Battle of Strasbourg] (1895)[48] was one of the first novels on the infamous theme of the "yellow peril." In it, a scientist uses telluric energy to fight the invading Asian hordes. In *L'Effrayante Aventure* [The Frightful Adventure] (1910),[49] Lermina uses Edward Bulwer-Lytton's vril-force (borrowed from *The Coming Race* (1871)) to create a vril-powered flying machine. The novel also features the resurrection of prehistoric monsters frozen in ice in caverns under Paris. His most interesting novel is *Mystère-Ville* [Mysteryville] (1905),[50] written under the pseudonym of William Cobb, and illustrated by Robida. In it, Lermina postulates that protestants who fled from French persecution created a secret, futuristic city in a hidden Chinese valley. The so-called "Mysteryville" uses advanced technology based on the properties of sound and light.

In *To-Ho Le Tueur d'Or* [*To-Ho and the Gold Destroyers*] (1905),[51] during the bloody Dutch-Aceh War in Sumatra at the end of the 19th century, ten-year-old George Villiers is about to be sacrificed by a Malay witch doctor when he is rescued by To-Ho, the member of a peaceful tribe of ape-men who secretly live hidden in the jungle. George is then raised among the ape-men, and meets a reclusive scientist who has developed a compound, phoebium, which destroys gold, hoping to save the tribe from hordes of invading prospectors who threaten their isolation. *To-Ho* was first published in *Le Journal des Voyages*. Its tribe of ape-men and the story of the human boy which they rescue and raise as their own predate Edgar Rice Burroughs' *Tarzan* by seven years.

---

[47] Black Coat Press, ISBN 978-1-935558-88-0.
[48] Black Coat Press, ISBN 978-1-61227-324-2.
[49] *Panic in Paris*, Black Coat Press, ISBN 978-1-934543-83-2.
[50] Black Coat Press, ISBN 978-1-935558-27-9.
[51] Black Coat Press, ISBN 978-1-935558-34-7.

In the traditional field of popular adventure serials, Jean de La Hire and Gustave Le Rouge dominated the period. La Hire created the first superhero, Leo Saint-Clair, a.k.a. the Nyctalope, which continued to delight audiences through pure, unbridled science fiction adventures until the mid-1950s. The Nyctalope made his first appearance in *Le Mystère des XV* [The Mystery of the XV] (1911),[52] in which a mad scientist called Oxus tries to conquer Mars; there is even a crossover with Wells' *War of the Worlds*. Technically, the series began with *L'Homme Qui Peut Vivre dans l'Eau* [The Man Who Could Live Underwater] (1908) in which Oxus grafts a shark's gills onto a man, christened the Hyctaner, and tries to conquer the world, but is foiled by Jean, Leo Saint-Clair's father. The Nyctalope returned in *Lucifer* (1920).[53] In it, another megalomaniacal scientist, Glo von Warteck, tries to take over the world by using his "Omega Rays" and "teledyname". In *Le Maître de la Vie* [The Master of Life] (1938),[54] Leo Saint-Clair faces a mysterious foe who has the power to kill remotely by the simple exercise of his will. In *Belzébuth* (1930), the villainous Mezarek sends the Nyctalope's wife and son into the future, to the year 2100. On the eve of World War II, in *Le Maître de la Vie* [The Master of Life] (1938),[55] the Nyctalope, faces one of his deadliest enemies: a mysterious and unidentified foe who has the power to kill remotely by the simple exercise of his will. To find, unmask and neutralize this "Master of Life", the Nyctalope and his friends must engage in a supreme battle of wits that takes them from a French spa to the far corners of the world—a forbidden lamasery in the heart of Tibet where the answers to all their questions lie. In *Le Roi de*

---

[52] *The Nyctalope on Mars*, Black Coat Press, ISBN 978-1-934543-46-7.
[53] *The Nyctalope vs Lucifer*, Black Coat Press, ISBN 978-1-932983-98-2.
[54] Black Coat Press, ISBN 978-1-64932-116-9.
[55] Black Coat Press, ISBN 978-1-64932-116-9.

la Nuit [The King of the Night] (1943),[56] the Nyctalope flies to Rhea, a wandering planetoid which has gotten close to Earth, and settles a war between day-siders and night-siders.[57]

La Hire was also the author of *La Roue Fulgurante* [The Fiery Wheel] (1908),[58] a proto- space opera in which five Earthmen are abducted by the eponymous "fiery wheel"—a flying saucer—and taken to Mercury by aliens who look like columns of light; and *Le Corsaire Sous-Marin* [The Underwater Corsair] (1912-13), a 79-issue Vernian serial.

Gustave Le Rouge's archetypal mad scientist saga, *Le Mystérieux Dr. Cornélius* [The Mysterious Dr. Cornelius], was serialized in 18 small volumes 1912-13.[59] Dr. Cornelius Kramm and his brother, Fritz, rule an international criminal empire called the Red Hand. Cornelius is a brilliant surgeon, nicknamed the "Sculptor of Human Flesh" because of his diabolical ability to alter people's likenesses through the science of "carnoplasty". His growing, global, evil web eventually causes the creation of an alliance of heroes, who band together to defeat the Lords of the Red Hand.

Prior to this, Le Rouge, with Gustave Guitton, had written *La Conspiration des Milliardaires* [The Billionaires' Conspiracy] (1899-1900),[60] in which American billionaire William Boltyn uses technology and the power of mediums to try to become master of the world. *Les Conquérants de la Mer* [The Conquerors of the Sea], *La Princesse des Airs* [Princess of the

---

[56] In *Return of the Nyctalope*, Black Coat Press, ISBN 978-1-61227-211-5.

[57] A companion volume, *Nyctalope! L'Univers Extravagant de Jean de La Hire*, edited by Emmanuel Gorlier, was published by Rivière Blanche in 2011.

[58] Black Coat Press, ISBN 978-1-61227-217-7.

[59] Three volumes, Black Coat Press, ISBNs 978-1-61227-243-6, 978-1-61227-244-3 and 978-1-61227-245-0.

[60] *The Dominion of the World* (four volumes), Black Coat Press, ISBNs 978-1-61227-095-1, 978-1-61227-096-8, 978-1-61227-097-5 and 978-1-61227-098-2.

Airs] and *Le Sous-Marin Jules Verne* [The Submarine Jules Verne], all written in collaboration with Guitton and published in 1902, were Vernian-inspired adventure serials featuring a variety of futuristic vehicles and colorful, larger-than-life villains. Without Guitton, Le Rouge also penned *L'Espionne du Grand Lama* [The Spy of the Great Lama] (1906), which featured a Lost World inhabited by prehistoric creatures, and *La Reine des Éléphants* [The Queen of Elephants] (1906) about a society of intelligent elephants.

Le Rouge's masterpiece, however, is without a doubt *Le Prisonnier de la Planète Mars* [The Prisoner of Planet Mars] (1908) and its sequel, *La Guerre des Vampires* [The War of the Vampires] (1909).[61] His Mars novel is sandwiched between the similarly-themed *Docteur Omega* (1906) by Arnould Galopin,[62] Henri Gayar's *Les Aventures Merveilleuses de Serge Myrandhal sur la Planète Mars* [The Marvelous Adventures of Serge Myrandhal on Mars] (1908)[63] and Edgar Rice Burroughs' *A Princess of Mars* (1912). Le Rouge's novel is a Martian Odyssey in which young engineer Robert Darvel is sent to Mars by the psychic powers of Hindu Brahmins. Once on the Red Planet, Darvel runs afoul of hostile, bat-winged, blood-sucking natives, a once-powerful civilization now ruled by a Great Brain. The entity eventually sends Darvel back to Earth, unfortunately with some of the vampires. The second volume deals with the war of the vampires back on Earth. Le Rouge's Mars is as elaborately described, with its fauna, flora and various races of inhabitants, as C. S. Lewis' Malacandra in *Out of the Silent Planet* (1938). Planetary romance blends with cosmic horror and Le Rouge's characters switch from swashbuckling he-men to helpless bundles of gibbering terror.

---

[61] Both collected in *The Vampires of Mars*, Black Coat Press, ISBN 978-1-934543-30-6.

[62] Black Coat Press, ISBN 978-0-9740711-1-4.

[63] Black Coat Press, ISBN 978-1-61227-265-8.

But on the eve of the Paris Universal Exposition of 1900 and, sadly, of World War I, the single author who best embodied the evolution of modern science fiction away from the juvenile scientific anticipations of Verne, or the pulp serials of d'Ivoi, La Hire and Le Rouge, towards a more mature, literary genre was Belgian author J.-H. Rosny Aîné ("Aîné" meaning the Elder, to distinguish him from his younger brother, also a writer).

Rosny was very much like Wells or Stapledon in his concepts and his way of dealing with them in his novels. He was, without a doubt, the second most important figure in in the history of modern French science fiction after Verne. As a member of the prestigious literary academy set up by Edmond de Goncourt in 1892, he was also the first writer to straddle the line between mainstream and science fiction literature, even though his genre fiction was unjustly, but not unsurprisingly, neglected by literary scholars.

Rosny's first science fiction tale was the short story "*Les Xipehuz*" (1887),[64] in which primitive humans (the story takes place a thousand years before Babylonian times) encounter inorganic aliens, with whom all forms of communication prove impossible. Men eventually drive away these strange invaders, but the hero mourns the loss of another life, another form of thought. This was the first time that science fiction had abandoned its usual anthropomorphic approach in the description of alien life. The story "*Un Autre Monde*" [Another World] (1895)[65] established that humans share the Earth with the land-bound Moedingen and the air-borne Vuren, two infinitely flat and invisible species who cohabit with us. Only a mutant whose vision is superior to that of ordinary men could see them. In "*Le Cataclysme*" [The Cataclysm] (1896),[66] an

---

[64] In *The Navigators of Space*, Black Coat Press, ISBN 978-1-935558-35-4.
[65] In *The Navigators of Space*, q.v.
[66] In *The Mysterious Force*, Black Coat Press, ISBN 978-1-935558-37-8.

entire region of France sees the physical laws of nature change as a result of the arrival of a mysterious electro-magnetic entity from outer space.

Rosny's short novel, *La Mort de la Terre* [The Death of the Earth] (1910),[67] took place in the far future, when Earth has all but dried out. In it, the last descendants of mankind become aware of the emergence of a new species, the metal-based "Ferromagnetals," fated to replace humanity. *La Mort de la Terre* is one of the most moving tales ever written about the eventual extinction of our species. One of the striking concepts of this poetic, evocative epic was that our disappearance was not the result of some kind of war or cataclysm, but merely that of natural evolution, the same evolution once responsible for the passing away of the dinosaurs. The Ferromagnetals were another of Rosny's strange and mysterious alien races, not evil, merely beyond communication, not unlike Abraham Merritt's *The Metal Monster* (1920).

Another novel, *La Force Mystérieuse* [The Mysterious Force] (1913),[68] told of the destruction of a portion of the light spectrum by the eponymous mysterious force, possibly aliens from outer space who, for a brief while, share our physical existence. This causes a great panic, then a progressive and potentially deadly cooling of the world. Social upheaval follows, before order is ultimately restored. *La Force Mystérieuse* was, coincidentally, published the same year as Arthur Conan Doyle's *The Poisoned Sky*.

L'Énigme de Givreuse [The Givreuse Enigma] (1917)[69] was another remarkable novel about the "bipartition" (some might say cloning) of a human being into two totally similar individuals, each naturally believing himself to be the original. The novella "*La Jeune Vampire*" [The Young Vampire] (1920)[70] was perhaps the first time that vampirism was de-

---

[67] In *The Navigators of Space*, q.v.
[68] Black Coat Press, q.v.
[69] Black Coat Press, ISBN 978-1-935558-39-2.
[70] Black Coat Press, ISBN 978-1-935558-40-8.

scribed as a genetic mutation, transmissible by birth, not unlike in Richard Matheson's *I Am Legend*. *L'Étonnant Voyage d'Hareton Ironcastle* [*Hareton Ironcastle's Amazing Adventure*] (1922) [71] was a more traditional adventure novel, in which explorers eventually discover a fragment of an alien world, with its fauna and flora, embedded into a far-off corner of Africa. *Dans le Monde des Variants* [The World of the Variants] (1939)[72] features a parallel world which certain privileged humans can inhabit.

Rosny's masterpiece was *Les Navigateurs de l'Infini* [The Navigators of Space] (1925) and its sequel *Les Astronautes* [The Astronauts] (written at the same time but published in a somewhat rewritten version in 1960)[73] in which the word "astronautique" was coined for the first time. In it, the protagonists travel to Mars in the *Stellarium*, a spaceship powered by artificial gravity and made of *argine*, an indestructible, transparent material, not unlike Larry Niven's ships in his *Known Space* series. Once on Mars, the human explorers come in contact with the gentle, peaceful, six-eyed, three-legged Tripeds, a dying race being replaced by the Zoomorphs, alien entities who bear more than a passing resemblance to the Ferromagnetals of *The Death of the Earth*. In the sequel, a young Martian female, capable of bearing children parthenogenically by merely wishing it, gives birth to a child after falling in love with one of the human explorers, undoubtedly the first romance ever penned between a man and an alien female. This heralds the rebirth of the Martian race and, with Man's help, their eventual reconquest of their planet.

Les Navigateurs de l'Infini was a colorful, poetic ode to the powers of love and science, a plea for understanding between races, and the view that all living creatures—men as well as aliens—are somehow connected in the greater scheme of things. This was a sharp departure from the xenophobic

---

[71] In *The Mysterious Force*, q.v.
[72] Black Coat Press, ISBN 978-1-935558-36-1.
[73] Both in *The Navigators of Space*, q.v.

approach shaped by Wells with *War of the Worlds* in 1898, which eventually came to dominate Anglo-Saxon science fiction, at least until Stanley Weinbaum's *A Martian Odyssey* (1934).

Like Verne, Rosny exerted a powerful influence on French science fiction. Finally, he was also, if not the creator, the author who virtually defined the sub-genre of the Prehistoric and Lost World stories in French literature. (These will be reviewed below.)

André Couvreur, a medical doctor turned writer, introduced the character of Dr. Armand Caresco, a conscienceless surgeon carrying out medical experiments, in *Le Mal Nécessaire* [The Necessary Evil] (1899).[74] Caresco sees himself as an intellectual superman whose discoveries might enable humankind to take a leap forward. This daring book dared to broach such shocking topics as the methodology and occasional necessity of hysterectomies., one of the first ever mad surgeons in genre literature, Caresco returns in *Caresco, Surhomme* [Caresco, Superman] (1904),[75] in which the brilliant mad scientist rules the body-shaped island of Eucrasia whose inhabitants have been transformed—improved—by advanced surgical techniques. The natives are addicted to sensual pleasures, subservient to the will of Caresco, whom they call the "Superman," for fear that he will castrate them—or worse.

Caresco also appeared in *La Graine* [The Seed] (1903)[76] was one of the most shocking works of its era, one that attempted more fervently than any other to push back the boundaries of the conventionally-unmentionable, such as contraception, abortion and eugenics, illustrated through the lives of the eighteen children of the Grignon family, afflicted by the ongoing social disasters of syphilis and alcoholism. To many contemporary readers it seems a truly bizarre novel, not so

---

[74] Black Coat Press, ISBN 978-1-61227-253-5.
[75] Black Coat Press, ISBN 978-1-61227-254-2.
[76] *Human Seed*, Black Coat Press, ISBN 978-1-61227-880-3.

much in putting forward the argument that it does, but in shaping the plot that illustrates and exemplifies said argument.

In 1909, with *Une Invasion de Macrobes* [An Invasion of Macrobes],[77] Couvreur embarked on a second series of adventures featuring yet another mad scientist, Professor Tornada. In it, Tornada unleashes a plague of giant microbes on Paris. In its sequel, *L'Androgyne* [The Androgyne] (1922),[78] Tornada turns a man into a woman. In *Le Valseur Phosphorescent* [The Phosphorescent Waltzer] (1923), he creates a phosphorescent android.[79] In *Les Mémoires d'un Immortel* [Memoirs of an Immortal] (1924), he tackles the concept of immortality.[80] Finally, in *Le Biocole* (1927),[81] Tornada does achieve a form of immortality through organ replacement and becomes the creator and virtual god of a utopian enclave called Biocolia, but it leads to social chaos, not unlike in Larry Niven's *A.R.M.* stories. The last Tornada story was *Le Cas de la Baronne Sasoitsu* [The Case of Baroness Sasoitsu] (1939),[82] in which the now-reformed mad genius solves a baffling murder case by using his psychovisor which translates thoughts into images. Before his death in 1944, Couvreur had started a new Tornada novel, *La Mort du Soleil* [The Death of the Sun], which sadly remained uncompleted. Another of his novels, *Le Lynx* (1911),[83] co-written with Michel Corday, was about artificial telepathy induced by a serum.

Couvreur's Caresco and Wells' Moreau undoubtedly influenced Maurice Renard in his creation of his own mad doc-

---

[77] In *The Exploits of Professor Tornada* (Volume 1), Black Coat Press, ISBN 978-1-61227-279-5.

[78] In *The Exploits of Professor Tornada* (Volume 1), q.v.

[79] In *The Exploits of Professor Tornada* (Volume 2), Black Coat Press, ISBN 978-1-61227-280-1.

[80] In *The Exploits of Professor Tornada* (Volume 2), q.v.

[81] In *The Exploits of Professor Tornada* (Volume 3), Black Coat Press, ISBN 978-1-61227-281-8.

[82] In *The Exploits of Professor Tornada* (Volume 3), q.v.

[83] Black Coat Press, ISBN 978-1-61227-273-3.

tor novel, *Le Docteur Lerne, Sous-Dieu* [Doctor Lerne] (1908),[84] which was dedicated to Wells. In it, a mad scientist transplants organs not from animals to men, but also from plants, and even machines. Renard's impact was more considerable in the 1920s and 1930s and will be discussed in more details later. However, he had already published several major collections of science fiction stories before World War I. "*Les Vacances de M. Dupont*" [Mr Dupont's Vacation]" (1905)[85] is a story about dinosaurs returning to life. *Un Homme chez les microbes* [A Man Among the Microbes] (1908)[86] features an "incredible shrinking man" who, through miniaturization, reaches an inhabited micro-world where he meets scientifically advanced aliens. *Le Voyage Immobile* [The Motionless Voyage] (1909),[87] a story about the "Aeroflix," an experimental anti-gravity flying machine.

In a 1913 short story, "*Le Brouillard du 26 Octobre*" [The Fog of October 26th],[88] Renard told how two scientists were transported back in time to the Miocene Era and encountered winged beings.

Renard's 1912 novel, *Le Péril Bleu* [The Blue Peril],[89] which many considered to be his masterpiece, postulated the existence of unimaginable, invisible creatures who live in the upper strata of the atmosphere and fish for men the way men capture fish. These aliens, dubbed "Sarvants" by the human scientists who have discovered them, feel threatened by our incursions into space the way men might be threatened by an invasion of crabs, and retaliate by capturing men, keeping them in a space zoo and studying them. Eventually, when the Sarvants come to the realization than these men are intelligent

---

[84] Black Coat Press, ISBN 978-1-935558-15-6.

[85] In *Doctor Lerne*, q.v.

[86] Black Coat Press, ISBN 978-1-935558-16-3

[87] In *A Man Among the Microbes*, q.v.

[88] In *The Doctored Man*, Black Coat Press, ISBN 978-1-935558-18-7.

[89] Black Coat Press, ISBN 978-1-935558-17-0.

beings, they release their captives. In the end, the bloodthirstiness and savagery were on the side of men, not the Sarvants.

Le Péril Bleu predated Charles Fort's *Book of the Damned* (1919) and other subsequent works in that same vein but retained a humanistic and tolerant rather than fearful and xenophobic philosophy. The conceptual leap taken in less than fifty years between Verne's first timid steps into space in 1865 and Rosny's and Renard's close encounter stories was staggering. By comparison with the United States, Gernsback had just published *Ralph 124C41+* in *Modern Electrics* in 1911 and *Amazing Stories* was still fifteen years in the future.

Other Notable Authors

In this section, we will review other notable genre works and authors published before World War I, along the same thematic lines as before.

Journeys to Other Worlds

In 1883, Alexandre Bessot de Lamothe published *Quinze Mois dans la Lune* [Fifteen Months on the Moon] (1883), a Vernian fantasy aimed at young adults.

In 1888, Charles Guyon published *Voyage dans la Planète Vénus* [Voyage to the Planet Venus],[90] a significant early planetary romance in which human explorers visit the colorful, prehistoric world of Venus via a hot air balloon. However, the Venusians have to build an enormous cannon to launch them back to Earth in an obvious tip of the hat to Verne.

In 1890, A. de Ville d'Avray wrote *Voyage dans la Lune avant 1900* [Journey to the Moon Before 1900], a small book-

---

[90] In *The Man with the Blue Face*, Black Coat Press, ISBN 978-1-61227-386-0.

let with fifty color plates which detailed a journey to the Moon, again made in a hot air balloon christened the *Intrépide*, and the adventures that its passengers had on our satellite.

Cybèle (1891)[91] by Adolphe Alhaiza does have authentic claims to being a significant contribution to the development of French futuristic fiction, as it contains a good deal of material that is still capable of stimulating the thought and imagination of the modern reader. One night, young Marius Foulane is mysteriously attracted by the light of the star Gemma and travels by astral projection to the planet Cybele which orbits it. He discovers a world identical to Earth, but historically displaced by 6000 years in the future. On Cybele, Marius discovers evolved dogs capable of speech, computers, and even peaceful relations with other alien species from the same Solar System.

In 1894, Jules Cahu penned *Perdus dans l'Espace* [Lost in Space].

In 1896, Pierre de Sélènes penned *Un Monde Inconnu, Deux Ans sur la Lune* [An Unknown World : Two Years on the Moon].[92] In this unauthorized sequel to Verne's *From the Earth to the Moon*, French astronomer Francois Mathieu-Rollere, Lord Douglas Rodilan and two brothers, Marcel and Jacques, purchase the giant cannon and shell once used by the Gun Club to send the first men into space and launch their own expedition to the Moon. Once there, they encounter the advanced, utopian civilization of the Meolicenes who live inside our satellite and are able to absorb in gaseous form the elements they need to feed themselves. *An Unknown World* is remarkable because of the author's ardent desire to imagine and describe things that no one had ever imagined or described before, in the quest to widen the horizons of human imagination.

---

[91] Black Coat Press, ISBN 978-1-61227-231-3.
[92] Black Coat Press, ISBN 978-1-61227-302-0.

The popular writer of adventure serials Arnould Galopin showed more imagination in his *Le Docteur Oméga - Aventures Fantastiques de Trois Français dans la Planète Mars* [*Doctor Omega, The Fantastic Adventures of Three Frenchmen on Planet Mars*] (1905),[93] in which in a quiet Normandy village, amateur violinist Denis Borel meets a mysterious white-haired scientist known only as Doctor Omega, who is building an amazing spacecraft, the *Cosmos*, a projectile-shaped vehicle built using an antigravitational substance called "repulsite", clearly influenced by Wells' cavorite. Doctor Omega invites Borel to accompany him on a voyage to Mars! The Mars they land on is a primitive planet, inhabited by savage reptilian warriors and macrocephalic gnomes who seize their ship. The *Cosmos* could also travel on land and under water. In a revised version published in 1908-09, Galopin changed the name of the ship to *Excelsior* and the substance to "stellite".

Mars remained in fashion in *Les Aventures Merveilleuses de Serge Myrandhal sur la Planète Mars* [The Marvelous Adventures of Serge Myrandhal on the Planet Mars] (1908)[94] by Henri Gayar. In it, the bold French Engineer Serge Myrandhal travels to Mars in a ship propelled by the power of thought, followed by his fiancée, the brave American novelist Miss Annabella Carpenter, and her guardian, the eccentric British millionaire Sir Washington Pickman. There, they make numerous wondrous discoveries including that of a race of small, red-furred anthropoids living underground, and beautiful winged humanoids called the Zoas, also referred to as the Elohim. The psychic-powered ship was named *Velox*. In a later version, published in 1927 as *Les Robinsons de la Planète Mars* [The Robinsons of Planet Mars] under the pseudonym of "Cyril," Gayar got rid of the psychic device and instead used planetary attraction; he also added German villains to the plot and prophetically rechristened his rocketships V1 and V2.

---

[93] Black Coat Press, 978-0-9740711-0-7.
[94] Black Coat Press, 978-1-61227-265-8.

Sylvain Déglantine's *Les Terriens sur Vénus* [*Earthmen on Venus*] (1907), on the other hand, was a rather naive story about a journey to and the exploration of Venus.

In Abbott Théophile Moreux' *Le Miroir Sombre* [The Dark Mirror] (1911), reprinted as *Mars va nous Parler* [Mars Will Talk to Us] in the *Journal des Voyages* (which Moreux briefly edited) in 1924, scientists learn to communicate with Mars through a radio-telescope-like device, the eponymous "dark mirror." Curiously, the novel postulates a link between sunspots and earthquakes.

Finally, popular adventure serial writer and engineer André Mas' novel, *Les Allemands sur Vénus* [The Germans on Venus] (1914),[95] was a rather chauvinistic novel, the first-ever published item in a series of propagandistic works of fiction by rocket enthusiasts. It is remarkable for its description of space travel, and its attempt to design a hypothetical biosphere for another planet. In it, the Germans used centrifugal force to launch a space expedition to take over the planet Venus. A year earlier, the author had, in fact, proposed launching a projectile from the rim of a spinning wheel. In his novel, Mas later divided the Solar System between the various Earth powers: Russia got the Moon, the United States, Saturn, Japan, Jupiter, France, Mars, etc.

Journey to Other Lands

Technically, the sub-genre known as the Prehistoric Novel was not the creation of J.-H. Rosny Aîné. That credit belongs to Samuel-Henry Berthoud and, most especially, Élie Berthet with his four-part serial, *Le Monde Inconnu* [The Unknown World] (1876), revised as *Paris Avant l'Histoire* [Paris Before History] (1885), which described in great detail the life of Parisians during the Stone Age, the building of the first Lake City and, finally, the foundation of Paris.

---

[95] Black Coat Press, ISBN 978-1-934543-56-6.

Ernest d'Hervilly's *Aventures d'un Petit Garçon Préhistorique en France* [*Adventures of a Prehistoric Boy in France*] (1887) was the first adventure-oriented prehistoric novel, although satirical in intent and aimed at a juvenile market.

But it was Rosny who gave that genre its nobility with several powerful classic novels: *Vamireh* (1892),[96] *Eyrimah* (1893),[97] *Nomai* (1897),[98] the world-renowned classic *La Guerre du Feu* [Quest for Fire] (1909), *Le Félin Géant* [The Giant Feline] (1918) (a.k.a. Quest of the Dawn Man)[99] and *Helgvor du Fleuve Bleu* [Helgvor of the Blue River] (1930).[100] In these novels, the author combined the notions of modern drama with the ability to depict Man's early days in a colorful, yet totally believable fashion. The conversations between prehistoric men and mastodons are not very different from the attempts at communicating with the Xipehuz. These prehistoric novels became so popular and widely respected that *Quest for Fire* was even included in schools' curriculum.

Other prehistoric novels of note included:

Raymond Auzias-Turenne, with *Le Dernier Mammouth* [The Last Mastodon] (1901-02).

Ray Nyst, with *La Caverne* [The Cavern] (1909).

Paul Max, with *Volcar le Terrible* [Volcar the Terrible] (1913).

Edmond Haraucourt with *Daâh, Le Premier Homme* [Daah, The Fist Human] (1914),[101] which begins with the proto-humans Dâh and his wives, Hock and Ta, living a solitary existence, and then sketches in episodic accounts, the story of their slow ascent towards civilization. With Daâh serving as a kind of collective hero, the novel proceeds through a sequence

---

[96] Black Coat Press, ISBN 978-1-935558-38-5.

[97] In *Vamireh*, q.v.

[98] In *Vamireh*, q.v.

[99] In *Helgvor of the Blue River*, Black Coat Press, ISBN 978-1-935558-46-0

[100] Black Coat Press, q.v.

[101] Black Coat Press, ISBN 978-1-61227-355-6.

of epiphanies that includes the invention of families, the axe, clothes, religion, fire and, ultimately, a burgeoning awareness of what will someday become our world. *Daâh* is a unique milestone in the genre of prehistoric fantasy, taking into account the then-new discipline of physical anthropology and attempting to bridge the gaps left by science. Haraucourt aspired to a kind of truthfulness in its depiction of the psychological and social processes involved in the pattern of change and discovery and was remarkable in his ability to portray characters who are not yet us, but will be someday.

Haraucourt wrote several ground-breaking science fiction stories, between 1888 and 1919, in which he variously described the rise of the Antichrist (*"L'Antéchrist"* [The Antichrist] (1893)), the cataclysmic consequences of the discovery of an immortality serum (*"La Découverte du docteur Auguérand"* [Doctor Auguérand's Discovery] (1910)), a journey across the ruins of Paris in the Year 6983 (*"La Traversée de Paris"* [A Trip to Paris] (1904)), the fall of the Moon upon the Earth (*"La Fin du Monde"* [The End of the World] (1893)), the last of the Great Wars that ends all life on Earth (*"Le Conflit Suprême"* [The Supreme Conflict] (1919)), and even *"Le Gorilloïde"* [The Gorriloïde] (1906), a futuristic *Planet of the Apes* where evolved gorillas wonder, "Are Apes descended from Humans?"[102]

In this genre, one should also include André Lichtenberger's *Les Centaures* [The Centaurs] (1904),[103] which chronicles the last days of the Era of the Beasts that preceded ours, when Fauns, Tritons and other now-mythical creatures shared the Earth. In that wild world, the balance of nature is maintained by the Centaurs, whose One Law is Thou Shalt Not Kill. But one day, Klevorak, the King of the Centaurs, learns that the One Law has been broken by the new creatures called Men, whom he calls The Accursed Ones. Meanwhile,

---

[102] All in *Illusions of Immortality*, Black Coat Press, ISBN 978-1-61227-075-3.

[103] Black Coat Press, ISBN 978-1-61227-184-2.

the beautiful Katilda, one of the few remaining female Centaurs, refuses to bear offspring with the males of her species and instead falls in love with a young hunter, who only sees in her a coveted prey. Soon, the Elder Races are slaughtered by Men. Klevorak saves the remnants of his people by taking them across the ocean to the legendary Sacred Isle. *The Centaurs* is a beautiful, timeless classic of fantasy.

In Gaston Danville's *Le Parfum de Volupté* [The Perfume of Lust (1905),[104] a ship is trapped in the waters of Atlantis when a submarine eruption returns the lost continent to the surface, and its crew and passengers are subjected to strange mental influences that stimulate their erotic impulses. The characters are haunted by memories, unconscious impulses and the poignant emotions provoked by those internal spurs. The author based his accounts of delusion and obsession on what he took to be sound theories of positivistic psychology which added an extra dimension of cruelty to his fiction and an extra dose of intensity to his eroticism.

Rosny was also a precursor of the "Lost World" novel. H. Rider Haggard's *She* dates from 1887 and Doyle's classic from 1912. *"Nymphée"* [Nymphaeum] (1893)[105] featured a Lost World located near the river Amour in Siberia inhabited by amphibious humans. *Les Profondeurs de Kyamo* [The Depths of Kyamo] (1896) and *La Contrée Prodigieuse des Cavernes* [The Wonderful Cave Country] (1896)[106] are more exotic Vernian excursions and feature giant, intelligent bats living in underground caverns. *Les Femmes de Setné* [*Setne's Women*] (1903)[107] features a Lost World in the days of Ancient Egypt. *Les Hommes-Sangliers* [The Boar Men]

---

[104] Black Coat Press, ISBN 978-1-61227-580-2.
[105] In *The World of the Variants*, Black Coat Prtess, ISBN 978-1-935558-36-1.
[106] Both in *The World of the Variants*, q.v.
[107] In *Pan's Flute*, Black Coat Press, ISBN 978-1-61227-755-4.

(1929),[108] later expanded as *La Sauvage Aventure* [The Savage Adventure] (1935), takes place on a mysterious Antipodean Island inhabited by savage Boar-Men, with locales called the Blue Forest, the Red Forest, The Infernal Rocks, the Vlugt Pass, etc.

The *Journal des Voyages* was, as its title indicated, the natural home for tales dealing with exotic lands and uncanny adventures in which daring heroes and their virginal girl-friends fought would-be masters of the world and mad scientists, often of Germanic or Asian origins. Among the authors of note published within its pages, and that of similar magazines, were:

Louis Jacolliot, who wrote adventure tales featuring exotic locations and/or futuristic vehicles such as *La Cité des Sables* [The City of the Sands] (1877), and *Les Mangeurs de Feu* [The Fire Eaters] (1885-87), which featured aerial battles between submersible planes.

François Teissier, who penned *Voyage Aérien de New York à Yokohama* [Aerial Journey from New York to Yokohama] (1878) and *Les Merveilles et Mystères de l'Océan, ou Voyage Sous-Marin de Southampton au Cap Horn* [Wonders and Mysteries of the Ocean, or Underwater Journey from Southampton to the Cape Horn] (1900).

Jules Gros, with novels such as *Un Volcan dans les Glaces* [A Volcano Under the Ice] (1879), the adventures of a scientific expedition at the North Pole, and the remarkable *L'Homme Fossile* [The Fossil Man] (1882),[109] a mildly satirical comedy describing the progress of an 1876 international scientific expedition to a fictitious island south-west of New Zealand, which comes across the existence of fossilized human remains. The theme was still very controversial when the story was set, especially in Catholic France, where religious opposition to the idea of the great antiquity of the human spe-

---

[108] In *The World of the Variants*, q.v.
[109] Black Coat Press, ISBN 978-1-61227-409-6.

cies, making nonsense of Biblical chronology, had been forceful. The notion that the human species had undergone a long, slow process of evolution was anathematized, and the gradual but enormous accumulation of evidence produced by excavations all over Europe, but particularly in France, was a hot topic. The discovery of quasi-Magdalenian remains in the southern seas would, indeed, have seemed as exciting and significant to real scientists then as it does to the fictitious ones in his novel.

Alphonse Brown, with novels such as *Les Conquérants de l'Air* [The Conquerors of the Air] (1875),[110] with its trip around the world in forty days in a steam-powered flying machine, significant in terms of its prediction of the development of future aviation; *Les Mohicans du Sahara* [The Mohicans of the Sahara] (1885); and *Une Ville de Verre* [A City of Glass] (1891),[111] in which a French scientific expedition to the North Pole becomes stranded in the ice. Because of their knowledge and local resources, they manage to build a super-scientific city dubbed Crystalopolis. However, rival American and Russian explorers threaten these new conquerors.

Before writing *La Ville Enchantée: Voyage au lac Tanganika* [The Enchanted City: A Journey to Lake Tanganyika] (1885),[112] Eugène Hennebert consulted Jules Verne; the result was a novel that combined exotic adventures with scientific discovery, with a buoyant tone and an action-packed narrative. Following on the trail of past heroic expeditions, a disparate band of French explorers, embark upon the quest for Kisimbasimba, the eponymous Enchanted City of Central Africa. During their epic journey, they will face dangerous native tribes, legions of hostile animals, trek through mysterious underground caverns before they finally reach their goal. Contemporary with Haggard's *King Solomon's Mines*, *La Ville Enchantée* is a somewhat didactic and earnest portrayal of the

---

[110] Black Coat Press, ISBN 978-1-61227-143-9.
[111] Black Coat Press, ISBN 978-1-61227-023-4.
[112] Black Coat Press, ISBN 978-1-61227-345-7.

heroic age of African exploration, celebrating the achievements of an era which, today, seems filled with nostalgia.

Gaston de Wailly, who wrote *Le Monde de l'Abîme* [The World of the Abyss], (1904), in which the Earth is revealed to be hollow and the protagonists discover a race of peaceful, scientifically advanced bat-like humanoids living under our feet. These spend their time hunting living dinosaurs which threaten their existence. In *Le Roi de l'Inconnu* [The King of the Unknown] (1905), we are introduced to another secret underground kingdom ruled by an enlightened scientist. Finally, in *Le Meurtrier du Globe* [The Murderer of the World] (1910),[113] the author imagines that the Earth is a living being, whose surface we inhabit as parasites. Moved by revenge against that "evil beast" which destroyed his family in an earthquake, a mad scientist schemes to literally murder the world by striking at its vital organs.

René Thévenin penned several pulpish yarns such as *La Cité des Tortures* [The City of Tortures] (1906), about an underground Australian city where the Chinese secretly prepared to take over the world; and *Le Collier de l'Idole de Fer* [The Necklace of the Iron Idol] (1912), about an idol of living metal created by Inca survivors to protect their Lost City.

Albert Bonneau, who also wrote under the pseudonym of Maurice Champagne contributed such genre novels as *Les Reclus de la Mer* [The Recluse of the Sea] (1907), a Captain Nemo variation; *Les Sondeurs d'Abîmes* [The Probers of the Abyss] (1911), in which brave explorers discover an evil Tibetan underground empire; *L'Âme du Dr. Kips* [The Soul of Dr. Kips] (1912) and *La Vallée Mystérieuse* [The Mysterious Valley] (1915).

Pierre Luguet's *Une Descente au Monde Sous-Terrien* [A Descent into a Sub-Terranean World] (1906) was another tale of underground exploration.

---

[113] Black Coat Press, ISBN 978-1-61227-408-9.

Charles Derennes was a notable addition to the genre with *Le Peuple du Pôle* [The People of the Pole] (1907),[114] in which, during an expedition to the North Pole, French aeronauts Jean-Louis de Venasque and Jacques Ceintras stumble upon an alien society of technologically advanced reptilian humanoids living in a secret enclave that has been isolated from the world for millions of years. The most original component of the novel is that the author, unlike Verne or Doyle, makes the assumption that progressive biological evolution would have continued, to the extent that the iguanodons isolated in the remote past would have developed a quasi-humanoid form, along with high intelligence and sophisticated technological capability. Derennes also penned *Les Conquérants d'Idoles* [The Conquerors of Idols] (1919),[115] about a hidden race of Incas who turned out to be descendants of Atlantis.

Jules Perrin & Henri Lanos' *Un Monde sur le monde* [A World Above the World] (1911)[116] described a utopian metal city built on giant pylons above Paris.

René-Marcel de Nizerolles' serial, *Les Voyages Aériens d'un Petit Parisien à travers le Monde* [The Aerial Voyages of a Little Parisian Across the World] (1910-12), serialized in 382 chapters, or 1776 pages in total, featured the fantastic globe-trotting adventures of a young hero named Tintin (no relation to Hergé's character).

Charles Malato was a notorious French anarchist and revolutionary once accused of plotting the 1905 assassination attempt against King Alfonso XIII of Spain. Malato was also a distinguished journalist and the author of exotic adventures serials such as *Perdus au Maroc* [Lost in Morocco] (1915).[117] Forced to hide in the still unexplored regions of Morocco, political prisoner and escapee Antonio Perez is caught in the

---

[114] Black Coat Press, ISBN 978-1-934543-39-9.

[115] In *The People of the Pole*, q.v.

[116] Black Coat Press, ISBN 978-1-61227-002-9.

[117] *Lost!* Black Coat Press, ISBN 978-1-61227-670-0.

grips of the most unexpected and most extraordinary predicaments. *Lost!* is original because of its Moroccan setting and contains the standard devices of lost world novels, each one more extraordinary than the last, piling mystery upon mystery, peril upon peril, such as an usurped throne, an enemy priestess, trial by combat, precious treasures, an ill-fated romance, but with unusual, original twists. Malato's heroes are not stereotypes, but subversive pariahs, marginal figures, escaping from society like Fantômas, Arsène Lupin and the real-life Bonnot Gang, bringing a radically different vision of the instability of the world around them.

Caresco, Tornada, Cornelius, Oxus, Lerne, etc., were not the only mad doctors who exemplified unfettered science in these early genre works.

The works of Jules Claretie were scientific anticipations based on the physiological and psychological research of the times. His *Jean Mornas* (1885) was about the criminal use of hypnosis. *L'Oeil du Mort* [Deadman's Eye] (1887) made use of the notion that the image of the murderer remained fixed on the victim's eye. Finally, in *L'Obsession* [*Obsession*] (1908),[118] artist André Fortis is the victim of a strange curse that suddenly and unexpectedly turns him into an entirely different man, splitting his existence into two separate lives. He will be cured by the mysterious Dr. Klipper who has invented a device that can read the human brain through the skull like an open book. *Obsession* deals with the psychological anomaly that would nowadays be called multiple personality syndrome in the tradition of Robet L. Stevenson's *Strange Case of Dr. Jekyll and Mr. Hyde* (1886). Although it remains an "evil twin" story, its representation of the personality of the inconvenient "double" is, however, unusual and striking.

---

[118] Black Coat Press, ISBN 978-1-61227-213-9.

In the short story "*Le Coeur de Tony Wandel*" [The Heart of Tony Wandel] (1884),[119] Belgian writer Georges Eekhoud was one of the first authors to postulate a personality transfer following a heart transplant. Even Alexandre Dumas, *fils* penned a short story entitled "*La Boîte d'Argent*" [The Silver Box] on the same theme.

L'Homme en Nickel [The Nickel Man] (1897)[120] by military historian and journalist Georges Espitallier features an eccentric scientist who uses galvanic technology to turn his body into a metal statue in an attempt to preserve it.

Notable adventure writers and novels in a similar vein included:

Albert Bleunard with *La Babylone Électrique* [The Electric Babylon] (1888), about an electric-powered city in Mesopotamia; *La Vengeance d'un Savant* [A Scientist's Revenge] (1890), about radio transmission; and *Toujours Plus Petits* [Ever Smaller] (1893),[121] the first modern novel on the theme of the "Shrinking Man," in which a group of scientists are shrunken down, first to insect-size, to explore an ordinary garden, which becomes as perilous to them as an alien world; then, to microbe-size inside a drop of water and, finally, into a rose bush.

Raoul Gineste was a scientist himself as well as a poet, and his attitude is far more balanced than some, infused with a genuine puzzlement and exploratory curiosity as well as a sense of inevitable tragedy. His *La Seconde Vie du Docteur Albin* [The Second Life of Doctor Albin] (1902)[122] belongs to a set of fictions that explore the supposed psychology typical of scientists with considerable analytical intensity. One of the central tenets of these is that scientific genius is incompatible with, and perhaps antithetical to, love between the sexes. The

---

[119] In *News from the Moon*, Black Coat Press, ISBN 978-1-932983-89-0.
[120] Black Coat Press, ISBN 978-1-61227-445-4.
[121] Black Coat Press, ISBN 978-1-61227-014-2.
[122] Black Coat Press, ISBN 978-1-61227-467-6.

novel provides what is perhaps the most searching analysis of that allegedly perverse emotional involvement with science to be found in the genre.

Henri Austruy's "*L'Eupantophone*" [The Eupantophone] (1904),[123] about a machine for reading text aloud that is spun off into a device transforming light into sound and which enables a blind man to see. Austruy, born in 1871, was a Parisian attorney, a writer and the editor of *La Nouvelle Revue* from 1913 until his unrecorded death during the Nazi occupation of France. Virtually forgotten today, he was the author of several remarkable, often humorous and imaginative works of science fiction in the vein of Robert Sheckley and R. A. Lafferty, featuring notions such as a global ecocatastrophe caused by soil erosion, and a new technology that enables the regeneration of souls as well as fantasy stories from remote epochs, abolished from human memory, such the bizarre city of Miellune and the fantastic land of Humania. Austruy's stories possess an idiosyncratic eccentricity that makes them highly unusual, a quality worthy of interest and high praise in the field of imaginative literature. Other notable works by him include "*L'Ère Petitpaon, ou La Paix Universelle*" [The Petitpaon Era, or Universal Peace] (1906),[124] a scathing pacifistic anticipation, put so comprehensively in the shade by the actual world war that followed it within a decade; and "*L'Olotélépan*" [The Olotelepan] (1925),[125] set in an alternative world but diverged as a result of the invention of a a wireless apparatus that instantaneously transports the senses to indefinite distance.

Danielle d'Arthez' *Le Trust du Soleil* [*The Sun Company*] (1906) was a prophetic novel about weather control.

Louis Forest (1872-1933) was a journalist for various Parisian newspapers, including *Le Matin*, for which he wrote a ground-breaking serial about the artificial creation of supermen through radium-based brain surgery. In *Le Voleur*

---

[123] Black Coat Press, ISBN 978-1-61227-293-1.
[124] Black Coat Press, ISBN 978-1-61227-294-8.
[125] Black Coat Press, 978-1-61227-295-5.

d'Enfants a.k.a *On Vole des Enfants à Paris* [Someone Is Stealing Children in Paris] (1906),[126] children are disappearing in full daylight, with diabolical cunning and monstrous audacity. The police being incapable of finding the perpetrators, the Government appoints a special scientific commission to investigate. Its leader is the notorious German doctor Professor Flax, who naturally turned out to be the villain. Coincidentally, the character returned to become the arch-enemy of the popular pulp detective hero *Harry Dickson*.

Pierre Giffard's Professor Lionel-Prospero Macduff, in *Le Tombeau de Glace* [The Tomb of Ice] (1908), succeeded in performing a heart transplant operation during a perilous mission to the Pole.

More interestingly, that same year, in *Le Mystérieux Dajann-Phinn* [The Mysterious Dajann-Phinn],[127] Michel Corday penned a variation on the Frankenstein theme, featuring a scientist who created a perfect humanoid.

Finally, in Jean de Quirielle's remarkably prescient *L'Oeuf de Verre* [The Glass Egg] (1912), androids were artificially grown in a glass container. This novel may well be the first use of the word "android," predating Karel Capek's *R.U.R.* by nine years. His *La Joconde Retrouvée* [*The Mona Lisa Recovered*] (1913) was based on yet another original concept: Leonardo da Vinci used "living paint" to paint the Mona Lisa, which was therefore "trapped" within the painting. The Mona Lisa was briefly stolen from the Louvre—historically true—merely to enable the young thief to free the young woman trapped inside the painting.

---

[126] Black Coat Press, ISBN 978-1-61227-252-8.
[127] In *The World Above the World*, Black Coat Press, ISBN 978-1-61227-002-9.

Jouneys to Other Times

Many scholars long considered *Prodigieuse Découverte et ses Incalculables Conséquences sur les Destinées du Monde Entier* [A Prodigious Discovery and its Incalculable Consequences on the Fate of the Entire World], credited to X. Nagrien and published by Hetzel in 1867 to be an uncredited Jules Verne novel. The book was even released under his name in Spain and Italy. However, it was a novel by A. Audois, in which in the near future, an inventor discovers two elements, dubbed "pos" and "neg" which, when brought together, nullify gravity. The inventor then builds a craft dubbed the *Negopos* which leads to a revolution in transports, like the introduction of regular air shuttles between Paris and Strasbourg. The consequences prove to be staggering since the new craft challenges the notion of national borders and leads to the redrawing of the political map of the world.

Didier de Chousy with *Ignis* (1883),[128] a novel about the industrial exploitation of Earth's central fire by a multinational cartel, penned a remarkable scientific anticipation which forecasted robot-driven cars, moving sidewalks, recorded music, as well as the use of geothermal energy as a power source and the manufacturing of robots, which were described as mechanical, metal beings whose various shapes were designed for specific tasks. These Atmophytes, or steam-powered men, eventually petition for human rights, almost forty years before Capek's *R.U.R. Ignis* also contains fanciful digressions into biological engineering, Utopian city planning, the possibility of brain control by means of electrical stimulation and the potential exhaustion of fossil fuels, all imagined at a time before the automobile was even invented!

Other notable scientific anticipations included:

Georges Pellerin's *Le Monde dans 2000 Ans* [The World in 2000 Years] (1878)[129] is a work of science fiction based on

---

[128] Black Coat Press, ISBN 978-1-934543-88-7.
[129] Black Coat Press, ISBN 978-1-61227-058-6.

economics. In the future it describes, the primary objective of economic policy is the prevention of the accumulation of money into the hands of relatively few individuals. While making money remains an objective, it is subsidiary to the determination to steer it in the right direction and redistribute it in such a way as to give every member of society the opportunity to earn a living free of hardship and strife. Whereas readers in 1878 could only make a simple comparison between their own world and the world of 3878 as it was glimpsed by the hero, contemporary readers can make a third comparison with the world of today, which adds an additional perspective of considerable significance to anyone interested in the future of our society.

Émile Calvet's *Dans Mille Ans* [In a Thousand Years] (1884)[130] paints a ground-breaking picture of a world transformed by prolifically distributed electric power and aerial transportation, demonstrating an attention to utilitarian detail rare among other constructors of futuristic utopias. The characters do not experience the future of the year 2880 as if it were a vision, but have the subjective impression that they have been physically displaced by suspended animation, even discovering ashes and records of their genealogy in the Necropolis of future Paris. Seen from the viewpoint of today, the book is a remarkable combination of innocence and ingenuity, unparalleled in its own time and rare even today. Contrasting the actual future that developed with the imagined future of a century ago, only adds to the reader's experience. a utopia in which three men used a drug to induce hibernation and travel to the future, where they discovered that compounded interest had made them rich.

A Swiss author signing "Verniculus" wrote *Histoire de la Fin du Monde, ou La Comète de 1904* [Story of the End of the World, or The Comet of 1904] (1882) in which the eponymous comet threatened to turn Earth's atmosphere into a

---

[130] Black Coat Press, ISBN 978-1-61227-192-7.

flammable gas. Verne himself appeared as a fictional character in the novel.

Léo Claretie, a cousin of Jules, wrote *Paris depuis ses Origines jusqu'en l'An 3000* [Paris From its Origins Until the Year 3000] (1886), in which the three final chapters detail the future of Paris: "*1987*," the self-explanatory "*Ruins of Paris*," and, finally, the more optimistic "*Year 3000*." In addition to Théophile Gautier's "*Future Paris*" (1851) and Alfred Franklin's "*The Ruins of Paris in 4875*" (1875), already mentioned, the grim future of the French Capital was also portrayed by Arsène Houssaye in "*Paris Futur*" (1856), Victor Fournel in "*Paris Futur*" (1865), and Maurice Spronck in "*L'An 330 de la République*" [The Year 330 of the Republic] (1894), subtitled "In the 22nd Century of the Christian Era," which may have been the first future history to use a non-Gregorian calendar and feature a Europe invaded by Africans.[131]

Poet Jean Rameau's 1887 collection, *Fantasmagories* [Phatasmagorias][132] described the mores and technology of the year 1987 in a satirical mode.

Alfred de Ferry's *Un Roman en 1915* [A Novel of 1915] (1889) was a political anticipation about a socialist politician who started a civil war.

Alain Le Drimeur's *La Cité Future* [The Future City] (1890)[133] postulates that the Conservatives left France in 1891 to emigrate *en masse* to the island of La Réunion, where they established a Roman Catholic kingdom that deliberately cut itself off from the homeland for a century. The book begins in the early years of the 21st century when two young men from the island decide to discover what happened to France since it was abandoned to secularist Republicans. The result is not a

---

[131] All in *Investigations of the Future*, Black Coat Press, ISBN 978-1-61227-106-4.

[132] In *The Mirror of Present Events*, Black Coat Press, ISBN 978-1-61227-486-7.

[133] Black Coat Press, ISBN 978-1-61227-114-9.

straightforward future projection so much as a kind of anticipatory alternative history.

A. Vilgensofer's *La Terre dans Cent Mille Ans* [Earth in 100,000 Years] (1893) postulates that all Earthmen speak French, because it is the only living language left on the planet, but is this conceited vision any more ludicrous than aliens all speaking English?

Gabriel Tarde's *Fragment d'Histoire Future* [Fragment of a Future History] (1894) was translated into English with a foreword by Wells; it depicted a utopian society which was forced to move underground as the sun's energy became depleted.

Camille Debans penned severa;l interesting futuristic stories in *La Science Illustrée*, such as "*Histoire d'un tremblement de terre*" [The Story of an Earthquake] (1892), "*L'Île en feu*" [Fire Island] (1893), "*Un duel à vapeur*" [A Steam Duel] (1895) and *Le Vainqueur de la Mort* [The Conqueror of Death] (1895).[134]

Han Ryner's *Un Roman Historique* [An Historical Novel] (1896) (published under his real name of Henri Ner), is dated from "Old Paris in the Year 2347 of the Abominable Social Era".

Paul Adam's *Lettres de Malaisie* [Letters from Malaisie] (1898)[135] presents a society that, although founded by utopians, has produced a compromised result, in which utopian and dystopian elements are fused, thus raising the question of whether any program of political reform could possibly produce the intended results, given the vagaries of human nature.

Joseph Déjacque's *The Humanisphere* (1899)[136] is set in dystopic future Paris.

---

[134] All in *The Conqueror of Death*, Black Coat Press, ISBN 978-1-61227-230-6.
[135] In *The Humanisphere*, Black Coat Press, ISBN 978-1-61227-511-6
[136] Black Coat Press, q.v.

In 1900, Guy de Téramond, one of the editors of the *Journal des Voyages*, wrote *L'Homme qui peut tout* [The Man Who Could Do Anything] in which brain surgery transforms a former criminal into a prodigious scientist who plans to forcibly transform Earth into a new utopia.

"Captain Cap" was the fictitious mouthpiece that humorist Alphonse Allais used in *Le Captain Cap, ses aventures, ses idées, sea breuvages* [The Adventures of Captain Cap] (1902)[137] to tell the tallest of his tall stories and develop his most exotic story ideas, including the majority of those that would nowadays be considered science-fictional. The author liked to keep up with contemporary developments in science and was ever ready to adapt ideas therefrom—especially ideas that seemed to pose a challenge to common sense—Into the humorous newspaper articles with which he made his living and his reputation. By virtue of this habit of picking up such trifles, and adding absurd twists to them, he became an influential figure in the development of French sf.

Fernand Kolney's *L'Amour dans 5000 Ans* [Love in 5000 Years] (1905, reprinted in 1928)[138] takes place in a futuristic post-apocalyptic world, thousands of years after the Martians, disgusted by Earth's bloody history, almost exterminated the Human Race. Births are all achieved through artificial insemination and love has been banished. But things start going awry when the Grand Procreator uses ancient corrupt seeds dating back to the 20th century and old human impulses reawaken, ultimately leading to the end of the world... Kolney, a polemicist, anarchist and specialist in the erotic literature of the 17th and 18th centuries, penned one of the most bizarre *romans scientifiques* ever, striving in every possible way to boggle the mind, and frequently succeeding.

Jean Grave published several anarchist utopias masquerading as children's books, such as *Les Aventures de Nono*

---

[137] Black Coat Press, ISBN 978-1-61227-218-4.
[138] Black Coat Press, ISBN 978-1-61227-155-2.

[The Adventures of Nono] (1901) and *Terre Libre* [Free Earth] (1908).

Gustave Guitton also wrote a number of novels speculating about the future: *Terre Abandonnée* [Abandoned Land] (1901), *Les Têtards (Futures Femmes)* [The Tadpoles (Future Women)] (1904) and *Ce Que Seront les Hommes de l'An 3000* [What Men from the Year 3000 Will Be Like] (1907), dedicated to Wells. The latter was a deliberately optimistic utopia, meant to contrast with the Englishman's pessimistic vision. In it, a young man awakens from a "belzevorine"-induced sleep in the year 3000 and discovers a technologically perfect utopia that features fiberglass, typewriters, computers, electronic showers, synthetic foods, etc. Earth has been turned into a vast garden with only two industrial zones at the poles, planetary weather control, and energy provided by the harnessing of its rotation.

Less optimistic was Jules Sageret's short story "*La Race qui Vaincra*" [The Race That Will Be Victorious] (1908),[139] an anticipation taking place in the "211st Year of the Second Cycle," and one of the first genre novels dealing with the theme of the mutants fated to replace the human race. Here, these mutants are called "Whistlers".

On a somewhat similar theme, Marcel Roland penned a series of books dubbed "novels of future times" which included *Le Presqu'Homme* [The Almost-Man] (1907), *Le Déluge Futur* [The Future Flood] (1911) and *La Conquête d'Anthar* [The Conquest of Anthar] (1914).

Émile Solari's *La Cité Rebâtie* [The Rebuilt City] (1907) also featured a universal flood.

In Jean Jullien's *Enquête sur le Monde Futur* [An Investigation of the World of the Future] (1909),[140] a reporter interviews scientists whose discoveries are in the process of laying the foundations for the transformation of human society.

---

[139] In *The Revolt of the Machines*, Black Coat Press, ISBN 978-1-61227-333-4.

[140] Black Coat Press, 978-1-61227-106-4.

Louis de Meurville's *La Cité Future* [The Future City] (1910) was another attempt at imagining what the future would look like.

The prolific Octave Béliard penned *Les Aventures d'un Voyageur qui Explora le Temps* [The Adventures of a Voyager Who Explored Time] (1909), which told the story of a scientist who invented a time travel machine which was then unwittingly hijacked by his two young sons and eventually discovered that they had gone on to become the founders of Ancient Rome; the aptly-named *La Journée d'un Parisien au XXIème Siècle* [A Day in the Life of a Parisian in the 21st Century] (1910), depicting a colossal, futuristic Paris where monuments like the Eiffel Tower are dwarfed by *Bladerunner*-like towers. Business is run by multinational corporations. The Moon has been terraformed since the 1950s and fitted with an artificial atmosphere; and *Une Exploration Polaire aux Ruines de Paris* [A Polar Exploration in the Ruins of Paris] (1911), which described a Europe buried under the ice and Paris being excavated by archeologists from Madagascar.

In 1911, the writing team of Victor Cyril and Dr. Eugène Berger, signing Cyril-Berger, penned *La Merveilleuse Aventure de Jim Stappleton* [The Wondrous Adventure of Jim Stappleton] (1911), the description of a future America and the story of a future boxer whose sparring partner is a robot.

Belgian writer, François Léonard, wrote *Le Triomphe de l'Homme* [The Triumph of Man] (1911), an odd Stapledon-like story that tgells how, ten thousand years in the future, under the leadership of a brilliant scientist, Earth is turned into a giant spaceship traveling towards Vega. After detailing the huge social upheavals created by the journey, the novel chronicles the survival of our species during its interstellar flight. After centuries of travel, the new men face the "Green Enemy" (intelligent plants) and the "Red Enemy," Vega itself, which ends up consuming the planet.

In 1912, René Lorraine penned the juvenile novel *Un Petit Monde d'Aviateurs en l'An 2000* [The Small World of

Aviators in the Year 2000] (1912) which portrayed the future as a flying utopia.

Another juvenile futuristic tale was *Le Déluge de Feu* [The Fire Flood] by Swiss author Eugène Pénard, which was serialized in the magazine *Les Pages Illustrées* in 1911-12.

In 1913, Belgian writer Alex Pasquier penned *Le Secret de ne Jamais Mourir* [The Secret of Never Dying] a tale about automata.

Charles Renouvier coined the term "Uchronia" to label alternate future histories of the type already imagined by Louis Geoffroy in his *Napoléon Apocryphe* (q.v). In his *Uchronie (L'Utopie dans l'Histoire): Esquisse Historique Apocryphe du Développement de la Civilisation Européenne tel qu'il n'a pas été, tel qu'il aurait pu être* [Uchronia (Utopia In History): Apocryphal Sketch of the Development of European Civilization, As It Was Not, But As It Could Have Been] (1876), Renouvier invented a parallel history of Europe, starting in the year 175 AD, then featuring the untimely death of Emperor Constantine, topsy-turvy Crusades where the Easterners attempted to take Rome back from the Western Church, and ending in the 8th century, dubbed the 16th century because in that world, years were counted from the date of the first Olympics.

In R.F. Géris' *Quo Vadimus?* (1903), sub-titled "A Story of Future Times", the Duke of Orleans restored French monarchy and saved France from the evil Freemasons.

In Louis Millanvoy's *Seconde Vie de Napoléon* [Napoleon's Second Life] (1913), Napoleon escaped his fate on Saint-Helena and ended up becoming a King in Africa after an unfortunate shipwreck.

During the 19th century, France had the dubious honor of fostering an entire sub-genre of scientific anticipation devoted to chauvinistic, militaristic tales of near-future wars pitting the French against pretty much the rest of the universe and often including super-weapons and vastly improved killing devices.

The major representative of that "school" was the prolific Émile-Auguste-Cyprien Driant, who wrote under the pseudonym of "Capitaine Danrit". Driant was a famous French military strategist and politician, who died heroically at Verdun during World War I. Like a 19th century Tom Clancy, he penned many very popular "techno-thrillers", which he used to develop his ground-breaking military theories, especially with regards to the application of then-new technologies to modern and future warfare. These bellicose anticipations included the eight-volume *La Guerre de Demain* [Tomorrow's War] (1889-96), in which the French fight the Germans; the four-volume *L'Invasion Noire* [The Black Invasion] (1895-96), in which the French fight the Muslims and the Africans; the three-volume *La Guerre Fatale* [The Fatal War] (1901-02), in which the French fight the British; the three-volume *L'Invasion Jaune* [The Yellow Invasion] (1905-06), in which the French fight the Asians; *L'Aviateur du Pacifique* [The Aviator of the Pacific] (1909-10), in which the French help the Americans fight the Japanese (which prophetically included an attempt by the Japanese to invade Midway); *L'Alerte* [The Alert] (1910), in which the French fight the Germans again.

Danrit also wrote a few less bellicose sagas, but still railing against anarchists and other Bolsheviks. In *Robinsons Sous-Marins* [Undersea Odyssey] (1907-08),[141] he tackled the use of the modern, 200-ton submarines which had just been introduced in the French Navy a few years earlier, campaigning for more safety measures through an harrowing and suspenseful tale of sailors trapped thirty fathoms below in the Mediterranean. The same dramatic template was repeated in *Robinsons de l'Air* [Robinsons of the Air] (1908-09), underground in *Robinsons Souterrains* [Underground Robinsons] (1912-13)) and even in the future with *La Révolution de Demain* [Tomorrow's Revolution] (1909-10), co-written with Arnould Galopin.

---

[141] Black Coat Press, ISBN 978-1-935558-81-1.

Danrit was awarded the Medal of Honor for the Promotion of Good in 1905, and a commemorative stamp was issued in 1956, forty years after his death. Nevertheless, he has been justifiably forgotten, remaining only as a curious footnote in the history of modern French science fiction.

Other works in this same vein included:

Les Malheurs de John Bull [The Misfortunes of John Bull] (1884),[142] by Camille Debans, in which a spurned lover seeking to avenge an insult by an English nobleman, becomes a billionaire and turns an improvised nation into a global empire, ultimately defeating and conquering England. This significant story anticipates warfare on a global scale, especially naval warfare, featuring battles between ironclad warships assisted by various fictional inventions.

Barillet-Lagargousse's *La Guerre Finale* [The Final War] (1885),[143] which takes the European arms race of the late 19th century to its logical end: a terrifying deadlock due to the political and social paralysis caused by weapons sufficiently powerful to be seemingly unbeatable. Based on a then-new idea, *La Guerre Finale* was the first elaborate extrapolation of the strangely modern notion is that peace can only be achieved through ultimate war, and the first novel to flesh it out with abundant detail.

La Guerre sous l'Eau [The Underwater War] (1890) and the rather candidly entitled *Mort aux Anglais* [Death to the British] (1892), by Georges Le Faure.

La Prise de Londres au XXème Siècle [The Taking of London in the 20th Century] (1891) by Pierre Ferreol.

L'Agonie d'Albion [The Agony of Albion] (1901) Eby ugène Demolder depicted an England conquered by the Boers.

La Patrie en Danger [*Our Homeland Under Threat*] (1905) by Colonel Royet and Paul d'Ivoi was the tale of yet another near future war; while their *Un, La Mystérieuse* [One, The Mysterious] (1905), featured a brilliant French inventor

---

[142] Black Coat Press, ISBN 978-1-61227-411-9.
[143] Black Coat Press, ISBN 978-1-61227-337-2.

using used a plethora of super-gadgets (including the "Proteus," a vehicle which could travel both in the air and underground) fighting the Bolshevik threat.

La Guerre Aérienne Berlin-Bagdad [The Aerial Berlin-Baghdad War] (1907) by Rodolphe Martini and *Haut les Ailes!* [Up The Wings!] (1914) by Marc Gouvieux both prophetically predicted that air power would win the next war.

Finally, *Le Capitaine Rex* (1910) by Roger Duguet & Georges Thierry depicted a Catholic France which allied itself with Spain and Italy to fight protestant anglo-saxon imperialism.

Four particularly remarkable authors deserve to be singled in this category:

Han Ryner, a French anarchist, philosopher and a startlingly original science fiction writer (who was once labeled the "Prince of Storytellers" by a popular magazine), and the only genre author to have stood for peace in these troubled times, for his *Le Sphinx Rouge* [The Red Sphinx] (1905) in which both Paris and Berlin are surrounded by their respective armies in an attempt to force peace, but the military leaders are captured, tried, convicted and executed, so that war can go on;. In *Les Pacifiques* [The Pacifists] (1914),[144] humans shipwrecked in the Sargasso Sea encounter peaceful Atlanteans who have domesticated the universal "pandyname" energy.

Pierre Giffard, with his thirty-issue serial *La Guerre Infernale* [The Infernal War] (1908), illustrated by Robida, which depicts with a prodigious wealth of details an apocalyptic world war opposing the West to the Chinese. In it, war is fought in the air, on and under water, and underground, with a multitude of superweapons capable of freezing the oceans or setting them on fire, of spreading vast clouds of toxic gases, etc.

Belgian writer François Léonard, with *La Conquête de Londres* [The Conquest of London], written in 1912 but not

---

[144] In *The Human Ant*, Black Coat Press, ISBN 978-1-61227-323-5.

published until 1917, which describes an Anglo-German war that featured radium-powered rockets, magnetic-powered flying dreadnaughts, and the discovery of the virus of death itself.

Arthur Bernède's *Chantecoq* (1916) foresaw yet another future war between France and Germany, this time using super-weapons.

Charles Dodeman with *La Bombe Silencieuse* [The Silent Bomb] (1916)[145] Once the subgenre of "war fiction" had been established, it was maintained, even in peacetime, by its inherent melodramatic potential. It is still thriving today, but its difficult birth took place in France and France was one of its pioneers. *La Bombe Silencieuse* is one of the earliest thrillers to be set during a war that was actually going on at the time of its publication, without the benefit of hindsight. In it, the author imagines a new, revolutionary type of bomb that, one that today, we would call a "dirty bomb" capable of spreading radioactive particles, delivered through radio-controlled miniature aircrafts, i.e.: "drones."

Mainstream Authors

Some literary works that would, by any standards, be regarded as science fiction, or at least containing sf elements, were published outside the field, and therefore not labeled as such, by non-genre authors.

The more notable of these was the distinguished astronomer-writer Camille Flammarion who, throughout the 19th century, continued his exploration of the cosmos in several brilliant, ground-breaking stories collected in *Récits de l'Infini* [Stories of Infinity] (1872), later revised as *Lumen* (1887), and *Rêves Etoilés* [Starry Dreams] (1888). In the story "*Lumen*", a man learns about the universe by conversing with an entity made of pure mind. In "*Un Amour des astres*" [Love Among

---

[145] Black Coat Press, ISBN 978-1-61227-319-8.

the Stars] (1896),[146] a man falls in love with an alien entity. Other stories dealt with the notion of an Earth where time runs backwards, extra-sensory perception enabling a man to see into other dimensions, and a description of the migration of human souls to the Sirian alien race.

Flammarion's masterpiece was a novel entitled *La Fin du Monde* [The End of the World] (1893), loosely adapted into an eponymous 1930 film by Abel Gance. Penned in an essay-like style, the book exposes in great detail the future history of Man in the 25th century, and the eventual disappearance of Earth's atmosphere in ten million years. Perhaps not surprisingly for someone so well versed in the history of the genre, the author's last man, like Grainville's, was named Omegar. Other notable works included the novels *Uranie* [Urania] (1889) and *Stella* (1897), in which a dying man and a woman found themselves reincarnated on Mars.

Flammarion's contribution to modern science fiction cannot be underestimated, including the fact that, like Verne, he was widely translated into English and, therefore, contributed to shaping the evolution of the genre.

Humorist Eugène Mouton's short story collection entitled simply *Nouvelles* [Short Stories] (1872) included a tale entitled "*La Fin du Monde*" [The End of the World] (1872),[147] a grim dystopia featuring monstrous cattle and sheep "modified" (genetically engineered) to better serve man's needs and depicting an ecocatastrophe precipitated by global warming generated by human industrial activity. His 1883 collection *Fantaisies* [Fantasies] included "*L'Origine de la Vie*" [The Origin of Life] (1877),[148] in which life on Earth is credited to a

---

[146] In *The World Above the World*, Black Coat Press, ISBN 978-1-61227-002-9.

[147] In *The Supreme Progress*, Black Coat Press, ISBN 978-1-935558-82-8.

[148] In *The Germans on Venus*, Black Coat Press, ISBN 978-1-934543-56-6.

collision with another world, and "*L'Historioscope*" (1883),[149] in which a scientist invents a device that can look into the past.

In 1860, French journalist and satirist Edmond About wrote *Le Cas de M. Guérin* [The Case of Mr. Guerin] in which a man becomes pregnant. His classic novel *L'Homme à l'Oreille Cassée* [The Man with the Broken Ear] (1862), adapted into an eponymous 1962 film, featured the reanimation in 1859 of a Napoleonic Army colonel who has been preserved in suspended animation since 1813. Finally, *Le Nez d'un Notaire* [The Notary's Nose] (1862) dealt with organ transplants, in this case in a humorous fashion since the organ is a nose.

Pierre Véron was a frequent contributor to two of the most popular Parisian humorous papers, *Le Charivari* (which served as the model for the English magazine *Punch*) and the *Journal Amusant*, until becoming editor-in-chief of both in 1874, retaining that position until a few months before his death. Although his *Les Marchands de Santé* [The Merchants of Health] (1862)[150] is set on the Planet Fantasia, it really is an ironic reflection on the French medical system of its time. Despite the fact that modern medicine is far more competent and better organized, it is disturbing to see how many of his observations regarding the psychology of patients and some of the tendencies of the "merchants of health" still ring a bell today. His *Monsieur Nobody* (1864) lavishly explored an immense future Paris of the 20th century and offered an ironic look at the future of Parisian life.

Writer, poet and inventor Charles Cros was a friend of Arthur Rimbaud, Paul Verlaine, Alphonse Allais, and others, literary and artistic celebrities and was a well-known literary figure of the times. His works later inspired the surrealists. His story "*Un Drame Interastral*" [An Interastral Drama]

---

[149] In *News from the Moon*, Black Coat Press, ISBN 978-1-932983-89-0.

[150] Black Coat Press, ISBN 978-1-61227-372-3.

(1872)[151] was about an unlawful love between an Earthman and a Venusian woman. Cros also invented an earlier version of the phonograph called paleophone.

In 1872, Auguste Blanqui, a notorious anarchist who spent about 30 years of his life in jail, penned *L'Éternité par les Astres* [Eternity Through the Stars], an elaborate cosmogony based on the universal repetition of some primordial pattern.

In 1873, Alphonse Daudet, a mainstream author famous for his series of Provencal tales, penned a remarkable short story entitled "*Wood's Town*" in which is plants revolt against men.

In 1883, the notorious anarchist Louise Michel was sentenced to six years of solitary confinement. Effectively deprived of communication, she had no refuge but writing. It is during that time that she penned *Les Microbes Humains* [The Human Microbes] (published only in 1887),[152] as a distraction from her awful circumstances. It was followed by a sequel, *Le Monde Nouveau* [The New World],[153] published in a truncated form in 1888, due to Michel being shot in the head that year. Both are modeled on the classic *feuilleton* serials of the 1840s and were intended to be part of a six-novel series, in which Mankind would build a new utopia on Earth before moving out into space. In the first novel, a man unjustly accused of a murder by an evil mastermind manages to escape the guillotine and embarks on a quest for revenge that will draw in its wake a cast of characters, including mad doctors, lost children, strange gypsies, Irish revolutionaries, Russian anarchists and Utopians. Containing graphic scenes of vivisection, rape, pederasty and necrophilia, the novel reads like a modern horror thriller. In the second novel, the Arctic Utopian community founded by Dr. Gaël, and comprised of the victims of tyranny rescued by Captain Josiah and his "phantom brig," is threat-

---

[151] In *The Supreme Progress*, q.v.
[152] Black Coat Press, ISBN 978-1-61227-116-3.
[153] Black Coat Press, ISBN 978-1-61227-117-0.

ened by the evil Judge Roll Wolff, intent on destroying it to cover his crimes.

Jean-Marie-Matthias Villiers de l'Isle-Adam, an important writer better known for his *Contes Cruels* [Cruel Tales], who will be reviewed at length in our companion volume on Supernatural Fiction, more than dabbled in science fiction. His short story "*La Machine à Gloire*" [The Glory Machine] (1874), featured the robot-like "andreids" manufactured by Edison. The author reused the idea in a more elaborate form in *L'Ève Future* [The Future Eve] (1886), a bitterly ironic novel in which a boorish young lord falls in love a female robot. His *Axel* (1890) was a prose poem in which the eponymous hero, a wealthy Rosicrucian scientist living in an impregnable fortress defies the armies of a dying world. *Axel* anticipated the effete, decadent universes of Jack Vance and Michael Moorcock. The hero's final words, "Live? Our servitors will do that for us!" summed up rather well the author's rejection of a future world in which there was no more room for effete aristocrats.

Some of the stories by Guy de Maupassant could just as easily be classified as science fiction: "*Le Horla*" (1887) about a man plagued by an invisible, other-dimensional entity, and "*L'Homme de Mars*" [Martian Mankind] (1888),[154] in which a man saw a Martian spaceship, described as a luminous, transparent globe, fall into the Atlantic Ocean near Etretat.

In 1893, André Gide penned *Le Voyage d'Urien* [The Voyage of Urien], an Extraordinary Voyage novel in which the hero discovers a utopia while exploring the Sargasso Sea and the North Pole.

The same year, novelist Paul Adam wrote *Le Conte Futur* [A Tale of the Future],[155] the tale of a future war that eventually led mankind to universal peace. One of the more interesting notions featured in that story was the creation of advanced machinery to take over farming labors.

---

[154] In *News from the Moon*, q.v.
[155] In *The Supreme Progress*, q.v.

Camille Mauclair, one of the younger recruits of the Symbolist Movement that was a highly significant feature of the Parisian fin-de-siècle and included Stéphane Mallarmé, Remy de Gourmont, Jean Lorrain and Marcel Schwob penned *L'Orient vierge, roman épique de l'an 2000* [The Virgin Orient, an Epic Novel of the Year 2000] (1897),[156] the account of a preventive strike by Europe, united under the government of Anarchism, against the perceived "Yellow Peril." Even though his accounts of two crucial battles fought in India are extended and bloody, the author's primary purpose is not to detail the war but rather to analyze the crisis of conscience suffered by the Anarchist "dictator" once it has been won.

Even the famous Émile Zola, the founder of the naturalist movement, wrote three novels before his untimely death in 1902 that could be classifiable as science fiction: *Fécondité* [Fecundity] (1899), *Travail* [Labor] (1901) and *Vérité* [Truth] (published posthumously in 1903). A fourth novel, *Justice*, was meant to complete that tetralogy, entitled *Les Quatre Evangiles* [The Four Gospels], but remained unwritten. The books followed the lives of four brothers in seemingly divergent futures, their events all taking place between 1925 and 1980: In *Travail*, for example, a workers' revolution succeeded, but the world was then destroyed by a cataclysmic war. There are other instances of scientific and social anticipations in the other two novels.

The advent of the 20th century brought several other notable works of "mainstream" science fiction.

Paul Vibert made several significant contributions to the early development of the genre. Published mostly in newspapers, his works were only recently rediscovered, and deserve much recognition alongside those of Alphonse Allais, Charles Cros, Alfred Jarry and Albert Robida. In his collection *Pour Lire en Automobile, Nouvelles Fantastiques* [To Read In A

---

[156] Black Coat Press, ISBN 978-1-61227-502-4.

Car, Fantastical Short Stories] (1901),[157] he explored such ground-breaking concepts as the artificial insemination of elephants with the seed of prehistoric mastodons found preserved in ice, the artificial production of microbe-sized humans, the existence of an underwater world inhabited by Ancient Jews, communication with Mars and other worlds via light signals, the power to look into the past, the electrical nature of the soul, the strange chemical lifeforms of the future, artificial Metempsychosis and the conquest of space.

La Force Ennemie [Enemy Force] (1903)[158] by John-Antoine Nau, an eccentric French poet and writer who led a marginal existence and whose works remained mostly unpublished until long after his death. *La Force Ennemie* won the first Goncourt literary award ever. "The best [novel] that we ever crowned," wrote Joris-Karl Huysmans. *La Force Ennemie* is a ground-breaking, surrealistic novel about a poet who is locked in a lunatic asylum and who mysteriously becomes possessed by an "Enemy Force," possibly an alien named Kmohoûn, originating from Tkoukrah, a hellish world orbiting the star Aldebaran, starkingly described by the author. Both tragic and satirical, emotional and visionary, it is considered by many to be a forgotten masterpiece of early science fiction.

Daniel Halévy's *Histoire de Quatre Ans, 1997-2001* [Four Years' History] (1903) was an attempt at creating a future history, including an invasion of Europe by the Arabic nations.

Nobel prize winner Anatole France contributed *Sur La Pierre Blanche* [The White Stone] (1905), in which a group of intellectuals theorized about the rise of socialism; and *L'Île des Pingouins* [Penguin Island] (1908), a *Planet of the Apes*-like novel in which mankind's evolution was paralleled in a

---

[157] The *Mysterious Fluid*, Black Coat Press, ISBN 978-1-61227-020-3.

[158] Black Coat Press, ISBN 978-1-935558-49-1.

satirical fashion through a race of penguins who, after having been baptized, become intelligent.

In 1909, Belgian writer Henry Kistemaekers, known mostly for his romance novels, penned *Aéropolis* (1909), subtitled "A Comic Novel of Aerial Life," the satirical tale of a Asian invasion of Europe.

In 1910, Jacques Constant also had fun in *Le Triomphe des Suffragettes* [The Triumph of the Suffragettes], a satirical novel taking place in 1995 when women have taken over. Amusingly, the same concept had been developed in Henri Desmarest's *La Femme Future* [Future Woman] (1890).

Léonie Rouzade, a combative and prominent woman author in the feminist cause, delivered a scathing social commentary in two tales from 1872: *Le Monde Renversé* [The World Turned Upside Down] and *Voyage de Théodosie à l'Île d'Utopie* [A Voyage to the Isle of Utopia].[159] *Le Monde Renversé* is the earliest fantasy of gender role reversal ever penned. An idealized woman, Celestine, climbs out of her circumscribed existence to rule a foreign kingdom, only to mandate the subjugation of men by women. Even today, its originality remains unsurpassed. It is a grandiose *conte philosophique*, taking satire to the edge of absurdity. In *Voyage de Théodosie,* a shipwreck strands a man in a perfect island civilization where, after confronting a parade of didactic lectures, he comes to accept that the rigors of logic have rendered obsolete human individuality.

Jean Richepin, a member of the French Academy, penned *L'Aile, Roman des Temps Nouveaux* [The Wing, Novel of the New Age] (1911),[160] the story of the "alerion," a flying machine capable of neutralizing gravity by harnessing Earth's telluric currents, powered by atomic disintegration and controlled by radio signals; but even more, it is the story of its inventors, their lives and loves, and the tragedies that bind

---

[159] Both in *The World Turned Upside Down*, Black Coat Press, ISBN 978-1-61227-346-4,

[160] Black Coat Press, ISBN 978-1-61227-053-1.

them. *L'Aile* is a significant text in the history of early French science fiction, being one of the few literary responses to the uniquely exciting combination of the simultaneous development of the wireless, radioactivity and aviation, which suggested the dawn of a "new age."

Finally, Gaston de Pawlowski, in his *Contes Singuliers* [Singular Tales] (1912) and especially in his *Voyage au Pays de la 4ème Dimension* [Journey to the Land of the Fourth Dimension] (1912),[161] written between 1895 and 1912, predates Stapledon's *Last and First Men* by almost 20 years. In this prodigious future history, we visit the singular era of the Leviathan, when a colossal entity envelops men like cells in a gigantic body; the time of the Scientific Tyranny, when the Savants rule supreme; and finally, the Great Idealist Renaissance, or the Age of the Golden Eagle, when the fourth dimension becomes familiar to all men. We hall meet homunculi and supermen, intelligent machines and giant microbes. As translator and critic Brian Stableford best describes it, "Much primitive futuristic fiction now seems banal and unadventurous in its anticipations, but there is nothing banal about Pawlowski's future history. The surreal quality of his futuristic vignettes-especially those dealing with 'atomic dissociation' and future biotechnologies in the Scientific Era has been given an extra edge by actual advances in modern science."

---

[161] Black Coat Press, ISBN 978-1-934543-37-5.

LES NAVIGATEURS DE L'INFINI

PAR
ROSNY Aîné
DE L'ACADÉMIE GONCOURT

LE RAYON
FANTASTIQUE

FOREST

The End of the Golden Age
(1918-1930)

World War I with its 2.3 million dead and crippled buried the 19th century and sapped the confidence of French society. Deep wounds were created in the collective psyche: on the one hand, France had won the war, and chauvinistic pride and xenophobic arrogance were at an all-time high. On the other, things could never be the same again. This almost schizoid conflict between the delusion of superiority that boosted the desire to preserve traditional values, and the emergence of new, and therefore threatening, ideas intending to break with the past was played out, with most dramatic results, in the field of science fiction.

Science fiction between the wars became the theater of a battle between the forces of conservatism and the forces of progress. Unfortunately, the contribution of science and technology to the slaughter of World War I was only too obvious: aviation, tanks, rockets, deadly gas, etc. Science had not carried people to the Moon or across the globe, but instead had killed millions of young Frenchmen. The emphasis being on "young," for one of the unintended consequences of World War I was that it polarized the conflict between "old" values and "young" ones, and the young ones lost.

Since Jules Verne, French science fiction had made prodigious conceptual leaps forward, not unlike what happened in the United States in the 1930s and 1940s. If the comforting, optimistic scientific anticipations of Verne had not entirely disappeared, they had nevertheless been replaced in a more ambitious, constantly expanding genre. By the time World War I erupted, the prodigious Rosny Aîné had evoked the end of our civilization; Le Faure & De Graffigny had explored the

Solar System; La Hire and Le Rouge had investigated the use of mind powers; Renard and Couvreur had worried about medical experiments; De Quirielle and Corday had created artificial life; Béliard and Robida had travelled through time. This was an unparalleled thematic record, unmatched by what was happening at the time in England and America.

After the war, however, because the new science fiction embodied the future and represented values that were perceived by the older French cultural elite as threatening the stability and conservatism of society, it was increasingly relegated to the shelves of juvenile fiction; and ultimately, even there, it was fought and driven out on philosophical and ideological grounds. The same reactionary forces that, in 1941, stood behind Marshal Petain and literally split France in half, the same conservative forces that equated science with Darwinism, thought that the Heavens "should be inhabited by angels, not aliens," (an actual quote!) and generally believed that their mission was to protect France as the Supreme Embodiment of the Christian West from the depraved forces of progress, anarchy, socialism, and more generally the outside world, and foreign influences pilloried the new science fiction.

Belgian scholar Jacques Van Herp found that, between 1923 and 1925, the publishers of the magazines *L'Intrépide* and *Sciences & Voyages* lost no less than five libel suits against various catholic organizations that had slandered them, their authors, and their publications. Other magazines, such as *Science & Voyages* and authors like Renard were also targeted by the same reactionary forces. The words of one of the judgments rendered against *Sciences & Voyages* in 1925 leave no room for doubt: the Court found that the magazine had exerted a "pernicious influence on the imagination and intelligence of children"!

Ideas, like men, can be killed in battle. This was exactly what happened to French science fiction. The conservatives' message was heard loudly and clearly throughout the French publishing establishment. The next few years saw a gradual end to the publication of ground-breaking novels about interplanetary exploration, biological experiments and mind powers. Instead, we saw a return to the tamer, non-threatening, Earth-based adventures of the late 19th century. Publisher Hachette sought refuge behind the politically correct name of Jules Verne and created a "Jules Verne Award" in 1926; with one exception, it was awarded to mediocre novels and was soon abandoned in 1933.

By the end of the 1920s, just as Hugo Gernsback's *Amazing Stories* (1926) was taking off on the other side of the Atlantic, the Golden Age of French Science Fiction had effectively ended, shot down on the ideological battlefield by the more powerful, conservative elements of a society which refused progress. It can be said with some degree of validity that French science fiction never recovered.

The Publishers

World War I had, directly or indirectly, been responsible for the cancellation of virtually all the major genre imprints. After the war, science fiction was mostly relegated to popular adventure imprints that carried little or no literary respectability.

Jules Tallandier was one of the most active publisher in the field with no less than a dozen imprints, including the long-lived *Bibliothèque des Grandes Aventures* [Library of Great Adventures] (1923-30), later renamed *Grandes Aventures-Voyages Excentriques* [Great Adventures & Eccentric Voyages] (1930-42), then simply *Grandes Aventures* [Great Adventures] (1949-53); *Les Romans Mystérieux* [Mysterious Novels] (1927-50); *Voyages Lointains-Aventures Étranges* [Far Voyages & Strange Adventures] (1927-32); *À Travers l'Univers* [Throughout the Universe] (1932-33 and 1952-53); *Les Chevaliers de l'Aventure* [The Knights of Adventure] (1930-34); *Les Meilleurs Romans d'Aventures* [The Best Adventure Novels] (1937-38); *Le Livre d'Aventures* [The Book of Adventures] (1937-38 and 1952-53); *Le Lynx* [The Lynx]

(1940-41); and *Univers-Aventures* [Adventure Universe] (1949-53). Among the writers published in these various imprints were Louis Boussenard, Paul d'Ivoi, André Falcoz, Albert Bonneau (writing as "Maurice Champagne"), Eugène Thébault, Léon Groc, Jean Petithuguenin, Gaston de Wailly, André Armandy, André Couvreur, and H.-J. Magog.

His main competitor was a Hungarian expatriate, Joseph Ferenczi, which published five competing imprints, *Les Romans d'Aventures* [*Adventure Novels*] (1921-29); *Le Livre de l'Aventure* [The Book of Adventures] (1929-31); *Voyages et Aventures* [Voyages & Adventures] (1933-41); *Le Petit Roman d'Aventures* [The Little Adventure Novels] (1936-39) and *Mon Roman d'Aventures* [My Adventure Novels] (1942-1956). Among the writers published by Frenczi were Jean de La Hire, René Thévenin, Max-André Dazergues (writing as "Mad"), Henry de Graffigny, and Maurice Limat

To this already impressive list should be added the imprint *Collection d'Aventures* [*The Adventure Collection*] (1918-27) published by the Offenstadt Brothers, featuring novels by Pierre Adam and José Moselli.

Publisher Pierre Larousse put out the *Contes et Romans Pour Tous* [*Tales and Novels For All*] (1927-36), featuring works by Henri Allorge, Henri Bernay and Gustave Le Rouge.

Publisher Fernand Nathan put out *Aventures et Voyages* [Adventures & Voyages] (1929-48).

Publisher Arthème Fayard put out *L'Aventure* [Adventure] (1929-30), featuring works by Jean d'Agraives and Eugène Thébault.

Publisher Jules Rouff put out *Romans pour la Jeunesse* [Novels for the Young] (1932-35).

The magazines also continued to fulfill their important function. In addition to the weeklies, *Le Journal des Voyages* and *L'Intrépide*, and the monthlies *Lectures Pour Tous* and *Je Sais Tout*, new magazines which started between the two wars included the very important *Sciences et Voyages* (1919-1935), published by the Offenstadt brothers (who already put out *L'Intrépide*), featuring new works by Léon Groc, José Moselli and René Thévenin; the short-lived *À l'Aventure* [To Adventure] (1920-21), which serialized some genre novels under the editorship of Louis-Frédéric Rouquette; and *Oeuvres Libres* [Free Works] (1921-40), published by Fayard, featuring works by André Couvreur, Claude Farrère and Tancrède Vallerey.

Major Authors

The two major science fiction authors of the period continued to be J.-H. Rosny Aîné, with the ground-breaking *Les Navigateurs de l'Infini* (1925) (q.v.), and Maurice Renard.

Renard had already made a powerful mark on the genre with his two classics, *Le Docteur Lerne* (1908) and *Le Péril Bleu* (1912). In 1920, he wrote the classic *Les Mains d'Orlac* [The Hands of Orlac], in which the hands of a killer are transplanted onto a pianist. *L'Homme Truqué* [The Doctored Man] (1923)[162] featured the graft of "electroscopic" eyes onto a man blinded during the war. The result was the strange description of a world perceived through artificial senses. *L'Homme Qui Voulait Être Invisible* [The Man Who Wanted To Be Invisible] (1923)[163] dealt excellently with the issue of invisibility; in it, the author exposed the scientific fallacy inherent in Wells' famous novel. Since, in order to function, the human eye must perform as an opaque dark room, any truly invisible man would also be blind! In the controversial *Le Singe* [The Monkey] (1925), co-written with Albert Jean, Renard imagined the creation of artificial lifeforms through the process of "radiogenesis," a sort of human electrocopying process. The novel was ferociously attacked by the Catholic press, which saw it as sacrilegious, and it was blacklisted by public libraries.

Un Homme chez les Microbes [A Man Among the Microbes] (1928)[164] was one of the first scientific novels on the

---

[162] Black Coat Press, ISBN 978-1-935558-18-7.
[163] Included in *The Doctored Man*, q.v.
[164] Black Coat Press, ISBN 978-1-935558-16-3.

theme of miniaturization. In it, the hero submits himself willingly to a shrinking process that eventually runs out of control. As in Richard Matheson's 1956 classic, he is first attacked by various insects, before eventually arriving on an electron-sized planet, where scientifically advanced people are able to reverse the process and send him home. It was certainly the first to introduce the concept of a micro-world where atoms fuction like microscopic solar systems.

Finally, *Le Maître de la Lumière* [The Master of Light] (1947)[165] anticipated Bob Shaw's notorious "slow glass" by introducing the concept of a glass that condensed time. Because of his understanding and knowledge of the genre—he even wrote an article on the *merveilleux scientifique* in 1914 for a major newspaper—Renard could have been a major literary breakthrough figure, comparable to an Arthur C. Clarke or an Isaac Asimov. Instead, because of the conservative pressures mentioned above, and the French context of the period, he remained a minor writer, known only to specialists.

The treatment accorded to José Moselli was ever more unjust, since all of his works were published only in magazine form, and none were collected in book form until the 1970s, even though all scholars agree that he was one of the most interesting genre authors of the 1920s and 1930s. Moselli was one of the most prolific and popular "house authors" published in the Offenstadt magazines *L'Intrépide* and *Sciences & Voyages*. Like Renard, Moselli could have become another Wells had the publishing opportunities existed. He embodied many of the qualities of modern science fiction writers: a seemingly endless variety of daring ideas, introduced seriously and not for satirical purposes, exploited logically and not serving merely as a pretext for a wild adventure, featuring fully developed, believable characters rather than cardboard hero figures.

A brief panorama of some of Moselli's genre output remains, even today, an impressive catalog of ideas: *Le Téléluz* (1918) was about a helmet that enables its wearer to see and

---

[165] Black Coat Press, ISBN 978-1-935558-19-4.

hear scenes that are taking place miles away. *La Prison de Glace* [The Ice Prison] (1920) dealt with a form of controlled hibernation. *Le Rayon Phi* [The Phi Ray] (1921) was about a powerful death ray. *La Corde d'Acier* [The Steel Rope] (1921) featured a gang of criminals whose scheme involves dropping corpses from the air. In *Les Conquérants de l'Abîme* [The Conquerors of the Abyss] (1922), a scientist devises a mean to modify the course of the Gulf Stream. In *Le Maître de la Foudre* [The Lightning Master] (1922), another mad scientist uses a death ray to destroy ships at a distance. *Le Voyage Éternel* [The Eternal Voyage] (1923) was the tale of the first Moon exploration venture in which a space prospector sadly realizes that he can never return to Earth. *La Cité du Gouffre* [The City in the Pit] (1925) featured an underwater city. *L'Archipel de l'Épouvante* [The Archipelago of Terror] (1926) was a lost world story.

Two works of this period particularly stood out. *Le Messager de la Planète* [*The Planetary Messenger*] (1924)[166] was not unlike John W. Campbell's classic *The Thing* in that it featured the discovery of an alien whose ship has crashed near the South Pole. But here, the alien turns out to be an advanced and peaceful being from Mercury. Unfortunately, the sled dogs kills him before he can share his knowledge with the Earthmen who rescued him.

The visionary *La Fin d'Illa* [*Illa's End*] (1925)[167] began with the emergence of a new Pacific Island on which are found a cache of ancient documents and a small fragment of "zero-stone." A San Francisco scientist managed to decipher the documents, which tell the tale of the final, apocalyptic clash between the ancient Gondwanan cities of Illa and Nour. Later, his maid unwittingly throws the "zero-stone" into the fireplace, causing the famous 1905 earthquake. *La Fin d'Illa* not only featured an array of impressive technological predictions, such as atom bombs, solar-powered cities, force fields,

---

[166] In *Nemoville*, Black Coat Press, ISBN 978-1-61227-070-8.
[167] Black Coat Press, ISBN 978-1-61227-031-9.

and flying saucers, but also a grim catalog of social predictions. The Illians are described as a technologically advanced race who have lost their will to fight and their feelings of humanity. They are served by Undermen, genetically manufactured from apes and used as slave labor. Their leader is Rair, a proto-Hitler with a fascist police force who violently suppresses any opponents to his regime. Rair's dreams of conquest eventually leads Illia to its total destruction after the dictator obtains the secret of nuclear desintegration (the "zerostone") and uses it on Nour. In *La Fin d'Illa*, Moselli not only anticipated the sociological and technological horrors of World War II and Naziism, but he was also the first to equate nuclear conflict—even one clearly won by one of the two combatants—with mutual destruction. *La Fin d'Illa* may well be one of the stories responsible for the harsh, unjust 1925 verdict rendered by the court against *Sciences & Voyages*, where it was published.

Moselli was a perfect example of self-censorship as a result of the pressures described above. His later works evidenced a return to safer, tamer ideas. Three novels ca n nevertheless be mentioned here: In *La Guerre des Océans* [The Oceanic War] (1929), Captain Fédor Ivanovitch Sarraskine, like a vengeful Captain Nemo, uses his advanced science to attack the British and American fleets; he also surgically turns his victims into fish-men, thereby ensuring their obedience. In *L'Empereur du Pacifique* [The Emperor of the Pacific] (1932-35), mad scientist Ambrose Vollmer turns a Pacific atoll into a nightmarish *Doctor Moreau*-like kingdom of radio-controlled zombies and human experiments. Finally, in *L'Île des Hommes Bleus* [The Island of the Blue Men] (1939), billionaire Wasili Tchorok uses the knowledge of scientist Antoine Chantour to build a giant floating city in a geostationary orbit; its "blue men" are men surgically modified to breathe in the upper atmosphere.

Renard and Moselli were, without a doubt, the two major genre authors of the 1920s. However, H.-J. Magog, while not as significant as they, deserves special recognition. He was the author of many popular adventure novels, many of which displayed a wild and unique imaginative streak, but from a literary standpoint, they were often marred with a pulpish nature. In his *Extraordinaire Aventures de Deux Fiancés à travers le Monde* [Extraordinary Adventures of Two Fiancés Across the World] (1922), which takes place in 2050, a Japanese mad scientist uses the heat from the Earth's core to cause the oceans to dry up, but the ensuing volcanic eruptions end up destroying Japan. In *L'Île Tombée du Ciel* [The Island Which Fell from the Sky] (1923), a chunk of a wandering planet falls near Australia; its first human explorers discover that it is inhabited by invisible aliens who, fortunately, turn out to be benevolent. *Trois Ombres sur Paris* [Three Shadows Over Paris] (1928) also takes place in the 21st century and features the artificial creation of a race of supermen, and their subsequent conflict with the political powers of the times. Its conclusion was remarkably similar to the 1935 Stapledon novel, *Odd John*, in which the supermen are exiled to an island where they eventually destroy themselves.

Magog also collaborated with the son of prolific serial writer Paul Féval Paul Féval, Fils on a sprawling, rambling serial entitled *Les Mystères de Demain* [The Mysteries of Tomorrow] published by Ferenczi as five volumes: *Les Fiancés de l'an 2000* [The Fiancés of the Year 2000] (1922), *Le Monde des Damnés* [The World of the Damned] (1923), *Le Réveil d'Atlantide* [The Awakening of Atlantis] (1923), *L'Humanité Enchaînée* [Humankind Enchained] (1923) and *Le Faiseur de Folles* [The Maker of Madwomen] (1924).[168]

Purporting to chronicle the early years of the 21st century, the saga takes place on a quasi-utopian Earth where war no longer exists, poverty has been banished, men no longer consume meat, and, thanks to the genius of master scientist Oronius, humanity has mastered natural forces. However, there

---

[168] All five volumes available from Black Coat Press, ISBNs 978-1-61227-945-9, 978-1-61227-948-0, 978-1-61227-966-4, 978-1-61227-971-8 and 978-1-61227-974-9.

exists a snake in this garden of Eden: Oronius' former colleague Otto Hentzen, a mad scientist who has allied himself with the beautiful, deadly enchantress Yogha. From their impregnable citadel located atop Mount Everest, they wish to crush the world and rule it. Oronius' pupil, Jean Chapuis, his fiancée, Cyprienne, Oronius' own daughter, ably assisted by his mechanic Laridon, her maid Turlurette, and their African manservant Julep, repeatedly thwart the evil duo's diabolical schemes.

The quest to find Oronius, seemingly slain at the end of Volume 1, takes the heroes into a vast, underground realm inhabited by giant vampire bats and homunculi who worship the great scientist as their god. But their foes push the Subterraneans to rebel. Giant moles, a sea of molten gold and the central fire feature in the action. Then, Hentzen unleashes a worldwide cataclysmic radioactive heat wave that dries up most of the oceans and awakens the ancient continent of Atlantis. Unfortunately, it is a savage world of cannibal warriors and monsters, ruled by the cruel Queen Atlantea.

After that worldwide cataclysm, Oronius and his friends discover an advanced civilization of giant insects long buried in Antarctica. These "Polars" launch an attack against Humanity, increasing the intelligence of animals, who then rebel and enslave mankind, turning the world into a "Planet of the Beasts." Oronius eventually escapes and enlists the help of the United States to fight the giant insects. In the last volume, the diabolical Hantzen, who has insidiously taken over another country under the alias of Professor Astaroth, plots to unleash a pandemic of madness on the women of the world. It is again up to Oronius' faithful and resourceful friends to thwart the demoniacal scientist.

Maurice Leblanc, the father of the popular gentleman-burglar Arsène Lupin, would undoubtedly have made an excellent science fiction writer, one to rival Renard and Moselli, if he had continued in that vein, but time only allowed him to write two excellent genre novels. *Les Trois Yeux* [The Three

Eyes] (1919)[169] was a remarkable novel about communication between alien races. In it, a scientist discovers how to receive images from Venus, whose inhabitants turn out to be three-eyed aliens. At first, the Venusians transmit images from Earth's past, then pictures of their own, almost incomprehensible alien society, seemingly based on triangular logic. Leblanc also wrote *Le Formidable Evènement* [The Tremendous Event] (1920),[170] in which an earthquake causes a new land mass to emerge between France and England.

Penned in 1927 before the Wall Street crash of 1929, Théo Varlet's *Le Roc d'Or* [The Golden Rock][171] was both a homage to Jules Verne and a novel with its finger firmly on the pulse of the real political issues and concerns of the 1930s, which it addresses with admirable verve and perspicacity. Shortly after the end of World War I, the fall of an asteroid in the Atlantic causes a tidal wave and gives birth to a new island. An expedition sent by the French government discovers that it is made of iron... and gold! The exploitation of the new island could upset the world's economic order and start a new World War, as forces from all across the globe converge upon the eponymous Golden Rock.

Finally, René Thévenin was another good example of a writer of popular but undistinguished adventure serials, such as *Le Maître des Vampires* [The Vampire Master] (1923), *La Jungle Insurgée* [The Insurgent Jungle] (1926), *Sous les Griffes du Monstre* [The Claws of the Monster] (1926) and *La Forêt Sanglante* [The Bloody Forest] (1927), who suddenly, like Moselli, rose above the pulpish nature of the medium and penned two genuine classics. *Les Chasseurs d'Hommes* [The Manhunters] (1930) takes place in Africa and tells the story of two superpowered mutants who hunt men to feed on their

---

[169] In *French Tales of Alien Encounters*, Black Coat Press, ISBN 978-1-64932-109-1

[170] In *French Tales of Cataclysms*, Black Coat Press, ISBN 978-1-64932-110-7.

[171] Black Coat Press, ISBN 978-1-61227-134-7.

lifeforce. The mutants use their psychic powers to create an Eden-like garden behind a force field, in which they study the humans. The male mutant is eventually killed by a free man ("wolf"); his mate, who may have been pregnant, disappears after being saved by a slave ("dog"). Thévenin also wrote an excellent prehistoric novel, *L'Ancêtre des Hommes* [The Ancestor of Men] (1932) and is credited by most scholars for *Sur l'Autre Face du Monde* [On the Other Side of the World] (1935), a novel written under the pseudonym of "André Valérie". Anticipating Clarke's classic *Against the Fall of Night*, this novel told the story of the confrontation between a city of civilized men who have survived an ice age and the savage hunters who, by contrast, have managed to survive on the surface of the planet. The man sent by the city to explore the outside world is eventually torn between the two societies that are not yet ready to cohabit peacefully.

Other Notable Authors

In this section, we will review other notable genre works and authors published in the 1920s and 1930s, grouping them along our usual thematic categories.

Journeys to Other Worlds

This section covers space travel as well as alien encounters.

Mars was still very much the preferred destination when it came to space travel. The oddly entitled *D'Amra sur Azulba* [Amra on Azulba] (1917) by Prince Louis de Bourbon, subtitled "Diary of a Marsian [sic] on Earth" was the satirical tale of a Martian who came to Earth (our world is called "Azulba" in his language) on a radium-powered spaceship during World War I.

Anthéa, ou l'Étrange Planète [Anthea, or The Strange Planet] (1918) was the work of Michel Epuy, pseudonym of Swiss writer Louis Vaury. Hailed by J.-H. Rosny Aîné when it was first published in a magazine, the story starts with a planetoid abandoned by a passing comet and orbiting around our globe. and its subsequent exploration by an astronaut. Anthea was revised for its publication as a book in 1923 and has successfully withstood the test of time.

In Marcel Laurian's *L'Étrange Voyage* [The Strange Journey] (1919), a Persian Magus transports an entire Earth and its inhabitants from Earth to Mars. Here, the red planet is inhabited by prehistoric monsters, electro-magnetic beings, black-skinned and red-skinned anthropoids, winged sphinxes, mermaids, and cyclops. For some reason, the heroes even met Nostradamus there!

Omer Chevalier with *L'Avatar d'Yvan Orel* [Yvan Orel's Avatar] (1919) featured an Earthman reincarnated on a utopian Venus.

That same year, Joseph-Louis Lecornu penned the very Vernian *De la Terre à la Lune* [From the Earth to the Moon].

In Miral-Viger's *L'Anneau de Lumière* [The Ring of Light] (1922),[172] a nuclear rocket-powered spaceship leaves France to explore the other planets of the Solar System. On board are the intrepid Marquis de Valsorres, the eminent Dr. Portier, the beautiful Zabeth and their loyal companion, Thomas. After a long stay on a utopian Mars, they reach the prehistoric world of Saturn. But in the meantime the Great War has started on Earth and a rival German expedition threatens their very survival… *L'Anneau de Lumière* first appeared as a serial in the daily newspaper *Le Petit Parisien* more than a year before Herman Oberth's seminal *By Rocket into Interplanetary Space* (1923), and Otto Willi Gail's *The Shot into Infinity* (1925). It is of considerable interest because it is one of the earliest responses to the popularizing of the notion that space travel might become practicable with the aid

---

[172] Black Coat Press, ISBN 978-1-61227-756-1.

of rockets, and particularly rockets propelled by atomic power derived from radium.

The writing team of Théo Varlet and Octave Jonquel wrote a two-volume epic, *Les Titans du Ciel* [The Titans of the Sky] (1921) and *L'Agonie de la Terre* [The Agony of Earth] (1922),[173] which was clearly influenced by Wells' *War of the Worlds*. In it, the Jovians intervene after another Martian attack on Earth and destroy Mars, using focused solar energy. But the Martians migrate to Earth *en masse*, our planet now being revealed as the place where Martian souls reincarnate. Souls are alleged to travel inward from Mars, to the Earth, to Venus, to Mercury, ending up one with the Sun. This was the reason for the original invasion. Curiously, the authors' Martians are described as creatures not at all like Wells' but more like Le Rouge's Martians. In the second volume, the Earthmen continue to fight the body-snatching Martians, but his time with the help of the Venusians. The novel turns into a post-cataclysmic epic, in which a handful of scientists battle hordes of cannibals and anarchists roaming a devastated Earth, while trying to rebuild our civilization.

Varlet alone also wrote *La Grande Panne* [The Great Breakdown] (1930),[174] which featured Aurore Lescure, the first woman astronaut to have gone into space, who returns to Earth with deadly alien spores which feed on electricity and threaten to utterly destroy our civilization. It is an exciting thriller which extrapolates ideas about dangerous alien lifeforms with considerable verve and polish and foreshadows many similar-themed novels of the 1950s. Its sequel, *Aurore Lescure, Pilote d'Astronef* [Aurore Lescure, Space Pilot],[175] was written in 1932 but not published (posthumously) until

---

[173] Both in *The Martian Epic*, Black Coat Press, ISBN 978-1-934543-41-2.

[174] *The Xenobiotic Invasion*, Black Coat Press, ISBN 978-1-61227-054-8.

[175] *The Castaways of Eros*, Black Coat Press, ISBN 978-1-61227-177-4.

1943. It describes the first successful interplanetary flight to the planetoid Eros. There, Aurore and her crew discover that evolution on Eros has taken a different turn than on Earth, producing a race of intelligent dinosaurs. The notion of a Japanese-financed space expedition led by a French female astronaut was a radical one. With this book, Varlet hoped to promote the potential of rocket technology to launch a "Space Age" of interplanetary colonization. Sadly, the advent of WWII and his untimely death in 1938 put an end to that dream, leaving only these two remarkable novels as a witness to a future that never was.

The writing team of Victor Cyril and Eugène Berger, signing Cyril-Berger, penned *L'Adversaire Inconnu* [The Unknown Adversary] (1922), in which the egg of a small, chameleon-like, vampiric alien lands on Earth in a meteorite and, after hatching, the creature begins to feed on humans.

Belgian author Pierre Nothomb penned *La Rédemption de Mars* [The Redemption of Mars] (1922), a Christian science fiction tale, a mystical story in which the issue of the encounter between Earthlings and Martians focuses on questions of faith. The novel begins with the arrival on Mars of a man who brings both God and sin there and it ends with his despair.

In André Mas' *Drymea, Monde de vierges* [Drymea, World of Virgins] (1923),[176] the author depicts a sexless world in which women reproduce parthenogenetically and man is unknown.

Henri Allorge, in *Ciel contre Terre* [Heaven vs. Earth] (1924), described an attack on our planet by Martians vampires who owed much to Le Rouge's *Prisonnier de la Planète Mars*. These Martians, however, were defeated by alcohol.

Henri de Graffigny stuck to the theme of space exploration with his *Voyage de Cinq Américains dans les Planètes* [Voyage of Five Americans on the Planets] (1925) and penned

---

[176] In *The World Above the World*, Black Coat Press, ISBN 978-1-61227-002-9.

Les Diamants de la Lune [The Moon Diamonds] (1930), which featured a rocket-plane and the mineral exploitation of our satellite. Another notable genre novel was *Electropolis* (1933).

René Trotet de Bargis followed in the same vein with *La Mission de Quatre Savants* [The Mission of Four Scientists] (1925).

The prolific Jean de La Hire penned the thirty-volume serial, *Les Grandes Aventures d'un Boy Scout* [The Great Adventures of a Scout] (1926), which included many interplanetary adventures with colorful titles such as *Les Hommes de Mars* [The Men From Mars], *Chasses Martiennes* [Martian Hunts], *Le Rayon-Ardent* [The Fiery Ray], *Vers le Tour du Monde Saturnien* [Across Saturn] and *Le Drame des Hommes-Taureaux* [The Tragedy of the Men-Bull].

Jean Petithuguenin in *Une Mission Internationale sur la Lune* [An International Mission to the Moon] (1926).[177] In it, the author attempted to produce realistic accounts of a voyage to the Moon effected by means of rocket propulsion. It boasts the most substantial literary pedigree, and is the most realistic, far closer to that eventual reality than other, more primitive efforts. The author's interest in technological advancement and the possibility of space travel are real and well-informed, taking into account acceleration, weightlessness, the use of lateral rockets to turn the ship prior to landing, airlocks, spacesuits, etc. Petithuguenin became one of the first experimenters in France with what would later come to be called hard science fiction.

In 1928, writer/illustrator Henri Lanos, whose art had graced the covers for *Je Sais Tout* since 1906 and *Lectures pour Tous* since 1911, wrote and illustrated *Le Grand Raid Paris-La Lune* [The Great Paris-Moon Race], serialized in *Pierrot*, a children's magazine.

Also in 1928, an unknown writer who used the nom-de-plume of Cabarel published the two-volume *Dans l'Étrange*

---

[177] Black Coat Press, ISBN 978-1-61227-466-9.

Inconnu [Into the Strange Unknown] (1928), an imaginative yet naïve novel in which the author, using hypnosis and astral projection, visits two unseen satellites of Earth, Ersa and Nemea, as well as other planets of the solar system and other star systems, including Sirius. The second volume includes a trip to Ancient Lemuria, or Mû, 60,000 years ago, and the resurrection of its ancient priestess, Oris.

In a more serious vein, Albert Bailly's *L'Éther-Alpha* (1929), the best novel to be awarded the Jules Verne Award, imagined a spaceship made of coagulated aether, the eponymous "ether-apha", a substance both hard and transparent. In it, the ship travels to the Moon where explorers encounter the "Radios," energy-based Selenites. After testing the humans, the Radios eventually decide they do not want to live next to them and take our satellite far away from Earth.

Another Martian novel was Paul Darcy's *La Conquête de la Planète Mars* [The Conquest of Planet Mars], serialized in *Le Petit Illustré* in 1929.

René Pujol was a journalist who branched out after the Great War into the production of popular fiction and librettos for comic opera. He went on to work prolifically as a screenwriter and director in French cinema during the 1930s. His *Le Soleil Noir* [The Black Sun] (1921),[178] offers an account of the planet-wide catastrophe that overwhelms the world when a collision with an errant dark star causes the sun's radiation to flare up dramatically, and tells of the heroes' battle for survival, hiding deep underground in an old quarry. In his *La Planète Invisible* [The Invisible Planet] (1931), a new planet is discovered in the solar system. Finally, in *Au Temps des Brumes* [*The Time of the Mist*] (1932), Earth is enveloped by a mysterious cosmic black cloud that stops all sunlight.

In Pierre Lavaur's *La Conquête de la Terre* [The Conquest of Earth] (1931), telekinetic Jovians attack our planet and are defeated through atomic power.

---

[178] In *The Chimerical Quest*, Black Coat Press, ISBN 978-1-61227-488-1.

Raoul Brémond's dry and rather academic *Par-Delà l'Univers* [Beyond the Universe] (1931) was undoubtedly one of the first novels ever written to deal with the theme of a journey through the fourth dimension based on purely scientific facts.

On the other hand, Étienne de Riche's *Le Raid Fantastique* [The Fantastic Raid] (1931) dismissed the notion of rocket-powered space travel because of the lack of atmosphere to push against!

"*Les Anekphantes*," one of the two stories contained in Roger Farney's collection *Deux Histoires Fabuleuses* [Two Fabulous Stories] (1931), featured microscopic, cell-like alien intelligences living among us on Earth, who suddenly become aware of man's existence after the discovery of radio.

Marcel Jeanjean's *La Merveilleuse Invention de l'Oncle Pamphile* [Uncle Pamphile's Marvelous Invention] (1930) was a juvenile novel illustrated by the author, who was the official painter of the Air Ministry, and was both a space and a time travel story, including the colonization of other worlds, the dangers of excess reliance on robots, and the modification of Earth's rotation.

Journeys to Other Lands

The tradition of the adventure serial that had been perfectly embodied before the war by writers such as Paul d'Ivoi continued with a vengeance between the wars. By then, the ingredients were familiar: fast-paced, globe-trotting adventures, centering around a single genre concept such as a super-powered vehicle, a futuristic weapon, the discovery of a Lost World, a Hidden Empire or a Secret City, all featuring brave heroes, demure girlfriends, and dastardly villains, megalomaniacal would-be world conquerors, mad scientists, all too often of Germanic or Asian origins.

Old hands at this craft included Gustave Le Rouge who, in 1923, penned *Les Aventures de Todd Marvel, Détective*

Milliardaire [The Adventures of Todd Marvel, Billionaire Detective] and Jean de La Hire, who continued his prolific serial writing career with adventure novels such as *La Prisonnière du Dragon Rouge* [The Prisoner of the Red Dragon] (1923), *La Captive du Soleil d'Or* [The Captive of the Golden Sun] (1926), *Les Dompteurs de Forces* [The Tamers of Powers] (1927), the six-volume *Aventures de Paul Ardent* [Adventures of Paul Ardent] (1928), *Les Amazones* [*The Amazons*] (1930) and many others.

Even Gaston Leroux, the father of Rouletabille and the Phantom of the Opera contributed *Les Aventures Effroyables de Herbert de Renich* [The Frightful Adventures of Herbert de Renich] (1917-20), an epic undersea saga which was his answer to Verne's *Twenty-Thousand Leagues*.

Other notable practitioners in this vein included:

Georges G. Toudouze who, in *Le Petit Roi d'Ys* [The Little King of Ys] (1914), featured a submarine tank whose crew was looking for the legendary sunken city. His *Les Sous-Marins Fantômes* [The Phantom Sub-Marines] (1921) also dealt with the exploitation of the ocean. *Les Compagnons de l'Iceberg en Feu* [The Companions of the Burning Iceberg] (1922) featured a frozen sailor from the Spanish Armada brought back to life. Other ocean-themed adventure novels by this author included *Le Corsaire du Pacifique* [The Corsair of the Pacific] (1929) and *Le Secret de l'Île d'Acier* [The Secret of Steel Island] (1934). His best work, however, was a loosely-connected series of novels entitled *Les Aventuriers de la Science* [The Science Adventurers], the first volume, of which, *L'Homme qui Volait le Gulf Stream* [The Man Who Stole the Gulf Stream] (1925), featured the descendent of an Aztec King who compelled a misguided scientist to create a new form of coral in order to divert the Gulf Stream; and *L'Éveilleur de Volcans* [The Volcano Whisperer] (1927), about a mad scientist who can control volcanos.

Pierre Adam, like Moselli, was a regular contributor to *L'Intrépide* throughout the 1920s and 30s. (According to some, it may have been a pseudonym of writer Antonin

Seuhl). His most notorious genre serials included *La Sirène aux Yeux Fauves* [The Mermaid with Fawn Eyes] (1916), *Les Yeux d'Acier* [Eyes of Steel] (1916), *L'Usine Infernale* [The Infernal Factory] (1919-20) and *Les Buveurs d'Espace* [The Drinkers of Space] (1922), in which the heroes use a superplane/submarine to explore a heretofore unknown land. Continuing in the same "Lost World" tradition, the author penned *Le Maître des Abîmes* [The Master of the Abyss] (1927), *Le Royaume du Silence* [The Kingdom of Silence] (1929) and *La Reine des Mayas* [The Queen of the Mayas] (1933). Adam also wrote *Le Grand Choc* [The Great Clash] (1922), in which a mad scientist tries to reverse Earth's magnetic poles, and *Le Gouffre aux Surprises* [The Pit of Surprises] (1932), in which another mad scientist brainwashes his victims in order to transfer other people's minds into theirs.

Marcel Rouff, the son of publisher Jules Rouff, published *Voyage au Monde à l'Envers* [Journey to the Inverted World] (1920)[179] in which, during a tropical storm over the Pacific, a French Air Force Captain is mysteriously transported to a utopia-like society of free love which rejected money and technology two thousand years earlier. But even that utopia has its dark side: the Accursed, a prison-state locked behind an impregnable magnetic barrier, where those who refuse to live in utopia are condemned to remain. His arrival obviously threatens the very foundations of the Inverted World... One of the most imaginatively ambitious works of this era, the novel is both a rare contemporary exercise in utopianism, as well as a ground-breaking work of science fiction depicting 2000 years of futuristic history.

The once-editor of the *Journal des Voyages*, Guy de Téramond contributed the sprawling 25-issue serial, *Vingt Mille Lieues à travers le Monde* [20,000 Leagues Across the World] (1923-24), which included a grab-bag of classic themes such as a Lost World located at the pole, a journey to the Center of the Earth, the flying island of Laputa, telepathy,

---

[179] Black Coat Press, ISBN 978-1-61227-039-5.

Hindu yogi, vampires, mad German scientists, and even a full-blown prehistoric novel insert, *À la Recherche du Plésiosaure* [In Search of the Plesiosaurus]. Other notable works by the author included *Ravengar* (1922), a novel on the theme of invisibility; *L'Homme qui Voit à travers les Murailles* [The Man Who Could See Through Walls] (1923), about a radium-powered superman; and *Le Faiseur de Monstres* [The Monster Maker] (1930), featuring a mad surgeon.

André Armandy with *Rapa Nui* (1923) explored the mysteries of Easter Island. His *Le Démon Bleu* [The Blue Demon] (1926) featured a race of powerful mole men. Other notable titles included *L'Île de Corail* [Coral Island] (1927) and *Le Satanic* (1928).

Jean d'Agraives wrote novels such as *La Cité des Sables* [The City of the Sands] (1924), which featured a giant flying ship armed with paralyzing rays; *Le Rayon Svastika* [The Swastika Ray] (1926); *Le Virus 34* [Virus 34] (1930); *Le Sorcier de la Mer* [The Wizard of the Sea] (1927), about a mad scientist who used radiation to control underwater monsters and threaten the world with mass starvation; (that novel also included some interesting notions like making oil from fish and an Inca Lost World located in Tierra del Fuego); and *L'Empire des Algues* [Empire of the Seaweed] (1935), in which a chemist discovers "algol", a new super-fuel made from algae, and is kidnapped by the Germans and the Japanese who force him to work for them in their secret Sargasso Sea base. The author also penned the more noteworthy *L'Aviateur de Bonaparte* [Bonaparte's Aviator] (1926), which claimed that Napoleon owed his many victories to secret aerial reconnaissance.

Albert Bonneau wrote various exotic adventures under the pseudonym of "Maurice Champagne." His best novels included *La Cité sans Soleil* [The City Without Sun] (1927), which told the story of a battle between two secret Egyptian kingdoms, and the six-volume *Les Samourais du Soleil Pourpre* [The Samurais of the Purple Sun] (1928-31), a sprawling "yellow peril" epic all too typical of the racial prejudices of the times. Other notable titles included *La Cité des Premiers Hommes* [The City of the First Men] (1929), featuring the descendants of the Hebrews who did not take refuge on Noah's Ark; *L'Île Engloutie* [The Sunken Island] (1929); *La Terre Perdue* [The Lost Land] (1930); *Le Complot des Météores* [The Meteor Plot] (1937) and *Le Piège sous la Mer* [The Underwater Trap] (1938).

André Falcoz also wrote novels under the pseudonyms of "Élie Montfort" and "L. Morvers." In *Le Soleil du Monde* [The Sun of the World] (1927), he told the tale of a lost Inca city with advanced technology. In *Les Rescapés de l'Île Verte* [The Survivors of the Green Island] (1929), he imagined a mad scientist manufacturing mutants. In *Le Semeur de Feu* [The Sower of Fire] (1925), he created another mad scientist, hidden in an underground Himalayan lair, who threatens the world with a death ray that can detonate explosives at a distance. Finally, in *La Poudre de Mort* [The Powder of Death] (1929), the author returns to the theme of the evil scientist who mutates children into gnomes with hypertrophied brains in order to build a death ray that will enable him to conquer an Asian kingdom.

Guy d'Armen (no information could be found about the writer who signed variously "Guy d'Armen," "Francis Annemary" and "Jacques Diamant") penned the classic *La Cité de l'Or et de la Lèpre* [The City of Gold and Leprosy] (1928)[180] which featured a secret Tibetan city ruled by an immortal mad scientist named Natas (Satan spelled backwards). Anyone who escaped immediately died of leprosy. Natas was eventually defeated by the heroic Doctor Francis Ardant. To the extent that all of D'Armen pulp heroes shared the same characteristics, Black Coat Press translated and released other novels by the same author under the inclusive imprint of "Doc Ardan", starting with *Les Troglodytes du Mont Everest* [The Troglodytes of Mount Everest] (1929) and *Les Géants du Lac Noir*

---

[180] Black Coat Press, ISBN 978-1-932983-03-6

[The Giants of Black Lake] (1931).[181] In the first novel, the villainous Mendax, headquartered at the top of Mount Everest, ransoms ocean liners with his super-plane/sub-marine; in the second novel, mad scientist Khyzil Kaya rules a secret city under the Gobi Desert with the help of giant spiders and other mutants. *La Fin d'Iramonda* [The Fall of Iramonda] (1935)[182] features one more hidden city inhabited by green-skinned men whose master controls various deadly rays. Other works scheduled to be translated and released as "Doc Ardan" novels include *Le Semeur de Cyclones* [The Hurricane Master] (1931), in which a mad scientist uses a captive volcano to control hurricanes in the Pacific; and *Le Secret de Frigidopolis* [The Secret of Frigidopolis] (1933) about a secret city located near Cape Horn.

Luc Alberny's *Le Glaive sur le Monde* [A Sword Over the World] (1928) may well be the first modern conspiracy novels. In it, it is revealed that the Cathars are secretly fomenting wars, and were responsible for World War I. In his *L'Étrange Aventure du Prof. Pamphlegme* [The Strange Adventure of Prof. Pamphlegme] (1933), music enables a man to travel into the Fourth Dimension. Finally, in *Le Mammouth Bleu* [The Blue Mastodon] (1935), the author postulates that the Basque language originated with a race of intelligent mastodons who still live in vast, underground caverns.

Jean Petithuguenin exploited the same vein with *Le Roi de l'Abîme* [The King of the Abyss] (1928-29) and *Le Secret des Incas* [The Secret of the Incas] (1931).

The father of Arnould Galopin, Dr. Auguste Galopin, wrote *Excursions du Petit Poucet à travers le Corps Humain* [Journeys of Tom Thumb Through the Human Body] (1928), a "Shrinking Man" novel anticipating the film *Fantastic Voyage*. Dr. Galopin was Van Gogh's doctor, and had his portrait painted by the now famous artist.

---

[181] Both Black Coat Press, ISBN 978-1-61227-483-6.
[182] Black Coat Press, ISBN 978-1-61227-977-0.

Max-André Dazergues wrote *Du Sang sur les Nuages* [Blood Over the Clouds] (1930) (under the pseudonym of "André Mad") about a gang of sky pirates led by a genius gnome and an android woman. The hero and the female android end up married and become the rulers of a race of Selenites on the Moon. *L'Île de Satan* [Satan's Island] (1931) featured an artificial island built by a mad scientist. *L'Île Aérienne* [The Aerial Island] (1931) (written under the pseudonym of "André Star") was about a flying city. Finally, *La Fusée des Glaces* [The Ice Rocket] (1938) featured a super-powered submarine able to navigate under the polar ice shelf.

Some other notable novels featuring Extraordinary Voyages of one kind or another included:

Pierre de La Batut's *La Jeune Fille en Proie au Monstre* [The Young Girl Who Became the Prey of a Monster] (1920) was about an archeologist who, while exploring the ruins of an ancient Assyrian city, discovers proof of the existence of an advanced antediluvian civilization, that of the Kirubim, a race of winged bulls with human faces. The hero's fiancée is then kidnapped by the Kirubim, who turn out to still live in a vast underground city where they keep men as their slaves and plot to conquer Earth. The author comes up with the rather fanciful notion that Earth's rotation around the Sun actually erodes the planet, and ultimately will condemn anyone living on its surface to extinction, releasing the species who live underground.

In engineer Léon Creux' *Le Voyage de l'Isabella au Centre de la Terre* [The Journey of the Isabella at the Center of the Earth] (1922), explorers use a mole machine, the *Isabella*, to travel to the center of the Earth. There, they find mountains of pure gold, copper, nickel, etc. At 6000 meters deep, they discover a giant radioactive cavern filled with aether. Finally, at the Earth's core, they find another cavity housing a miniature solar system, composed of a sun-like liquid platinum sphere, surrounded by miniature satellites including a 40-km in diameter "Anti-Earth."

Two more novels on the "Earth Core" theme included Jean Duval's *Au Centre de la Terre* [At the Earth's Core]

(1925), in which giant ants live at the Earth's Core; and Camille Audigier's *La Révolte des Volcans* [*The Revolt of the Volcanos*] (1935), where the underworld, this time, is inhabited by ancient Romans who found refuge there after the fall of the Empire.

Paul Vimereu's *César dans l'Île de Pan* [Caesar on Pan's Island] (1923) featured Napoleon who has managed to avoid imprisonment by substituting a lookalike, and who, after being shipwrecked in the Pacific, ends up on a "Lost World" island inhabited by primates and prehistoric beasts. Coincidentally, in Pierre Veber's *La Seconde Vie de Napoléon 1er* [Napoleon's Second Life] (1924), Napoleon secretly escapes and goes on to live a secret life in France until his natural death at age 80.

In the tradition of Rosny, prehistorian Max Begouën penned two well-documented novels about life in prehistoric times, *Les Bisons d'Argile* [The Clay Buffalos] (1925) and *Quand le Mammouth Ressuscita* [When the Mastodons Returned] (1928), which won the Jules Verne Award. In the latter, a mastodon and seven cavemen trapped in ice were revived.

Other notable prehistoric novels included:

André Legrand's *L'Île sans Amour* [The Loveless Island] (1921).

André Lichtenberger's *Raramené* (1921).[183] In the midst of World War I, German and French explorers discover a mysterious Pacific Island where they encounter a race of "missing links" that time forgot. But they also bring to that peaceful utopia the ravages of the bloodiest war ever fought. *Raramené* shares some common themes with Edgar Rice Burroughs' *The Land That Time Forgot* (1918). It depicts a lost island culture, halfway between nature and civilization, made up of intelli-

---

[183] *The Children of the Crab*, Black Coat Press, ISBN 978-1-61227-200-9.

gent anthropoids in an intermediate state between humans and apes.

Claude Anet's *La Fin d'un Monde* (1922) describes the end of an advanced prehistoric civilization.

Victor Forbin's *Les Fiancés du Soleil* [The Fiancés of the Sun] (1923).

René Trotet de Bargis' *Kh'ia, la Fille des Gorilles* [Kh'ia, Daughter of Gorillas] (1923).

Fernand Mysor's *Les Semeurs d'Épouvante, Roman des Temps Jurassiques* [The Sowers of Terror, A Novel of the Jurassic Times] (1923), in which two persons travel back in time to the Jurassic era, where they end up eaten by a prehistoric monster, and *Va'Hour l'Illuminé* [Va'Hour the Mad] (1924).

Pierre Goemaere's *Le Pèlerin du Soleil* [The Pilgrim of the Sun] (1927).

Léon Lambry's *Rama, Fille des Cavernes* [Rama, Daughter of the Caves] (1928) and *La Mission de Run le Tordu* [The Mission of Run-the-Twisted] (1929).

Jean de Kerlecq's *Urfa, l'Homme des Profondeurs* [Urfa, the Man of the Depths] (1931).

René Thévenin's *L'Ancêtre des Hommes* [The Ancestor of Men] (1932).

H.-J. Proumen's *Ève, Proie des Hommes* [Eve, the Prey of Men] (1934).

Charles de L'Andelyn's *Nara le Conquérant* [Nara the Conqueror] (1936).

Guy de Larigaudie's *Yug* (1945) and *Yug en Terres Inconnues* [Yug in the Unknown Lands] (1946).

Raymond de Rienzi's startingly original *Les Formiciens* [*The Ant-Men*] (1932), sub-titled "A Novel of the Secondary Era," which told the detailed story of the life of an ant-man named Hind in a semi-barbaric civilization of insect-men that existed during Earth's Secondary Era.

Atlantis, too, proved to be a fertile ground for inspiration. After Pierre Benoît's classic novel *L'Atlantide* (1919) (filmed as *The Queen of Atlantis*), it became the theme of numerous pulpish novels written during the 1920s and 1930s, such as:

Paul Féval, Fils & H.-J. Magog's *Le Réveil d'Atlantide* [*Atlantis Awakens*], the third volume of their serial *Les Mystères de Demain* [*The Mysteries of Tomorrow*] (1922-23) (see above).

Georges Grandjean's *Antinéa, La Nouvelle Atlantide* [*Antinea, The New Atlantis*] (1922).

Georges Spitzmuller and J.-A. Barbier-Daumont's *Héliodora en Atlantide* [Heliodora in Atlantis] (1923).

Jean d'Esme's *Les Dieux Rouges* [*The Red Gods*] (1923), in which the survivors of the lost continent of Gondwana find refuge in Vietnam.

Léon Groc's *2000 Ans Sous la Mer* [2000 Years Under the Sea] (1924).

Jean Carrère's *La Fin d'Atlantis* [The End of Atlantis] (1926)[184] was more sophisticated than most Atlantean fantasies of the timers. Its account of the fall of Atlantis echoes that of the Roman Empire, and contains an elaborate criticism of contemporary European society, whose own crisis of degeneration is supposedly reflected therein.

Noelle Roger's *Le Soleil Enseveli* [The Buried Sun] (1928).

P. Couteaud's *Chez les Atlantes* [With the Atlanteans] (1928).

Roger Devigne's *Mon Voyage en Atlantide* [*My Journey to Atlantis*] (1929).

Charles Magué's trilogy, comprised of *Les Survivants de l'Atlantide* [The Survivors of Atlantis] (1929), *La Cuve aux Monstres* [The Vat of Monsters] (1930) and *L'Archipel des Demi-Dieux* [The Archipelago of the Demi-gods] (1931).

Pierre Legendre's *Le Dernier des Atlantes* [The Last of the Atlanteans] (1930).

---

[184] Black Coat Press, ISBN 978-1-61227-618-2.

Eugène Thébault's *Nira, Australe Mystérieuse* [Nira, The Mysterious Australian] (1930), which described a secret Atlantean civilization in the Antarctic that uses magnetic power and anti-gravity discs.

Paul-Adolphe de Cassagnac's *Le Couloir de Lumière* [The Corridor of Light], a "Lost World" story serialized in *L'Intrépide* in 1932.

Claude Saint-Yves' *Le Marabout des Atlantes* [The Priest of Atlantis] (1932).

Annette Godin's *La Dernière Atlante, ou Le Second Péché d'Ève* [The Last Atlantean, or Eve's Second Sin], published in Algiers in 1933.

Jean Fardet's *Dans l'Éclatante Atlantis* [The Shimmering Atlantis] (1935),

Alin Monjardin's colorful *L'Extraordinaire Voyage* [The Extraordinary Journey] (1934), in which the Atlantean survivors live in an underwater city also inhabited by octopus-men and dinosaurs.

H. de Volta's twenty-part serial, *L'Île Merveilleuse* [The Marvelous Island], published in 1921 by Tallandier, featured a grabbag of every popular theme, with chapters entitled "*Cinq Cent Lieues sous la Terre*" [500 Leagues Underground], "*Ressuscités après 100.000 Ans*" [Brought Back to Life After 100,000 Years], "*Vers les Mondes Inconnus*" [Towards Unknown Worlds], "*La Découverte de l'Atlantide*" [The Discovery of Atlantis] and "*Scientific City*".

Jules d'Ottange wrote a four-volume serial, *La Chasse aux Milliards* [The Hunt for Billions] (1926-31), in which a billionaire builds new cities at the bottom of the sea.

Other popular adventure writers liked to craft pseudo-scientific thrillers such as:

Jules Hoche was one of the more interesting writers who dabbled in speculative fiction in the first quarter of the 20th century. He was a genuinely original thinker, both in his inventions and his attitudes, and never failed to produce food for thought, although one cannot help but regret that he was gradually strangled by the relentless dullness of the popular demand. *Le Faiseur d'hommes et sa formule* [The Maker of Men and His Formula] (1906)[185] was amongst several notable novels inspired by H. G. Wells, in this case *The Island of Doctor Moreau*. In it, the author tried to go further, featuring a much bolder project in the manufacture of human beings, with more complex results. Whereas Moreau confined himself to surgical methods, Dr. Brillat-Dessaigne starts from primordial slime, subjecting it to a process of accelerated evolution to produce the "Pure Ones" who are not merely human, but anticipations of the ultimate humankind. The addition to the plot of the "Unclean Ones", in contrast to the Pure Ones, opens numerous interesting biological and philosophical questions, and adds an element of horrific bizarrerie that culminates in a garish, violent climax.

The speculative motif featured in his *Le Mauvais Rêve* [The Bad Dream] (1923)[186] was the possibility of suspended animation achieved by means of refrigeration. The author's depiction of this technology was, however, much closer in spirit and speculative technological depiction to modern development in "cryonics" than anything that had gone before, and it deserves to be reckoned a significant precursor of the many modern works featuring that theme.

Jean Bonnéry with *1 = 2 = 3* (1927), *Le Visage de Lumière* [The Face of Light] (1927) and *La Ville Invisible* [The Invisible City] (1933).

Gaston Pastre followed more blandly in Verne's footsteps with titles such as *La Ville Aérienne* [The City in the Air] (1928); *Le Secret des Sables* [The Secret of the Sands] (1928) (which won the Jules Verne Award); *Le Palace à la Dérive* [A Palace Adrift] (1929) and *L'Île d'Épouvante* [The Island of Terror] (1932).

Georges Simenon, before he became the creator of the world-famous Commissaire Maigret, penned several pulp ad-

---

[185] Black Coat Press, ISBN 978-1-61227-426-3.
[186] Black Coat Press, ISBN 978-1-61227-904-6.

venture novels under the pseudonym of "Georges Sim", such as *Le Roi des Glaces* [The King of the Ice] (1928), *Les Nains des Cataractes* [The Dwarves of the Waterfalls] (1928) and *Le Secret des Lamas* [The Secret of the Lamas] (1928).

Pierre Demousson contributed pulp-like adventure novels with genre elements such as *Le Destructeur du Monde* [The Destroyer of the World] (1929), *Les Compagnons du Dragon Noir* [The Companions of the Black Dragon] (1929) and *Le Secret de l'Antarctide* [The Secret of Antarctica] (1930).

Louis-Frédéric Rouquette, the editor of *À l'Aventure*, wrote *L'Homme qui Vint...* [The Man Who Came...] (1921), *Le Grand Silence Blanc* [The Great White Silence] (1921), *L'Épopée Blanche* [The White Epic] (1926) and *Le Secret du Pôle* [The Secret of the Pole] (1926).

Paul-Yves Sébillot penned the four-volume *L'Île Volante* [The Flying Island] (1923), *Les Aventures de Gobe-la-Lune* [The Adventures of Moon-*Gulper*] (1924) and *Le Roi de l'Épouvante* [The King of Terror] (1930).

Other novels of the period featuring mad scientists, mutants and various perversions of science included:

Henri Falk's *Le Maître des Trois États* [The Master of Three States] (1917),[187] tells of a scientist who creates a machine that can transform the human body into a liquid or a gas.

Jules Chancel's *Sous le Masque Allemand* [Under the German Mask] (1917) featured the notion of advanced cosmetic surgery; his *L'Étreinte de la Main de Fer* [The Grip of the Iron Hand] (1925), a device that enables one to see through walls, and *Le Tour du Monde Involontaire* [The Involuntary Journey Around the World] (1929), a death ray.

The brother-sister writing team of Marie and Frédéric Petitjean de la Rosière, who later became famous as the renowned authors of *Harlequin*-like romance novels under the

---

[187] In *The Age of Lead*, Black Coat Press, ISBN 978-1-935558-42-2.

pseudonym of "Delly", wrote *Les Maîtres du Silence* [The Masters of Silence] (1918-19), a two-volume serial about a good Chinese secret society (for a change!) which uses its paranormal powers to fight tyranny.

Another renowned romance novelist, Max du Veuzit, wrote *L'Automate* [The Automaton] in 1935.

Raoul Bigot's *Nounlegos* (1919),[188] sub-titled "The Man Who Could Read Brains", was a remarkable short novel about telepathy. In collaboration with E.-M. Laumann, the author also penned *L'Étrange Matière* [The Strange Matter] (1921), about the discovery of the "crystallopyr", a substance that can generate extreme heat and cold; and *Le Visage dans la Glace* [The Face in the Ice] (1922).

Laumann and Henri Lanos wrote *L'Aérobagne 32* (1920)[189] about a futuristic aerial prison.

Léon Baranger's *Le Maître de la Force* [The Master of the Force] (1919) featured a hate-focusing ray, a mental collector, and other deadly inventions.

Jean de La Hire's *Rolon, l'Autre Homme Invisible* [Rolon, The Other Invisible Man] (1919), written under the pseudonym of "Edmond Cazal," was another variation on Wells' classic.

Les Voleurs de Cerveaux [The Brain Stealers] (1920) by Jean de Quirielle featured a mad scientist who coupled human brains together to create a giant power battery.

Henry Du Roure's *Le Secret de l'Or* [The Secret of Gold] (1920) featured a scientist who, having discovered the secret of gold-making, uses it to ruin France.

J. Bruno-Ruby (the pseudonym of female author Madame Jean Vignaud) with *Celui Qui Supprima la Mort* [He Who Got Rid of Death] (1921) crafted a Christian allegory in which Satan is depicted as a 30th century scientist who seeks

---

[188] In *On the Brink of the World's End*, Black Coat Press, ISBN 978-1-61227-474-4.

[189] In *The Mirror of Present Events*, Black Coat Press, ISBN 978-1-61227-486-7.

the secret of immortality but is ultimately defeated by the power of the Cross.

Pierre Desclaux' *Les Morts de Bronze* [The Dead Men in Bronze] (1921) featured criminals who use a special death ray to turn their victims into metal statues. His *Le Maître du Monde* [The Master of the World] (1921) was about an invisible mastermind named Robur (like Verne's character). And his *Le Secret d'Hermano* [The Secret of Hermano] (1926) (written under the pseudonym of "Jean Frick") was about an evil secret society which uses brain surgery to turn people into zombies.

In Gabriel Bernard's *La Volonté de John Harry Will* [The Will of John Henry Will] (1921), a tycoon's mental energy is used as an energy source. His *Satanas* (1922) featured men with telepathic powers. In *Les Compagnons de la Haine* [The Fellowship of Hate] (1928), a scientist devises a machine that can accurately predict people's actions.

In Cyril-Berger's *L'Expérience du Dr. Lorde* [The Experiment of Dr. Lorde] (1922), the eponymous hero discovered the scientific reality of the soul, which he calls the "odic fluid", and for revenge, transferred that of a murderer into another man.

In 1923, Clément Vautel imagined *La Machine à Fabriquer des Rêves* [The Dream-Making Machine].

In 1924, Noelle Roger wrote *Le Nouvel Adam* [The New Adam] (1924), about an artificial man.

In Raoul Gain's *Le Donneur de Jeunesse* [The Youth Giver] (1927), a mad scientist uses organ transplants to prolong life.

Gaston Danville's *Double Tête* [Double-Head] (1927)[190] was a bold narrative about stock-market manipulation, extrapolating the notion of technologically assisted telepathy while detailing a quest to rediscover the alchemists' fabled philosopher's stone. The novel is sufficiently innovative and intelligent to transcend its deliberately popular format, has consider-

---

[190] Black Coat Pres, ISBN 978-1-61227-912-1.

able imaginative substance, and deserves to be reckoned a significant contribution to the genre.

Paul Féval, Fils penned *Miriakris, Amie d'Enfance de Jésus* [Miriakris, Jesus' Childhood Friend] (1927), with Henri Allorge, which featured an Egyptian priest awakened from suspended animation. His *Félifax* (1929)[191] took on the perhaps impossible task of trying to bring two archetypes together, Sir Eric Palmer, the great British detective, successor of Sherlock Holmes, against jungle-born Felifax, the tiger-man, a clone of Tarzan, in the hope of generating a singular literary synergy. But unlike the vast majority of Tarzan imitations, Felifax was not a feral child but the result of a biological experiment. This element of the plot is particularly interesting, because it forges a thematic link with today's comic-book superheroes. Felifax is brand new as a significant anticipation of the Incredible Hulk and others. Féval, Fils' *La Lumière Bleue* [The Blue Light] (1930), co-written with Henri Boo-Silhen, featured a machine that could print thoughts like photographs.

Henri Bernay's *La Pastille Mystérieuse* [The Mysterious Pill] (1927) featured controlled nuclear explosions. In his *On A Volé Un Transatlantique* [They Stole a Transatlantic Ship] (1928), "lambda rays" are used to control people's wills. *Le Secret de la Sunbeam Valley* [The Secret of Sunbeam Valley] (1928), co-written with René Pujol, featured the notion of solar energy being used to grow food in the Australian desert.

Roger Fribourg's *Des Éclairs dans la Nuit* [Lightning Bolts in the Night] (1927) featured a man who, after having been struck by lightning, develop the ability to see magnetic waves.

In Arnould Galopin's *Le Bacille* [The Bacillus] (1928), initially published as *L'Homme à la Figure Bleue* [The Man with the Blue Face] (1907),[192] the author of *Doctor Omega* describes in frightfully realistic terms how a scientist driven

---

[191] Black Coat Press, ISBN 978-1-932983-88-3.
[192] Black Coat Press, ISBN 978-1-61227-386-0.

mad by grief uses deadly germs to revenge himself on the inhabitants of Paris. The author also penned several pedestrian Vernian serials, such as *Le Tour du Monde en Sous-Marin* [Around the World in a Sub-Marine] (1925-26), *Les Aventures d'un Apprenti Parisien, ou Le Tour du Monde en Hydroplane* [The Adventures of a Parisian Apprentice, or Around the World in an Hydroplane] (1928) and *Le Tour du Monde en Aéroplane* [Around the World in an Airplane] (1929), the latter co-written with Henri de la Vaulx.

In Henri Darblin's *La Horde des Monstres* [The Horde of Monsters] (1928), a lost valley in the Rocky Mountains was inhabited by giant insects created by a mad scientist. This one of the first novels on the theme of giant insects, along Jean Duval's *Au Centre de la Terre* [At the Earth's Core] (1925) mentioned above.

That same year, Norbert Sevestre published the far more elaborate *La Révolte des Monstres* [The Revolt of the Monsters] (1928), in which mankind must fight giant insects on a planetary scale. Sevestre was the creator of the character of *Sâr Dubnotal* and had previously written Vernian novels such as *Le Tour du Monde en 14 Jours* [Around the World in 14 Days] (1926) and *Trois Jeunes Aéronautes au Pôle Sud* [Three Young Airmen at the South Pole] (1927).

In Étienne Gril's *La Machine à Guérir de la Vie* [The Machine That Could Cure Life] (1929), co-written under the pseudonym of "Stéphane Corbière" with J. Fouquet, a scientist invents a ray that can just as easily kill cancer as it can kill people.

Octave Béliard's *Les Petits Hommes de la Pinède* [The Little Men in the Pine Forest] (1929) was the tale of an impossible love between a man and an ant-sized woman genetically created by a mad scientist. The sop-called "Little Men" developed at a faster pace than man and would eventually have threatened our species had a fire not destroyed the pine forest in which they lived. The author won the first Jules Verne Award with the rather unremarkable, non-genre novel *La Pe-*

tite Fille de Michel Strogoff [Michel Strogoff's Grand-Daughter] (1927)).

Eugène Thébault's *Radio-Terreur* [*Radio-Terror*] (1930)[193] was translated by Fletcher Pratt for *Wonder Stories* in 1933. In it, the mad Marquis de Saint-Imier attempts to blackmail France and create a reign of terror through his control of atomic forces and electromagnetic waves. But against him stand the indomitable Professor Mazelier and his assistant Monsieur Gribal. In *Le Soleil Ensorcelé* [The Spellbound Sun] (1933), another mad scientist, Colquorès, uses a red diamond star which emits the mysterious "Rays 55" to alter the very shape of the Earth and turn Paris into a jungle.

Michel Corday's *La Flamme Éternelle* [The Eternal Flame] (1931) and its sequel *Ciel Rose* [Pink Sky] (1933)[194] were two of the few novels about scientific discovery to focus on the economic implications of such discoveries, including publicity, capitalization and the conflict of vested interests. It was a pioneering work in its development of those themes, especially with regard to the harnessing of atomic energy. They were also original in the manner in which they posed the question of the ultimate objectives of scientific and social progress. The author's experiences during World War I caused him thereafter to become an ardent propagandist for pacifism.

In Maurice Landay's *L'Antenne Mystérieuse* [The Mysterious Aerial] (1931), the hero is transformed into a living radio, and is thus able to defeat the evil scheme of a German super-villain who was plotting to drive the French out of Vietnam (!).

L'Ombre Inaccessible [*The Unreachable Shadow*], published in *L'Intrépide* in 1931-32 under the pseudonyms of Mettra & Nubé, was a colorful Fu-Manchu pastiche in which the villainous Karma, Lord of the Tulpakhangs, reigns over a city of "ice ghosts".

---

[193] Black Coat Press, ISBN 978-1-61227-007-4.
[194] Black Coat Press, ISBN 978-1-61227-189-7.

Finally, Hervé de Peslouan's *L'Étrange Menace du Prof. Iouchkoff* [The Strange Threat of Prof. Iouchkoff] (1931), which also won the Jules Verne Award, brought together a school monitor and the eponymous Russian mad scientist, a Robur-like engineer who had created a formidable flying machine called the "Menace".

Journeys to Other Times

Novels trying to predict what life would be in the year 2000 or 3000 continued to be in fashion. Amongst the most notable titles published during the period were:

Joseph-Louis Lecornu's *Cinquante Ans Après: Une Exposition à Verdun en 1967* [Fifty Years Later: An Exhibit at Verdun in 1967] (1918).

Gérard d'Houville's *En l'An 2000* [In the Year 2000] (1921).

André Lebey's *Tenue du... 16 Septembre 5924* [Review of... Sept. 16th, 5924] (1922).

Pierre Mille's *Dans Trois Cents Ans* [In 300 Years] (1922),[195] which postulated a future that reverted to barbarism after global war.

Georges Spitzmuller's *Une Expédition aux Ruines de Paris* [An Expedition in the Ruins of Paris] (1923).

Théo Varlet (see above) also penned *La Belle Valence* [Beautiful Valencia] (1923),[196] in which a squadron of World War I soldiers from the Trenches is transported back to the Spanish town of Valencia in the 14th century where they ally themselves with the Moors to fight the Spanish Inquisition. While it is one of several French novels inspired by H. G. Wells' *The Time Machine*—purporting, in fact, to be its sequel—It has more in common with Mark Twain's *A Connecti-*

---

[195] In *Nemoville*, Black Coat Press, ISBN 978-1-61227-070-8.
[196] *Timeslip Troopers*, Black Coat Press, ISBN 978-1-61227-078-4.

cut Yankee... in that its time-slipped protagonists set out to use the advantages of modern civilization, but eventually cannot prevail against Dark Age obduracy. *Timeslip Troopers* is one of the finest time travel novels of the period and holds up remarkably well as an exploratory endeavor. The quality of its cynical black humor is still as fresh as ever.

Edmond Caraguel's *Napoléon V, Dictateur* (1926).

Charles Rivet & Michel Goriellof's *Le Triomphe de Lénine (Anno Diaboli 310) 2227 - Roman Soviétique* [The Triumph of Lenin (Anno Diaboli 310) Yr. 2227 – A Soviet Novel] (1927).

Bernard Audry's *La Dictatrice* [The Female Dictator] (1928), about a woman taking power in France.

Lucien Banville d'Hostel's *Z, Anticipation Dramatique sur le Dernier Jour de la Terre* [Z, A Dramatic Anticipation About the Last Day on Earth] (1929).

Henri Bernay's *L'Homme qui Dormit Cent Ans* [The Man Who Slept for a Hundred Years] (1929), in which a new Rip Van Winkle wakes up in the 21st century.

Catholic writer Louis Artus deserves here a special mention for a series of stories collected in *La Maison du Fou* [The House of the Madman] (1918), *La Maison du Sage* [*The House of the Wise Man*] (1920), and *Les Chiens de Dieu* [God's Dogs] (1928), which portrayed with chilling details a future dystopian Europe where communism and technology have triumphed and Christians are persecuted.

These novels about the future were supplemented by a variety of novels dealing with catastrophes and social revolutions befalling our world, such as:

As early as 1913, Henri Allorge had predicted the dire consequences after the disappearance of iron in *La Famine de Fer* [The Iron Famine]. His more elaborate *Le Grand Cataclysme* [The Great Cataclysm] (1927)[197] takes place in the Age of Science in the year 9978 when Earth has cooled down and a

---

[197] Black Coat Press, ISBN 978-1-61227-026-5.

population of scientists and artists live in a handful of great cities scattered across the globe. They spend their time studying the ruins of the great cities of the past (our present) and are served by a population of advanced apes. But the stability of this utopia is threatened when electricity suddenly vanishes... *Le Grand Cataclysme* won a literary award due to the stridency of its pacifism, but the more interesting aspect of its moralistic argument is probably its ardent condemnation of waste in the exploitation of natural resources. Interestingly, in the future depicted by the author, love has long been found to be caused by a virus!

The disappearance of iron was also explored in Raoul Bigot's *Le Fer qui Meurt* [The Iron that Died] (1918)[198] and Serge Held's *La Mort du Fer* [The Death of Iron] (1931), in which alien spores carried to Earth by a meteorite destroy all iron. This story was later translated into English by Fletcher Pratt.

In Colonel Royet's *La Tempête Universelle de l'An 2000* [The Global Storm of the Year 2000] (1921), a solar eruption killed all life on Earth, except for an American man and a French woman; these new Adam and Eve then fight giant worms for possession of the world. The author also penned the eloquent *À Deux Doigts de la Fin du Monde* [On the Brink of the World's End] (1929)[199] which explores in a colorful fashion how a mad scientist threatens the stability of the world.

In Henri Falk's *L'Âge de Plomb* [The Age of Lead] (1922),[200] the Sun's increased emission of gamma rays causes a universal scourge, the only remedy of which is lead, which suddenly becomes more valuable than gold. Mostly forgotten today, the author was a comedy writer who, not unlike Thorne Smith in America, penned several sardonically humorous speculative fiction stories.

---

[198] In *On the Brink of the World's End*, Black Coat Press, ISBN 978-1-61227-474-4.
[199] Black Coat Press, q.v.
[200] Black Coat Press, ISBN 978-1-935558-42-2.

Noelle Roger (see above) penned *Le Nouveau Déluge* [The New Flood] (1922).

Aslan's *Adieu, Britannia!* (1923) depicted the British Isles submerged by a giant tide.

Pierre Dominique's Le Feu du Ciel [Fire from the Sky] (1926) was a vision of a new apocalypse caused by fiery meteors.

André Armandy's *Le Grand Crépuscule* [The Great Twilight] (1929) prophetically dealt with the exhaustion of petroleum resources.

Charles de L'Andelyn's *Les Derniers Jours du Monde* [The Last Days of the World] (1931) featured a new ice age which threatened mankind's survival.

Social upheavals occurred in Antonin Seuhl's *La Grève des Machines* [The Machines on Strike] (1924) and Étienne Gril's *Les Chevaliers de l'Incertain* [*The Knights of Uncertainty*] (1929), about a world subjected to rampant anarchy.

In *Jean Arlog, Le Premier Surhomme* [Jean Arlog, The First Superman] (1921), Georges Lebas featured a self-made superman who tries to stop the rotation of the Earth through sheer telekinetic power, but dies in the process. The same author then described how Earth was captured by a wandering star in *L'Heure Perdue* [The Lost Hour] (1930).

Further in the future, Han Ryner in *Les Surhommes* [*The Superhumans*] (1929)[201] told stories of the Time of the Mad Sun, a second sun which lights the Earth in the far future, when a race of giant and super-intelligent Mastodons has arisen to rule the world and enslave Mankind...

In *Tréponème* (1931), by Dr. Marc La Marche, it is a virus that turns men into supermen.

Then, there was the ever-constant flow of stories about future wars:

As early as 1915, Louis-Jules Gastine's 18-issue serial, *La Guerre de l'Espace* [The Space War] (1915) depicted a

---

[201] Black Coat Press, ISBN 978-1-935558-77-4.

worldwide war between the West and Asia that reached the upper strata of the atmosphere. The author continued to exploit the "Yellow Peril" theme with *La Ruée des Jaunes* [The Yellow Rush] (1933).

Roger Chanut's *Les Ombres de Demain* [Tomorrow's Shadows] (1920) predicted a futuristic war conducted with deadly super-weapons.

Doctor Rochard, using the pseudonym of "Professor Motus" penned the grimly prophetic *L'Offensive des Microbes, Roman d'une Guerre Future* [*The Microbian War, Novel of a Future War*] (1923), a.k.a. *La Guerre Microbienne, La Fin du Monde* [*The Microbian War, The End of the World*], in which Germany attacked France with bacteriological weapons.

Anarchist Victor Méric's *La Der des Der* [The Next Last War] (1929) described the next war in bitter and cynical tones.

In Charles Duhemme's *Français, Garde à Vous!* [Frenchmen, To Arms!] (1930), co-written with Hubert-Jacques, Germany staged an "Aero-Chemical War" against France.

Jean Petithuguenin's *Le Grand Courant* [The Great Current] (1931) was about a future war between a technologically advanced Europe and an ecologically conscious Asia.

The same fear of Asians could be found in Pierre-Barthélemy Gheusi's *Le Mascaret Rouge* [The Red Tide] (1931).

Colonel Royet's twenty-issue serial, *1932: La Guerre est Déclarée* [*1932: War Is Declared*] (1931) anticipated the real war by less than ten years.

More novels in this vein followed until World War II actually broke out.

Finally, the period saw the publication of two interesting uchronias by René Jeanne: *Napoléon-Bis* (1932), in which it is revealed that the real Napoleon had been kidnapped and replaced by a look-alike during the Russian Campaign, hence its failure; and *Si le 9 Thermidor...* [If on 9 Thermidor...] (1929), co-written with E. M. Laumann, a "What if Robespierre had not died."

The definitive time travel novel of the period was Jacques Rigaut's *Un Brillant Sujet* [A Brilliant Subject] (1921), in which a scientist built a time machine and traveled seven years back into the past. There, he meets an old flame and his younger self. Going on, he meets his mother and, unlike in *Back to the Future*, may well be his own father. The daring hero pursues his journey into the past, is not afraid of killing Jesus, cut off Cleopatra's nose and teaches the Incas the use of steam power and electricity. He finally dies of old age before reaching Genesis.

Mainstream Authors

As before, a number of writers generally catalogued as mainstream authors penned works that, for all intents and purposes, belonged to the genre.

One of the best was Claude Farrère, the first recipient of the literary Goncourt Award. His *Les Condamnés à Mort* [Those Condemned to Die] (1920) featured machines leading men into a communist dystopia, but its revolutionaries were eventually defeated by a scientist and his disintegrating ray. His collection *Histoire de Très Loin ou d'Assez Près* [Tales of Very Far or Near Enough] (1923) included the classic short story *"Où?"* [Where?], a remarkable exploration of a fourth dimension which obeyed different laws of time and space. His story *"Fin de Planète"* [End of a Planet] (1927) featured a disgruntled chemist who, unable to marry the aristocratic girl he loves, instead causes the disintegration of his world—which is ultimately revealed to be the missing fifth planet of our solar system.

André Arnyvelde's *L'Arche* [The Ark] (1920)[202] was begun shortly after the author was conscripted during the Great

---

[202] Black Coat Press, ISBN 978-1-61227-432-4.

War and finished after he was demobilized. A deliberately extravagant fantasy, it is a psychological Ark meant to carry him through the Deluge of the war, permitting him—as long as he avoids being killed—to endure the devastation of his personal happy valley. The novel features a race of superhuman mutants, the "Arcandres", born from ordinary men and women and gifted with extrasensory perception. Arnyvelde had previously penned *Le Roi de Galade* [The King of Galade] (1910),[203] a fantasy in which the eponymous hero emerges from his idyllic valley kingdom, surrounded by seemingly insurmountable mountains, to explore the outside world and investigate its wonders and vicissitudes. In 1922, Arnyvelde wrote *Le Bacchus Mutilé* [The Mutilated Bacchus],[204] in which a young genius, severely mutilated after a plane crash, still manages through sheer will power to turn his home valley into an Eden-like utopia dedicated to the search for Joy; but a twist of fate leads to a cruel end, full of disillusionment. "*On Demande un Homme*" [They Ask for a Man] (1924)[205] is a bittersweet chronicle of a competition between suitors to determine who will win the hand of a particularly desirable bride.

Nicolas Ségur's *Une Île d'Amour* [An Isle of Amour] (1921)[206] is interesting addition to a sequence of French utopian novels that attempted to get to grips with the thorny question of how best to organize sexual relations in a utopia, and what the social consequences would be of instituting a system of "free love."

Henri Barbusse, a novelist famous for his award-winning *Le Feu* [Under Fire] (1916), a novel about a soldier's life during World War I, penned *Les Enchaînements* [One Thing Af-

---

[203] In *The Ark*, q.v.
[204] Black Coat Press, ISBN 978-1-61227-433-1.
[205] "*The Strange Tournament of Love*" in *The Mutilated Bacchus*, q.v.
[206] In *The Human Paradise*, Black Coat Press, ISBN 978-1-61227-617-5.

ter Another] (1925), which featured a hero whose visionary experiences enable him to travel through time.

The first professional woman writer of science fiction was Swiss author Noëlle Roger, already mentioned several times. Her real name was Hélène Pittard and she was the daughter of a literary scholar and the wife of a famous anthropologist. She began writing proto-feminist tales at age 22 and served as a nurse during World War I. She traveled with her husband to the Middle East and Asia and wrote a number of genre works published by mainstream publishers such as Calmann-Lévy and Albin Michel, and recognized by the French Academy. Her *Le Nouveau Déluge* [The New Flood] (1922) showed the entire European continent sinking, and the waters of the Atlantic Ocean flooding France. The ensuing exodus and fight for survival are narrated with uncharacteristic sobriety and subtlety, anticipating the novels of John Wyndham and Edmund Cooper. Her *Le Nouvel Adam* [The New Adam] (1924) was about the deliberate attempt to scientifically create a superior race of men. Her *L'Hôte Invisible* [The Invisible Host] (1926) was about a monster who appeared every century or so, and *Celui Qui Voit* [He Who Sees] (1926) was a variation on the theme of invisibility. *Le Livre qui fait Mourir* [The Book That Kills] (1927) featured a cursed book. *Le Soleil Enseveli* [The Buried Sun] (1928) told of the reemergence of Atlantis. *Le Chercheur d'Ondes* [The Wave Seeker] (1931) dealt with parapsychological themes, and *Le Nouveau Lazare* [The New Lazarus] (1935) with resurrection. Her later works included *La Vallée Perdue* [The Lost Valley] (1940), a worthy prehistoric novel in which the eponymous Lost World is located in a hidden Swiss Valley, and *Au Seuil de l'Invisible* [On the Threshold of the Unseen] (1949), a collection of genre stories that initially appeared in the 1930s.

Another woman author of the period was Renée Dunan, whose first book, *Baal ou La Magicienne Passionée, Livre des Ensorcellements* [Baal or The Impassioned Magician, Book of

Spells] (1924)[207] was a science fiction treatment of ESP powers, magic and alchemy. In it, the sorceress Madame Palmyre teaches her female assistant Renée the secret of her magic, including the ability to travel from one dimension to another. They meet a Lovecraftian entity Baal whose octopus-like form is described as a three-dimensional projection of some incomprehensible multi-dimensional entity. Her *La Dernière Jouissance* [The Ultimate Pleasure] (1925)[208] is a dystopia that describes in stark, uncompromising terms a future tyranny and the struggle of its heroine, known only as B 309. In that world, a small technocratic elite uses deliberate terror in a desperate attempt to preserve the last remnant of the human race from a worldwide disaster precipitated by a massive disruption of the San Andreas Fault that unleashed a deadly underground gas called Necron. The rebel leader uses a powerful new explosive, the Klazzite, whose explosion can only be triggered by the detonation of the less powerful Klazzite-2. Her *Kaschmir, Le Jardin du Bonheur* [Kaschmir, The Garden of Happiness] (1925)[209] was an engagingly idiosyncratic variation on the exotic femme fatale, the beautiful but deadly Zenahab of Kashmir, likely inspired by Haggard's *She*. *Metal* (1920),[210] one of the author's earliest works, is a prehistoric Atlantean fantasy inspired by the works of J.-H. Rosny Aîné. Other notable novels included *La Montagne de Diamants* [The Mountain of Diamonds] (1934) and *L'Épouvantable Secret* [The Awful Secret] (1934).

Félicien Champsaur penned the novella *Le Dernier Homme* [The Last Man] (1885),[211] in which a comet increased the oxygen in Earth's atmosphere, causing the forests to take over Paris and man to revert to an ape-like condition. His *Les*

---

[207] Black Coat Press, ISBN 978-1-61227-046-3.
[208] Black Coat Press, ISBN 978-1-61227-406-5.
[209] In *The Ultimate Pleasure*, q.v.
[210] In *The Ultimate Pleasure*, q.v.
[211] In *The Human Arrow*, Black Coat Press, ISBN 978-1-61227-045-6.

Ailes de l'Homme [*The Human Arrow*] (1917/27),[212] initially written just prior to World War I, was the story of the first non-stop Paris-to-New York flight by rocket-powered plane as it never happened. French engineer Henri Rozal faces tough competition from rivals for the hand of his fiancée, as well as shady dealings from financiers trying to steal his invention. But as the shadow of war looms, Rozal's utopian dream of a peaceful planet traversed by powerful flying machines turns into an apocalyptic nightmare. The original 1917 edition was rewritten in 1927, to take into account Charles Lindbergh's flight and the horrors of World War I.

Champsaur also penned *Ouha, Roi des Singes* [Ouha, King of the Apes] (1923),[213] the thematic "missing link" between Edgar Rice Burroughs' *Tarzan of the Apes* (1912) and Edgar Wallace's *King Kong* (1933). Ouha, an exceptional ape from the jungles of Borneo, is educated and transformed into the "Napoleon of Apes" by a well-meaning American scientist. But tragically, he eventually falls victim to a "Beauty and the Beast"" doomed romance. There is an archetypal quality to the character of Ouha, as there is to Tarzan and King Kong; if he is no more plausible than Jules Lermina's To-Ho (see above), he is no less relevant as a specter at the feast of civilization and modern morality.

In *Homo Deus, le Satyre Invisible* [Homo Deus, The Invisible Satyr] (1924),[214] Dr. Marc Vanel, the son of a scientist and a beautiful exotic spy, polymath, engineer, gifted with prodigious strength and intelligence, trained by the Brahmins of India, acquires the power of invisibility and, he becomes "Homo-Deus," invisible but for his emerald-green eyes, haunting the dreams of evil men and lovely women alike. This is a ground-breaking novel which combines biomedical and superhero speculative fiction. It is a milestone in the evolution of the superhero, dealing with its fundamental problem: to what

---

[212] Black Coat Press, q.v.
[213] Black Coat Press, ISBN 978-1-61227-115-6.
[214] *Homo-Deus*, Black Coat Press, ISBN 978-1-61227-351-8.

extent a person who can act with total impunity is likely to admit any constraints stemming from morality?

Nora, La Guenon Devenue Femme [Nora, The Ape-Woman] (1929)[215] is a sequel to both *Homo Deus* and *Ouha*. It is the story of two hybrids: a beautiful dancer sired by an orangutan and a human scientist, further humanized by surgery, and the son of a native woman and the partly human orangutan Ouha. The novel is about evolution and the true nature of the simian and human species; it deals with the scientific modification of such species by means of surgery, thus enhancing the human condition, ultimately leading to the creation of supermen and the conquest of death. Despite various critical claims, *Nora* refuses to be racist and proudly claims that supposedly civilized white men are not superior to other races, or even species. It is a story of the triumph of animality and argues that such triumph is not something of which we should be ashamed.

Gabriel de Lautrec's ground-breaking collection *La Vengeance du Portrait Ovale* [The Vengeance of the Oval Portrait] (1922),[216] which borrows its title from Edgar Allan Poe, owes as much to the author's predilection for dark humor, Grand Guignol and the mixing of genres, as it does to the influence of alcohol and hashish, which he used regularly. De Lautrec was a disciple of Alphonse Allais and the winner of the 1920 Humorists' Award. While he hid behind a smiling mask, his troubled personality is on display in this series of mysterious and thrilling tales. Reviewers have compared them variedly to Mark Twain, Edgar Allan Poe, H. G. Wells and Maurice Renard. It included such science fiction tales as "*Dans Le Monde Voisin*" [In the Next World], which features creatures from the Fourth Dimension, and "*Fragment de Conte Futur*" [Fragment of a Tale of the Future], about the slow disappearance of oxygen.

---

[215] Black Coat Press, ISBN 978-1-61227-403-4.
[216] Black Coat Press, ISBN 978-1-61227-009-8.

Jacques Chenevière, with *Jouvence, ou la Chimère* [Jouvence, or The Chimera] (1922) wrote about a scientist who left an immortality formula behind after his death.

The first two volumes of Victor Margueritte's famous trilogy, *La Garçonne* [The Bacheloress] (1922), and *Le Compagnon* [The Companion] (1923), featured two couples, focusing primarily on their children and the broad social implications of an international socialist revolution attempting to overturn the depredations of capitalism. The final volume, *Le Couple* [The Couple] (1924)[217] was set in the near-future. The author skillfully orchestrated a tangle of frustrated relationships in a way that allowed the hope of security, freedom, and love to be transferred to outcomes of politics and war. The heightened sense of anxiety about the future, amid uprisings and political coups, picked up momentum toward a confused and conspiratorial rush to a war that was "nothing but a financial game, in which every proletarian cadaver consolidates the bourgeois strong box!"

Playwright Alexandre Arnoux wrote *Le Règne du Bonheur* [The Reign of Happiness] (1924), a modern utopia in which space voyagers who travel faster than light return to a future Earth which has reverted to its primitive innocence; and *Petite Lumière et l'Ourse* [Little Light and The She-Bear] (1923), about a superhuman, self-aware robot.

Ernest Pérochon, another Goncourt Award winner and usually the author of novels extolling the glory of French farmers, wrote a remarkable scientific anticipation and a prescient warning against unchecked technology, *Les Hommes Frénétiques* [The Frenetic People] (1925).[218] The novel takes place in our 30th century, the 5th century of the new Universal Era, after a global bacteriological war with Asia won thanks to a young female physicist, Noelle Roger (an homage?). The secrets of radium and aether has been discovered by the great

---

[217] All three volumes, Black Coat Press ISBNs 978-1-61227-360-0, 978-1-61227-361-7 and 978-1-61227-362-4.

[218] Black Coat Press, ISBN 978-1-61227-118-7.

French scientist, Averine. (In the future, French is, of course, the universal language.) Limitless energy is provided by the controlled disintegration of potassium salts, and great cities stretch like conducting wires along the meridians that form a planet-wide grid. But another, even more cruel war starts between rival meridians, using new weapons that mutate men and turn them into monsters: in Australia, their skeleton become soft; in South America, they become blind; in Central America, cannibals; in the Middle East, beast-like creatures; some grow new organs; others, new senses... The novel ends with a new Adam and a new Eve.

Pérochon suggests that the desire for impossible justice, honor and liberty has always been the motive compelling people to slaughter one another, and that mindless courage has always provided them with the psychological means. That supposition makes *Les Hommes Frénétiques* distinctive in the tradition of utopian literature, posing a moral and pragmatic question with respect to the desirability and practicality of such lofty goals. It is an important work which remains well worth reading today.

In *L'Homme qui lit dans les âmes* [The Man Who Read Souls] (1928),[219] Paul Gsell's protagonist, Jean Pilgrim, manufactures strange spectacles that permit the observation of what is happening in the minds of others. The novel begins as a Voltairean satire, but soon changes both tone and direction as it progresses from relatively amiable exploration of the hypocrisies of art and science to scathing accounts of contemporary science and politics, before the comedy turns jet black in its account of modern warfare. The book combines a striking philosophical vision with a unique love story and a brief but graphic utopian fantasy.

---

[219] *The Man Who Could Read Minds*, Black Coat Press, ISBN 978-1-61227-860-5.

Odette Dulac's *(L'Amour)...Tel qu'il est* [(Love)...As It Were] (1926)[220] was a colorful esoteric novel postulating the existence of an ancient, technologically and psychically advanced civilization, a Gaia-like sentient Earth, with secret initiates living hidden among us for thousands of years. It describes a strangely fanciful sexual biology, combined with insectile analogies and an astrological theory of evolution. It incorporates an idiosyncratic mysticism based on Buddhist and Hindu ideas, filtered through the reinterpretations of theosophist feminism. The result of that triple layering of fantastic notions is a unique literary construct that has no parallel in literary history. It foreshadows, in many ways, such endeavors as *Men are from Mars, Women are from Venus*. The author was one of the most popular cabaret singers in Paris during the first few years of the 20th century. She quit the stage in 1904, launching an entirely new career as a sculptor and a writer, active in the cause of women's rights.

The son of Alphonse Daudet, Léon Daudet, a noted right-wing political editorialist, wrote *Le Napus, Fléau de l'An 2227* [The Nomore, The Plague of the Year 2227] (1927), in which people start disappearing without explanation and war ensues. His *Les Bacchantes* (1931) featured the discovery of "time waves" which enable scientists to bring images back from the past. His *Ciel de Feu* [Sky of Fire] (1934) described a futuristic Franco-German war.

Finally, the renowned essayist, biographer and novelist André Maurois, the author of the satirical, best-selling World War I novel, *Les Silences du Colonel Bramble* (1918), penned several science fiction satires such as the Swiftian *Voyage au Pays des Articoles* [A Voyage to the Island of the Articoles] (1927); *Deux Fragments d'Une Histoire Universelle - 1992* [Two Fragments of a Universal History - 1992] (1928), in which the inhabitants of Uranus fail to understand Earthmen.

---

[220] *The War of the Sexes*, Black Coat Press, ISBN 978-1-61227-405-8.

A Period of Transition
(1930-1950)

During the late 1930s and 1940s, while science fiction in the United States blossomed, the genre was allowed to flounder in France, the victim of censorship and spiraling economic pressures, attributable to a loss of readership, an increase in the cost of paper and, from 1935 on, the competition of magazines publishing translations of American stories and comic-strips.

By the start of World War II, the field was severely depressed. *Sciences et Voyages* had stopped publication in 1935, *L'Intrépide* in 1937, *Je Sais Tout* in 1939, *Lectures Pour Tous* and *Oeuvres Libres* in 1940. Only the *Journal des Voyages* carried on until 1949.

Five years of war and Nazi occupation completed the devastation of what had been the Golden Age of French science fiction. Quantitatively, the field was severely hit. Qualitatively, however, there were a few glimmers of hope. However, these came not from the authors of the previous decades, like Maurice Renard and José Moselli, whose spirits had been effectively crushed, but from new voices, often originating from mainstream culture. The flame was kept alive, if only barely, by André Maurois (see above), René Barjavel and Jacques Spitz, writers who were influenced by and followed the Surrealists.

In the field of popular literature, a few new names emerged, such as Maurice Limat, Yves Dermèze and the talented B.-R. Bruss, who followed in the footsteps of J.-H. Rosny Aîné.

Finally, it was during that period of transition that the first elements of a true French science fiction fandom began to emerge, with names like Georges H. Gallet, Jacques Bergier,

Jacques Van Herp, and Pierre Versins, who eventually not only preserved the rich heritage of the Golden Age, but were instrumental in orchestrating a revival of science fiction in the 1950s, when the genre finally reemerged from its long slumber.

Major Authors

Léon Groc embodied the evolution of French science fiction between the wars, with a career that began in 1913 with *Ville Hantée* [The Haunted City] (1913) and *L'Autobus Évanoui* [The Vanished Bus] (1914), two stories influenced by Maurice Renard that dealt with paranormal powers in a pseudo-scientific fashion. In *L'Autobus Évanoui*, for example, an artificial form of telepathy was created through the use of radioactivity and the appropriate thought-harnessing equipment. His *2000 Ans Sous la Mer* [2000 Years Under the Sea] (1924) was typical of its times, featuring the descendants of ancient Phoenicians who lived underwater in great domed cities. The same was true of *Le Chasseur de Chimères* [The Hunter of Chimeras] (1925), which anticipated the concept of nuclear disintegration.

Groc's works began to evolve with the more original *La Révolte des Pierres* [The Revolt of the Stones] (1930), in which the inhabitants of the Moon are portrayed as mineral, radio-active beings who live in gestalt-like triads. A Norwegian scientist succeeds in transporting a Selenite to Earth. Eventually, a madman kidnaps one of the Selenites and uses his power to control stones and cause much havoc, such as the overthrowing of the Paris Obelisk, the demolition of Notre-Dame and the destruction of the Alps, before being stopped. Another notable work of the period is *Le Maître de l'Étoile* [The Master of the Star] (1933).

After the war, Groc was once again at the forefront of popular anticipation with *La Planète de Cristal* [The Crystal Planet] (1944), which featured two-dimensional beings living on a quasi-invisible crystal moon above the Earth. They perish when men touch them, but in a *Flatland*-like twist, so do men who come into contact with four-dimensional beings! Finally, *L'Univers Vagabond* [The Wandering Universe] (1950), co-written with his wife Jacqueline Zorn, featured a generation starship *en route* to Alpha Centauri. Once there, the human colonists are defeated by radioactive mineral aliens and forced to return to Earth. Other notable works of this period include *La Fuite du Radium* [The Escape of Radium] (1944), *Le Maître du Soleil* [The Master of the Sun] (1946) and *L'Émetteur Inconnu* [The Unknown Transmitter] (1949), also co-written with Zorn.

During this period, notorious Belgian writer Raymond Jean Marie De Kremer a.k.a. Jean Ray penned many stories which often straddled the line between horror and science fiction, such as the novella "*La Ruelle Ténébreuse*" [The Dark Street] (1932), about a street that led into another, frightening dimension, and many *Harry Dickson* tales, such as "*L'Homme au Masque d'Argent*" [The Man In The Silver Mask] (No.151, 1936), about a death-dealing silver android.

Belgian writer Henri-Jacques Proumen was more characteristic of the evolution of the genre during the 1930s and 1940s. He wrote *Sur le Chemin des Dieux* [The Path of the Gods] (1928), in which a scientist discovers the secret of mind control; at first, he uses it for peace, but then he succumbs to his megalomaniacal impulses. *La Boîte aux Marionnettes* [The Puppet Box] (1930) is a superb collection of genre stories, including "*Surhommes*" [Supermen] (1926), a satirical look at men with hypertrophied brains. His *Le Sceptre Volé aux Hommes* [The Scepter Stolen From *Men*] (1930) was a novel in which the next race of supermen, the "hyperanthropes", enslave mankind and live on an island, just like in Stapledon's *Odd John* and Magog's *Trois Ombres sur Paris* [Three Shadows Over Paris] (1928) (see above). While some men serve the mutants of their own free will, others revolt and eventually destroy the island. *Eve, Proie des Hommes* [Eve, Prey of Men] (1934) was a prehistoric novel featuring a cave woman. *La*

Brèche d'Enfer [The Hell Breach] (1946) was a warning written initially about a new, fictional weapon of mass destruction called "fulgurium", but the bombing of Hiroshima overtook the author and he had to rewrite it to make it about the atom bomb. His genre tales were collected in *L'Homme qui a été mangé* [The Man Who Was Eaten] (1950).

After Maurice Renard, the French writer who most characterized the pre-World War II period, and one of the few original voices of that time, was Jacques Spitz. His novels were generally dark and pessimistic, but they also contained some fierce satirical observations and were always extremely well documented, contrasting the realistic attention brought to the description of the details of everyday's life with the outlandishness of their events. In term of literary influences, the author had come out of Surrealism, as evidenced by his first novels, *La Croisière Indécise* [The Indecisive Cruise] (1926) and *Le Vent du Monde* [The Wind of the World] (1928). His genre career really began with *L'Agonie du Globe* [The Agony of the Globe] (1935), in which Earth was bisected into two hemispheres, one of which eventually crashed into the Moon. That novel established the use of realistic details that became characteristic of his style. The more pedestrian *Les Évadés de l'An 4000* [The Escapees from the Year 4000] (1936) told of a new ice age which drove men underground, subject to the ensuing scientific dictature before finally escaping to Venus. *La Guerre des Mouches* [The War of the Flies] (1938) featured the conquest of Earth by mutated flies animated by a gestalt intelligence. At the end, the flies keep only a few men (among them the narrator) in a reserve. In *L'Homme Élastique* [The Elastic Man] (1938), one of his best novels, a means to compress and decompress atoms is found, enabling the creation of tiny super-soldiers and flaccid giants. *L'Expérience du Dr. Mops* [*The Experiment of Dr. Mops*] (1939) and *L'Oeil du Purgatoire* [*The Eye of Purgatory*] (1945)[221] both explored the

---

[221] Both in *The Eye of Purgatory*, Black Coat Press, ISBN 978-1-935558-64-4.

theme of seeing into the future. In the former, a man's vision is modified so that he can peer into the future at an accelerated rate, giving his entourage foreknowledge of events yet to come. It asks the questions: Can the future be changed? And what will the subject see after his own death? The unhappy protagonist of *L'Oeil du Purgatoire* sees not the real future but an increasingly aging present, where death and decay became overpowering sights. This dark, introspective novel is a powerful reflection of the notion of time and aging and is unique in the annals of science fiction. The author's concerns anticipated the so-called "New Wave" of the 1960s and writers like J. G. Ballard and Thomas Disch by thirty years.

Later Spitz works included *La Parcelle "Z"* [Particle Z] (1942) and *Les Signaux du Soleil* [The Signals from the Sun] (1943), in which Martians and Venusians mine Earth's atmosphere for its components, but stop once they realize our planet is inhabited by intelligent beings; this was achieved by encrypting "pi" into the ionization of the atmosphere. *Ceci Est Un Drame* [This Is a Tragedy] (1947) was a play taking place in the far future. Finally, and most regrettably, two of his novels, *Alpha du Centaure* [Alpha Centauri] and *La Troisième Guerre Mondiale* [World War III], remained unsold and unpublished, a perfect illustration of the difficulties encountered by science fiction writers in the 1940s.

Another notable author of the late 1930s was Régis Messac. Less prolific than others, he was nevertheless a groundbreaking writer as well as an editor who launched a short-lived science fiction imprint, *Les Hypermondes* [The Hyperworlds] in 1935. He would undoubtedly have contributed even more significant works to the field had he not died in the concentration camps in 1943. As it was, he only wrote three novels, one of which was not published until 1973! A veteran of World War I, Messac had foreseen the evils of World War II in his classic *Quinzinzinzili* (1935), which featured a society of children who reverted to savagery after a chemical world war. Written twenty years before William Golding's *Lord of the Flies*, *Quinzinzinzili* postulated that a party of school children, isolated from the outside world, saw civilization as we know it collapse amongst them. The narrator is a lone, embittered adult. Since the children quickly develop a new simplified language, he progressively finds himself incapable of understanding his former charges. For him, there is no happy ending, only an inescapable tragedy. For the author, not only is the veneer of civilization brittle, but Man is, by nature, amoral. The book's title came from the name of the children's totemistic god, derived from a mangled, badly remembered Latin prayer, *Pater Noster Qui es in coelis*—Quinzinzinzili. The relationship of religion to myth and ritual is carefully described as the children revert to a more primitive stage of development. Messac's other ground-breaking novel is *La Cité des Asphyxiés* [*The City of the Asphyxiated*] (1937), which begins with a "chronoscope" enabling its protagonists to peer into the future. One of them is then accidentally transported to the eponymous underground futuristic city, where air itself has become a rare commodity. The book then becomes a biting satire of contemporary society.[222]

---

[222] Brian Stableford's note: "The English translations of the various Messac works indicated and cited above do exist, and their publication was scheduled by Black Coat Press for 2016. Even though the works are all in the public domain, the author having been dead for seventy years, that publication was blocked by the threat of legal action by his grandson, Olivier Messac, which BCP could not afford to defend no matter how certain the eventual victory might be. Evidently, Olivier Messac feels that the best way to conserve his grandfather's legacy is to extend the inaccessibility of his work in the English language for as long as humanly possible. We can, of course, only speculate as to what the fervently anti-capitalist utopian Régis Messac might have thought of copyright trolls, although we do know that the Nazis murdered him in order to prevent him communicating his ideas to his fellow human beings, not because he posed any kind of military threat to them."

René Barjavel was the last "grandmaster" of the period and the first to emerge during World War II. His works formed a bridge between the popular science fiction of the 1930s and the mainstream literature of the 1940s. His vision of the world was also pessimistic and firmly positioned against progress and science, which was precisely the kind of ideology that made him respectable with the cultural elite. In his Rousseauist vision of the world, Man is born good, Machine is what made him evil. His novels showed how science fiction themes could be incorporated in mainstream literature, to the extent that, through a peculiar form of circular logic, they became not-science fiction. Science fiction being by its nature badly written and pro-technology, since Barjavel was a good writer and against technology; therefore his works could not be science fiction.

His first novel, *Ravage* (1943), took place in 2052 and portrayed a post-holocaust France turning away from the evils of technology and returning to an agricultural utopian-like setting after the mysterious disappearance of electricity, a theme already explored in Allorge's *Le Grand Cataclysme* (see above). *Le Voyageur Imprudent* [The Imprudent Traveler] (1944) was a time travel story that took his Wellsian protagonist through various dystopic futures, before ending on what was then a new idea: a time paradox where the hero erases himself by accidentally killing one of his ancestors. *L'Homme Fort* [The Strong Man] (1946) featured an artificial superman who, like Philip Wylie's *Gladiator*, tries to impose peace upon the world but failed. *Le Diable l'Emporte* [The Devil Takes It] (1948) introduced the character of Mr. Gé, a powerful billionaire who has built a giant, underground Noah's Ark under Paris to preserve the human race. Destruction comes in the form of "thick water", a substance which raises the freezing point of water above even a human body's temperature and, like Kurt Vonnegut's Ice-9 from *Cat's Cradle*, kills off all life on Earth. However, a desperate couple of survivors manage to flee in a rocket. The novel's dedication summed up the author's belief in our future self-destruction: it was dedicated to our ancestors and our descendants, the cavemen.

Barjavel, even more so than Rosny, was the first genre writer to break out of the science fiction ghetto. Like Vonnegut in the United States, he became one of the most distinguished purveyors of both science fiction and fantasy tales under the guise of mainstream literature.

The author known as "B.-R. Bruss" (a pseudonym of writer René Bonnefoy) came to represent a transition between the popular science fiction of the 1930s and that of the 1950s and 1960s. His first genre novel was *Et la Planète Sauta...* [And the Planet Exploded...] (1946), which told of the self-annihilation of a world that turned out to be the fifth planet. The novel begins with the discovery of a cache of documents found in a meteor, like Defontenay's *Star* (see above). Once deciphered, these are revealed to be the diary of an alien nuclear scientist who ultimately chose to disintegrate his own world rather than allow its population to be totally enslaved by a tyrant with mind-controlling powers. *Apparition des Surhommes* [The Coming of the Supermen] (1953) was another novel on the theme of the coming race of supermen fated to replace men. Like in Thévenin's *Les Chasseurs d'Hommes* and Proumen's *Le Sceptre Volé aux Hommes*, the mutants are portrayed as beautiful, angelic beings whose existence split Mankind into two camps: the "dogs" who serve them faithfully, and the "wolves" who dream of destroying them. Bruss then went on to become one of the best authors of Éditions Fleuve Noir throughout the 1950s, 1960s and 1970s.

Two other notable works also stand out during this period:

Belgian writer Marcel Thiry's *Échec au Temps* [Time in Check] was written in 1939, but not published until 1945. The author had already penned collections of surreal poetry in the 1920s. *Échec au Temps* was an alternate history novel about Napoleon winning the battle of Waterloo. Coincidentally, the same theme was explored by mainstream author Robert Aron in *Victoire à Waterloo* [Victory at Waterloo] (1937).

Journalist Marc Wersinger's *La Chute dans le Néant* [The Fall into Nothingness] (1947) was an odd novel featuring a man who discovers that he has the power to materialize and control a mysterious, ectoplasmic substance. At first, he uses his powers to become a stage magician, but the ectoplasm eventually escapes his control and begins to cause much havoc and destruction. The hero's desperate attempts to regain control of his powers causes him to start shrinking. From that point on, the ending of the novel is very much like Matheson's 1956 classic *The Incredible Shrinking Man*.

Other Notable Authors

Journeys to Other Worlds

One of the most nefarious consequences of the self-censorship imposed on science fiction in the 1930s was the virtual suppression of space opera as a sub-genre. While in America, the unbridled imagination of authors was given free rein, in France, writers wisely preferred to remain Earth-bound. Works like Gustave Le Rouge's *Le Prisonnier de la Planète Mars*, Arnould Galpoin's *Doctor Omega*, or Jean de La Hire's *La Roue Fulgurante*, which were the French equivalent of Edgar Rice Burroughs, could have inspired others to follow and helped the genre to blossom—but it was not to be.

Nothing illustrated this fact better than Alin Monjardin's 1934 novel, *L'Extraordinaire Voyage* [The Extraordinary Journey] (see above), which was rewritten by the author to change its initial interplanetary setting into an Atlantean story.

Henri Duvernois' *L'Homme qui s'est Retrouvé* [The Man Who Found Himself] (1936)[223] was a cosmic journey with a unique twist. In it, a starship transports the protagonist to a

---

[223] Black Coat Press, ISBN 978-1-935558-04-0

world orbiting Proxima Centauri. After a three-year journey at the speed of light, the hero discovers that that planet is identical to Earth in every respect, except that its history is unfolding 40 years behind. His arrival offers the 60-year-old hero the opportunity of "finding himself" at age 20. The novel is one of the earliest French texts to feature interstellar faster-than-light travel and to combine the notions of a trip in time and in space.

One of the last, grand masters of space operas was René-Marcel de Nizerolles with his 108-issue serial, *Les Aventuriers du Ciel: Voyages Extraordinaires d'un Petit Parisien dans la Stratosphère, la Lune et les Planètes* [The Adventurers of the Sky: The Extraordinary Voyages of a Little Parisian in the Stratosphere, The Moon and the Planets] (1935-37), a belated sequel to his 1912 *Les Voyages Aériens d'un Petit Parisien à travers le Monde* [*The Aerial Voyages of a Little Parisian Across the World*], featuring the adventures of the indomitable Tintin (no relation to the comic book character). In it, Tintin used the hydrogen-powered spaceship "Bolide" to explore the solar system. On Venus, he found descendants of the Greek Gods ruling a race of giant cyclops. On Mars, he came across a race of little men served by giant robots. The saga also included time travel; and, anticipating Pierre Boulle's *Planet of the Apes*, Tintin discovered that apes had replaced men five thousand years in the future.

Other notable authors and works included:

Félix Celval, with *Les Robinsons de l'Espace* [The Space Robinsons] (1934), and *Les Flibustiers de l'Espace* [The Space Corsairs] (1938).

Jean Loisy, with *Un Français dans la Lune* [A Frenchman on the Moon] (1935)

Jacques Loria, with *La Visite des Martiens* [The Visit of the Martians] (1935).

Maurice Limat, with *Les Fiancés de la Planète Mars* [The Fiancés of Mars] (1936). The author, like Bruss, would go on to become one of the regular contributors of Éditions Fleuve Noir in the 1950s, 1960s and 1970s. Limat followed in the footsteps of Gustave Le Rouge with novels such as *L'Avion Mystérieux* [The Mystery Plane] (1937) and *Les Naufragés de la Voie Lactée* [The Castaways of the Milky Way] (1939), but this was still science fiction following the templates of 1914 being published almost in 1940.

Maurice Pérot, with *Les Explorateurs de l'Espace* [The Explorers of Space] (1938).

Robert Jean-Boulan, with *Les Aventuriers de la Planète Mars* [The Adventurers of Planet Mars] (1941).

Louis Grivel's *À la Conquête de Venus* [The Conquest of Venus] was published in Tunis in 1942 and depicted Venus as a prehistoric planet.

Finally, a few notable juvenile/YA genre novels were published just before World War II. These included:

Le Mystère de la Nuit Sans Lune [The Mystery of The Moonless Night] (1942), about the explosion of the Moon, by Christiane Fournier.

Panique sur le Monde [Panic Over the World] (1942), *S.O.S.! Ici Paris* [SOS! Paris Calling] (1942) and *Le Rayon du Sommeil* [*The Sleep Ray*] (1943), by Henri Suquet

By the early 1940s, American science fiction had welcomed the talents of Isaac Asimov, Robert A. Heinlein and A. E. Van Vogt, to name but a few, while in France, Maurice Renard, José Moselli and René Thévenin had virtually deserted the genre, while Jacques Spitz was a lonely voice.

Journeys to Other Lands

One of the last and most remarkable authors to come out of the adventure magazines and popular imprints of the 1920s and 1930s was Tancrède Vallerey. In his *Celui qui Viendra* [He Who Shall Come] (1929), a young scientist and his mentor, Dr. Fauster, are visited by a mysterious being who looks like the Invisible Man from the 1933 film, but turns out to be an alien from Aldebaran. The alien tells them that his world is willing to share its scientific wonders with Earth, but he can only take one man back with him. Fauster goes, but because of the time factor, he won't be able to return before several centuries have passed. The novel ends with the young hero's tragic plight, wondering about the wonders he will never know and telling his successors to wait for Fauster's return. His *L'Île au Sable Vert* [The Island with Green Sand] (1930) won the Jules Verne Award but was a more pedestrian adventure novel featuring underground tunnels linking various parts of the globe. *L'Avion Fantastique* [The Fantastic Plane] (1936) featured a remote-controlled plane. Far more interesting was *Un Mois sous les Mers* [A Month Undersea] (1937), in which it is revealed that a piece of Mercury has fallen to the bottom of the Pacific Ocean and created an underwater alien eco-system, complete with intelligent, giant ants and a crystalline vegetation. The ant-like aliens are at war with each other ("just like men") and use weapons that harness radioactivity.

J.-H. Rosny Jeune, Rosny Aîné's younger brother, with *L'Énigme du Redoutable* [The Enigma of Redoutable] (1930), in which a lost underwater Briton colony was discovered; and *Le Destin de Martin Lafaille* [The Fate of Martin Lafaille] (1945), featuring a brilliant mathematician who solved the mysteries of the universe.

Fernand Fleuret's *Jim Click* (1930)[224] was written at a time when androids were much in fashion throughout Europe, thanks to the widespread distribution of Karel Capek's play *R.U.R.* (1920) and Fritz Lang's film *Metropolis* (1927), and, like those works, it is both a significant reflection of the spirit of its era and a work of enduring appeal and value. In it, the protagonist, Jim Click, invents a robot in the image of his friend, Admiral Horatio Gunson, on the eve of a great battle. Everything starts going wrong when the robot kills his model. Frightened, the inventor then sets up a fabulous hoax, in which his automaton will act as if he were the real admiral. And after the fake Gunson wins the battle, no one discovers the deception, not the king nor his sailors, or even his mistress...

---

[224] Black Coat Press, ISBN 978-1-61227-442-3.

Giant insects were back in Charles de Richter's *La Menace Invisible* [The Invisible Threat] (1934), in which a mad scientist leads an invasion of termites to destroy Paris and almost conquers the world. That novel was translated by Fletcher Pratt in *Wonder Stories* under the title of *The Fall of the Eiffel Tower*. Other notable works by the same author included *Le Signe de la Bête* [The Mark of the Beast] (1930) and *L'Homme qui Voulut le Déluge* [The Man Who Wanted a Flood] (1945), about a mad scientist trying to create a new flood.

Also in 1934, Jean Cotard's *Le Flot d'Épouvante* [The Flood of Terror] featured an invasion of the French coastline by giant crabs. Another notable mad scientist was Raoul Lortac's *Demonax* (1938). And in Jean-Pierre Besson's *Le Monstre de St. Basile* [*The Monster of St. Basile*] (1941), a giant, mutated fly attacked Paris.

In 1936, the prolific Maurice Limat began his career with *La Montagne aux Vampires* [The Mountain of Vampires] (1936), about a man who could control vampires. It was followed by *L'Araignée d'Argent* [The Silver Spider] (1936), featuring a spider-robot created by an ancient civilisation, *Les Hommes d'Acier* [The Men of Steel] (1936), *L'Empereur des Scaphandriers* [The Emperor of Deep-Sea Divers] (1937), *Le Septième Cerveau* [The Seventh Brain] (1939), *Le Zodiaque de l'Himalaya* [The Zodiac of the Himalaya] (1942), *Les Rescapés de la Préhistoire* [Escape From Prehistory] (1947) and *La Comète Écarlate* [The Scarlet Comet] (1948), to name but a few.

Also in 1936, Paul Alpérine wrote *L'Île des Vierges Rouges* [The Island of the Red Virgins] (1936), about a Lost World of Amazons hidden in the Brazilian jungle. Other notable novels by the same author included *Ombres sur le Thibet* [Shadows Over Tibet] (1945), about a peak made of radium; *La Citadelle des Glaces* [The Ice Citadel] (1946); *Les Secrets de la Mer Morte* [The Secrets of the Dead Sea] (1949) and Demain dans le Soleil [Tomorrow Inside the Sun] (1950).

Finally, Paul Bérato, who wrote under the pseudonyms of "Paul Béra" and "Yves Dermèze", began a prolific career as a writer of juvenile adventure novels with *La Cité dans les Glaces* [The City in the Ice] (1942), soon followed by *Les Buveurs d'Océan* [The Ocean Drinkers] (1943), *Le Pays sans Soleil* [The Sunless Land] (1948) and *Les Pirates du Ciel* [The Sky Pirates] (1949), all appearing in children's magazines. Like Bruss and Limat, Béra eventually joined the team of Éditions Fleuve Noir.

Other notable authors or works of the 1930s and 1940s in the popular adventure vein included:

Raoul Le Jeune, with *Prisonniers au Fond des Mers* [Prisoners at the Bottom of the Sea] (1931), *Le Pays de la Mort* [The Land of Death] (1931), *Le Maître des Sargasses* [The Master of the Sargasso Sea] (1932) and *Prisonnier des Invisibles* [*Prisoner of the Invisibles*] (1933).

V. Géraud, with *Sous les Sables du Sahara* [Under the Sands of the Sahara], serialized in *Le Petit Illustré* in 1932, told of the exploration of the underground sea and vast oil fields that lie hidden under the Sahara, which was rather prophetic considering that no one suspected the existence of oil there at the time.

Maurice Boué and Édouard Aujay, with *Le Tour du Monde en... Un Jour* [Around the World in One Day] (1933), which featured a method of travel which involved remaining motionless while letting the Earth rotate underneath one's feet.

Georges Delhoste, with *Le Maître du Jour et du Bruit* [The Master of Day and Noise] (1933), which featured the television-like transmission of sounds and images; and *La Science Folle* [Science Gone Mad] (1934), in which a mad scientist transformed the Sahara into a futuristic empire.

Gustave Gailhard, with *La Cité Fantôme* [The Phantom City] (1934), *Les Yeux du Fauve* [The Eyes of the Beast] (1935) and *Le Lac des Mirages* [The Lake of Mirages] (1938).

Félix Celval, with *Le Rayon Infernal* [The Hell Ray] (1935), and *Le Monstre de l'Île sans Nom* [The Monster of the Nameless Island] (1936).

Félix Léonnec, with *Le Secret de l'Immortalité* [The Secret of Immortality] (1934), *L'Île d'Épouvante* [Island of Terror] (1936) and *Le Dragon Volant* [The Flying Dragon] (1937).

René Duchesne, with *Le Maître de la Mort* [The Master of Death] (1936), *Les Forbans de l'Océan* [The Oceanic Bandits] (1936), *L'Extraordinaire Voyage du Loriot* [The Extraordinary Voyage of the Loriot] (1937) and *Les Hommes sans Visage* [The Faceless Men] (1938).

Michel Darry, with *La Course au Radium* [The Race for Radium] (1936), *La Chambre de la Mort Lente* [The Chamber of Slow Death] (1937), *La Vallée de la Mort Rouge* [The Valley of the Red Death] (1937) and *L'Île des Singes Rois* [The Island of the Monkey Kings] (1939).

Robert Jean-Boulan, with *L'Île des Centaures* [Centaur Island] (1936), La Ville des Tritons [The City of Tritons] (1937), and *Au Paradis des Étoiles* [A Paradise of Stars] (1938).

André Michel, with *Le Mystère de la Pyramide* [The Mystery of the Pyramid] (1936), *L'Oiseau du Pôle* [The Bird of the Pole] (1937), *Au Coeur du Cyclone* [In the Heart of the Hurricane] (1938) and *Le Secret des Huit* [The Secret of the Eight] (1939).

Maurice Pérot, with *L'Expérience du Dr. Hortner* [The Experiment of Dr. Hortner] (1937), *Le Royaume de l'Épouvante* [The Kingdom of Terror] (1937), and *La Cité des Réprouvés* [The City of the Reprobates] (1939).

Mona Gloria, with *Au Pays des Géants Rouges* [In the Land of the Red Giants] (1937), *Les Mystérieuses Catacombes* [The Mysterious Catacombs] (1938) and *Au Pays des Demi-Hommes* [In the Land of the Half-Men] (1941).

Jean Normand, with *La Cité du Mystère* [The City of Mystery] (1937), *Le Maître de l'Étoile* [The Master of the Star] (1938) and *Le Vengeur des Incas* [The Inca Avenger] (1941).

George Fronval, with *Le Mystère du Temple en Ruines* [The Mystery of the Ruined Temple] (1938), *L'Énigmatique*

Fen-Chu [The Enigmatic Fen-Chu] (1944) and *Le Maître des Robots* [The Robot Master] (1946).

Pierre Olasso, with *Le Sorcier de la Jungle* [The Wizard of the Jungle] (1938) and *Le Monstre Préhistorique* [The Prehistoric Monster] (1952).

Léopold Frachet, with *Mille Lieues sous les Terres* [A Thousand Leagues Under the Earth] (1939), *La Guerre des Robots* [War of the Robots] (1939) and La Reine de l'Amazone [*The Amazon Queen*] (1939), a colorful Lost World story.

Jean Kery, with *Les Conjurés de l'Île Secrète* [The Conspirators of the Secret Island] (1939), *La Secte Infernale* [The Infernal Sect] (1949), *La Reine du Pôle* [The Queen of the Pole] (1950) and *Les Mystères d'Atomeville* [The Mysteries of Atom-City] (1951).

Roger-Henri Jacquart, with *Cet Étrange Docteur Lang* [That Strange Dr. Lang] (1940), *La Prison sous l'Océan* [The Underwater Prison] (1944) and *Le Dernier Couple* [The Last Couple] (1945).

Swiss writer Jacques Chable, with *Le Maître du Soleil* [The Master of the Sun] (1942) and the juvenile *Flammes dans le Ciel* [*Fire in the Sky*] (1943).

Xavier de Langlais, with *L'Île sous Cloche* [The Domed Island], first published in Breton as *Enez ar Rod* in 1944 and translated into French by the author in 1946.

Jean Bucline, with *Fabrique d'Hommes* [Man Factory] (1946) about a secret Master of the World living on an artificial island, who uses agents to sow discord and foment wars.

Émile Couture, with *Les Rayons M.V.* [The M.V. Rays] (1947).

Journeys to Other Times

The perspective of a new conflict with Germany continued to fill the pages of the science fiction imprints and magazines throughout the 1930s and 1940s, with novels such as

Jean Bardanne's *L'Allemagne Attaquera Le...* [Germany Will Attack On...] (1932), followed by the grimly prophetic *La Guerre et les Microbes* [War and Microbes] (1937).

In Colonel Brat's *Paris Sera-t-il Détruit en 1936?* [Will Paris Be Destroyed In 1936?] (1933), the French thwarted a sneak German attack. This book was written as an explicit response to a German novel *How Paris Will Be Destroyed in 1936* (1932) by German author Major von Helders, in which France was attacked by the British.

Albert de Pouvourville's *Pacifique 39* (1934) and the thirty-issue serial *La Guerre Prochaine / L'Héroïque Aventure* [The Next War / The Heroic Adventure] (1934-35) were military anticipations of World War II, just as Danrit's novels had been military anticipations of World War I. What was especially ironic in this case was that reality overtook fiction and the real war forced the author to stop writing in the middle of his story.

Gaston Pastre was another provider of adventure novels and military anticipations such as *L'Île Z* [Z Island] (1936), *Le Grand Complot de 1950* [The Great Plot of 1950] (1938), *Les Avions de la Mort* [The Planes of Death] (1939) and *Les Sous-Marins Fantômes* [The Ghost Submarines] (1939); what made his military fiction rather lame was that he "cheated" by boosting the performances of French machines, unrealistically lowered that of German equipment, and did not hesitate to employ transparent *deus ex machina* plot devices to let the French win.

More serious was the five-issue serial *La Guerre! La Guerre!* [*War! War!*] (1939) written by Jean de La Hire under the pseudonym of "Commandant Cazal". Written on the eve of the war, it prophesied the enormously important role played by oil in the future conflict.

The same year, a writer using the pseudonym "Commandant Verdun" released two volumes of *Face à l'Ennemi* [Facing the Enemy], which included an underground war and a "tornado squad."

Other novels about the future included:

E.-G. Perrier's *En l'An 2000* [In the Year 2000] (1931).

Georges Duhamel's *Les Jumeaux de Vallangoujard* [The Twins from Vallangoujard] (1931), a YA novel about the discovery of the secret of happiness, which ends up standardizing mankind.

Pierre de Nolhac's *Saison en Auvergne* [A Season in the Auvergne] (1932), in which an earthquake creates an inland sea in the center of France.

Jean Quatremarre's *Alors la Terre s'arrêta...* [Then the Earth Stood Still] (1934), in which an asteroid crashes into the Moon, which falls to Earth, killing everyone except a couple of humans.

Belgian writer Ege Tilms' *Hodomur, l'Homme de l'Infini* [Hodomur, Man of Infinity] (1934).

Charles de L'Andelyn's *La Prodigieuse Découverte de Georges Lefranc* [Georges Lefranc's Prodigious Discovery] (1935) was about an immortality serum and a future where perfumes are personalized and food come in tablets.

Elga Dimt's *Et La Vie Continue* [***And Life Goes On***] (1941) was sub-titled "An Idyll in Lausanne in the Year 2234."

Étienne Gril's *L'Ovipare* (1942) described an odd near-future in which women start laying eggs.

Pierre Devaux' *Uranium*, written in 1944 but not published until 1946, was a prophetic warning against the atom bomb.

Belgian author Stéphane Hautem's *Le Retour au Silence* [The Return of Silence] (1945) was a dystopia subtitled "Diary of the Homo Citroensis No. K228b" after the famous car make.

Aimé Blanc's *Le Drame de l'An 3000* [The Drama of the Year 3000] (1946).

In Christophe Paulin's *S'il n'en reste qu'un* [If Only One Is Left] (1946), a young French physicist and an American girl become the only survivors on an Earth "purified" of all living matter by a mad scientist; together, they restart civilization.

Finally, a special place should be reserved for Swiss writer Léon Bopp, whose unique and unclassifiable *Jacques*

Arnaut et la Somme Romanesque [Jacques Arnaut & The Sum of His Novels] (1933) was a literary hoax about a fictional writer. His four-volume *Liaisons du Monde* [World Relations] (1938-44) was a detailed uchronia that told the story of a parallel France under Soviet domination from 1935 to 1944. His genre stories were collected in *Drôle de Monde* [Funny World] (1940).

Mainstream Authors

The renowned novelist André Maurois, remained the most notable mainstream writer dabbling with science fiction themes during the period. His *Relativisme* [Relativity] (1930) was a collection of fantastic tales. The classic *Le Peseur d'Âmes* [The Weigher of Souls] (1931), featured a scientist who discovers that the soul is a gas that escapes the body upon death and attempts to posthumously blend his soul with that of his lover. His *La Machine à Lire les Pensées* [The Thought-Reading Machine] (1937) dealt with a machine capable of recording thoughts like photographs.

Another novel on the same theme was A. Clouet's *La Machine à Capter la Pensée* [The Machine for Capturing Thoughts] (1941).

Nicolas Ségur's *Le Paradis des Hommes* [The Human Paradise] (1930)[225] was a scathingly sarcastic satire in which God offers to grant wishes expressed unanimously by the entirety of humankind. The wishes voiced are carefully extrapolated in such a way as to suggest that, however effective individuals might be at screwing up their wishes, a committee composed of the whole human race could do a far more comprehensive job.

Raymond Desorties' *Le Tétrabie* (1933) was about a fantastic machine that could travel in the air, on land and under

---

[225] Black Coat Press, ISBN 978-1-61227-617-5.

the sea and symbolized how the Vernian spirit of invention had eventually infiltrated the field of mainstream litterature.

Another notable futuristic allegory was Jean Talabot's *R'Adam et R'Eve ou Le Vestige* [R'Adam And R'Eve or The Remains] (1934).

Belgian thriller writer Stanislas-André Steeman, the author of the character of *Monsieur Wens*, penned two novels dealing with robots, *Ennemi sans Visage* [Faceless Enemy] (1938) and *Monsieur Wens et l'Automate* [Mr. Wens & The Automaton] (1943).

In *Voyage au Pays des Bohohoms* [Voyage to The Lands of the Bohohoms] (1938), Luc Durtain told the story of a man who discovers that the clouds are inhabited by nearly insubstantial beings. He also penned *La Guerre n'existe pas* [War Does Not Exist] (1939) and a collection of genre tales, *Histoires Fantastiques* [Fantastic Stories] (1942).

In 1946, André H. Balnec described the colonization of the Moon in *Séléné*. In it, the first man to land on the Moon is a Frenchman, Émile Durand. The Moon, now dubbed the Satellite and its inhabitants the Satellians, is then partitioned in various colonies, each affiliated to a different nation. The novel goes on to examine in great detail the social, economic, religious and political problems created by the existence of a Moon colony.

Finally, the names of Romain Gary, Henri d'Amfreville, Yves Gandon and Raymond Abellio should be added here as they began to contribute genre novels in the late 1940s, but their works will be more appropriately reviewed in our next chapter.

Les Dieux Verts

C. HENNEBERG

LE RAYON FANTASTIQUE

The Silver Age
(1950-1970)

Until the early 1950s, French science fiction was limping along, not having recovered from the double blows of the censorship of the late 1920s and World War II.

Maurice Renard and José Moselli were lost for the genre. Jacques Spitz had not created any followers. And René Barjavel was on his way to becoming a full-fledged mainstream author.

All the magazines, except for the now outmoded *Journal des Voyages* were dead, and it, too, stopped publication in 1949. A short-lived *Anticipations* was started in Brussels in 1945 but lasted only fifteen issues.

The situation was just as bleak with the popular paperback imprints. Fernand Nathan's *Aventures & Voyages* was cancelled in 1948; Tallandier's *Grandes Aventures* only lasted from 1949 to 1953) and *Le Livre d'Aventures* from 1951 to 1954;, Ferenczi's *Mon Roman d'Aventures* limped along from 1942 to 1956, but published a type of science fiction that had basically not changed since 1914, and could even be said to have regressed compared to the heights of the late 1920s. A small imprint, *Horizons Fantastiques* [Fantastic Horizons] by publisher Le Sillage only released four titles between 1949 and 1953.

All this began to change in 1951.

As was the case in the previous chapters, we have divided the next fifty years into chronological sub-divisions, but in this instance, four instead of three. The first, dubbed the "Silver Age", started in 1950 and ended approximately in 1970, just after the cultural revolution of May 1968. It was a period of rebirth, growth and consolidation. It was during that period that a new slate of major, modern authors began to emerge.

It was also, unfortunately, a period during which French science fiction, which had been in a literary coma since the 1930s, discovered in one massive, collective blow the best of American science fiction of the 1940s and 1950s. As a result, and for the next thirty years or so, French science fiction lived under the shadow of American science fiction, always comparing itself to it and playing catch up. More subtly, the very themes and modes of expression of the genre were now defined according to American criteria. Even at its best, French science fiction was forced to play by the literary rules established by American science fiction, and if it did not always lose in quality, it often did in originality.

The Publishers

The notion that an allegedly new literary genre dubbed "science fiction" was about to emerge was first broached in a series of articles published in the press: in 1950, in the major daily newspaper, *Le Figaro*; in 1951, in literary magazines such as *Critique*, *Les Temps Modernes*, *Cahiers du Sud* and *Esprit*; and, finally, in 1952, as a full-page blast in the major popular daily newspaper, *France-Dimanche*. Science fiction had arrived. It was naturally linked to the great pioneers, Jules Verne and H. G. Wells, but in a surprising act of collective amnesia, all the prodigious works of the first half of the century, which had not been labeled science fiction since that label had not yet existed, were completely forgotten and left unmentioned.

The idea of a dedicated, adult science fiction book imprint had been pitched to various publishers by notable fans such as Jacques Bergier, Georges H. Gallet and Michel Pilotin since after the war.

In January 1951, publishers Hachette and Gallimard, rather than competing, joined forces to create the first, modern French science fiction imprint, *Le Rayon Fantastique* [*The Fantastic Bookshelf*], jointly edited by Gallet and Pilotin. The

Rayon Fantastique published both golden age American classics selected by Gallet) and more contemporary works selected by Pilotin, such as novels by Isaac Asimov, Arthur C. Clarke, A. E. Van Vogt, Theodore Sturgeon, Edmond Hamilton, Robert A. Heinlein, Fritz Leiber, Jack Williamson, Catherine L. Moore, etc. It also introduced French authors such as Francis Carsac, Nathalie C. Henneberg, Albert Higon a.k.a. Michel Jeury, Gérard Klein, and Philippe Curval. The *Rayon Fantastique* books sported attractive covers by noted French artist Jean-Claude Forest, the creator of *Barbarella*. The imprint eventually became a victim of lukewarm sales, as well as a tug of war between its two rival co-owners, and stopped publication in 1964 after having released 124 titles. During its existence, it also resurrected the Jules Verne Award.

Eight months later, in September 1951, publisher Marc de Caro whose company, Fleuve Noir, was specialized in pulpish paperback imprints, such as police thrillers (*Special-Police*), espionage novels (*Espionnage*), adventure stories (*L'Aventurier*) and (later) war stories (*Feu*), decided to launch a science fiction imprint called *Anticipation*. (A horror imprint entitled *Angoisse* followed in 1954.) The new imprint was entrusted to editor François Richard who, with young author Henri Richard Bessière, became half of the writing team of Richard-Bessière. The particularity of *Anticipation* was that it cultivated its own school of in-house authors: Richard-Bessière, Jean-Gaston Vandel (another writing team better known as "Paul Kenny", creator of a French *James Bond*-like hero, *Francis Coplan*), Jimmy Guieu, Stéfan Wul and B.-R. Bruss, to which were later added Maurice Limat, Max-André Rayjean, Kurt Steiner, Peter Randa, Gérard Klein (writing as "Gilles d'Argyre"), Pierre Barbet and Jean-Louis & Doris Le May. Another particularity was that the authors' style owed relatively little, at least at first, to their American counterparts. The early volumes of the imprint followed the literary traditions established by Rosny and Renard. *Anticipation* also published a few selected novels by American or British authors, such as Poul Anderson, Isaac Asimov (the first of his *Lucky*

Star novels), Leigh Brackett, Arthur C. Clarke, John Russell Fearn (writing as "Vargo Statten"), L. Ron Hubbard, Murray Leinster, E. C. Tubb (also writing as "Volsted Gridban"), A. E. Van Vogt and John Wyndham, as well as translations of the successful German *Perry Rhodan* series.

In 1953, an exhibit entitled *Présence du Futur* [*Presence of the Future*] was held at the bookstore La Balance, owned by Valerie Schmidt, which had become a meeting place for well-known fans and professionals of the period: established figures such as Jacques Bergier, Michel Pilotin, Jacques Sternberg and Boris Vian met newcomers such as Philippe Curval, Francis Carsac, Pierre Versins, André Ruellan (a.k.a. "Kurt Steiner"), Jacques Sadoul and Gérard Klein. La Balance, later renamed L'Atome, closed in 1962.

The following year, in March 1954, publisher Denoël borrowed the name to launch its own *Présence du Futur* imprint, edited by Robert Kanters. With a first slate of titles initially selected by Pilotin, *Présence du Futur* introduced Ray Bradbury, H. P. Lovecraft, Alfred Bester, Richard Matheson, James Blish, Fredric Brown, Brian W. Aldiss, Kurt Vonnegut, Clifford D. Simak, J. G. Ballard, Daniel F. Galouye, and others, to the French public. It also published early works by Gérard Klein. In terms of French authors, during this period, *Présence du Futur* concentrated on works by mainstream-oriented writers, such as Jérôme Sériel (a pseudonym of Jacques Vallée), Jacques Sternberg, René Barjavel, Marianne Andrau, Jean-Louis Curtis, Jean Hougron and René Réouven, a.k.a. René Sussan.

In October 1953, publisher Maurice Renault, whose company O.P.T.A. (an acronym for Office de Publicité Technique & Artistique) had been putting out *Mystère-Magazine*, a French edition of *Ellery Queen's Magazine* since 1948, decided to launch *Fiction*, a French edition of the American *Magazine of Fantasy & Science Fiction*. *Fiction* was at first edited by Renault, with the help of his partner Daniel Domange until his death in 1971. *Fiction* published many stories by French genre authors from the start.

In 1959, under the direction of writer Alain Dorémieux, who had joined the team in 1957, OPTA began publishing a series of yearly, book-length *Specials*, several of which were entirely devoted to French authors. In 1964, Renault added a French edition of *Galaxy* to his line. An earlier edition had previously been published from 1953 to 1959 by a smaller publisher. In 1965, it launched the hardcover imprint *Club du Livre d'Anticipation*, at first co-edited with Jacques Sadoul) and the paperback imprint *Galaxie-Bis*. Both published mostly American classics until the 1970s.

Other short-lived imprints of the mid-1950s included:

Visions Futures [*Future Visions*] (1952-53), by publisher La Flamme d'Or, which published ten volumes including works by Henri Keller & Grégoire Brainin and Kurt Steiner writing as "Kurt Wargar".

Grands Romans-Sciences-Anticipations [Great Novels of Science & Anticipation] (1953-54), by publisher Le Trotteur, which published eight volumes including works by Henri Keller & Grégoire Brainin.

Série 2000 (1954-56), by small publisher Métal, which published twenty-five volumes including works by Nathalie & Charles Henneberg, Maurice Limat, Pierre Versins and Paul Béra writing as "Yves Dermèze".

Cosmos (1955-57), by publisher Grand Damier, which published twelve volumes including more works by Henri Keller & Grégoire Brainin and Maurice Limat.

In January 1958, a new magazine entitled *Satellite* was launched by Michel Benâtre and Hervé Calixte (also assisted by Jacques Bergier) to compete with *Fiction*. It lasted only forty-seven issues, until January 1963, but during that time, it published stories by Francis Carsac, Nathalie Charles Henneberg, Gérard Klein, Philippe Curval, Michel Demuth and Pierre Versins. *Satellite* also published a short-lived paperback imprint, *Les Cahiers de la Science-Fiction* [*The Science Fiction Notebooks*] (1958-60), which published ten volumes.

Pierre Versins also published the remarkable fanzine *Ailleurs* [*Elsewhere*] from 1956 to 1963. Other notable fanzines of the 1960s included Jacqueline H. Osterrath's *Lunatique* (Osterrath was also the translator of the *Perry Rhodan* series for Fleuve Noir) and Jean-Pierre Fontana's *Mercury*.

Three more short-lived genre imprints made their appearance in the 1960s:

Science-S-Fiction by Ditis, which released only eight titles in 1960; *Espions de Demain* [Tomorrow's Spies] by Arabesque, which published ten novels in 1960; and *Science-Fiction Suspense* (1960-61) by Daniber, which published seventeen volumes, including works by Lester Del Rey, and Donald A. Wollheim.

Finally, Belgian publisher Marabout began publishing science fiction novels regularly as part of its *Fantastique* imprint, starting in 1964 with an anthology by Hubert Juin, followed by novels by Poul Anderson, George Langelaan, A. E. Van Vogt, and Norman Spinrad, before giving the genre its own dedicated imprint, *Science-Fiction*, under the editorship of Jean-Baptiste Baronian in 1969.

Major Authors

Gérard Klein was the first among a new wave of science fiction fans turned writers, inspired by American science fiction. He began to publish a series of short stories in *Satellite* in 1955 when he was 18, which were later collected in *Les Perles du Temps* [The Pearls of Time], for *Présence du Futur*. In 1958, he published two minor space operas, *Agent Galactique* [Galactic Agent] under the pseudonym of "Mark Starr" in *Satellite*, and *Embûches dans l'Espace* [Ambushes in Space], co-written with Richard Chomet and Patrice Rondard, for the *Rayon Fantastique*. He also wrote a major novel, *Le Gambit des Étoiles* [Starmasters' Gambit] (1958)[226] for the *Rayon Fantastique*. In it, the secret immortal masters of the federa-

---

[226] In *Starmasters*, Black Coat Press, ISBN 978-1-61227-712-7.

tion play galactic chess with the human agent of mysterious cosmic powers, who turn out to be sentient stars. *Le Gambit des Étoiles* established the author as a major new talent, and from that point on, he has remained one of the best French science fiction writers.

Klein followed up with the popular *Argyre* saga, describing the future history of Man's conquest of the Solar System. Written for Fleuve Noir's *Anticipation*, and originally published under the pseudonym of "Gilles d'Argyre", these were comprised of *Chirurgiens d'une Planète* [The Planet Surgeons] (1960; revised in 1987 as *Le Rêve des Forêts* [A Dream of Forests]), which described the terraforming of Mars by the enterprising Georges Beyle; *Les Voiliers du Soleil* [The Solar Sailors] (1961), in which Beyle, now linked to a giant computer, defeats an alien invader; *Le Long Voyage* [The Long Journey] (1964), in which Beyle returns to launch a plan to turn a terraformed Pluto into a starship. Other notable works of the period included another time-thriller, *Le Temps n'a pas d'Odeur* [Time Has No Scent] (1963)[227] for *Présence du Futur*, and *Les Tueurs de Temps* [The Time Killers] (1965)[228] for *Anticipation*, which reprised the theme of a chess game spanning time and space. The author also published a collection of literary stories, *Un Chant de Pierre* [A Song of Stone] (1966), and *Le Sceptre du Hasard* [The Scepter of Chance] (1968), a political space opera of the far future, in which Beyle is mentioned in passing.

In 1969, Klein, who by then had become a renowned critic and essayist, launched the prestigious *Ailleurs & Demain* [*Elsewhere & Tomorrow*] science fiction imprint at publisher Robert Laffont. There, he published one major new novel, *Les Seigneurs de la Guerre* [The Overlords of War] (1971) (later translated by John Brunner), and another excellent short story collection, *La Loi du Talion* [The Law of Retaliation] (1973). *Les Seigneurs de la Guerre* was a sophisticated space-time

---

[227] *The Day Before Tomorrow* in *Starmasters*, q.v.
[228] *The Mote in Time's Eye* in *Starmasters*, q.v.

opera incorporating challenging philosophical implications. Its hero, Colson, is a lone warrior caught in a future war who finds himself thrown back and forth between two segments of time separated by 6000 years. The prime movers are the mysterious Gods of Aergistal, omnipotent chess players who live a complex "hyper-life" (infinitely replaying their own existence) at the end of time, and have built a simulated battlefield where all the various wars of time are being waged again and again. Their goals are both simple and complex: war is to be abolished, war is to be understood, war is to be preserved (in case the universe needs it someday). War is depicted as a negative, yet indispensable factor in human evolution, almost a biological imperative. It is interesting to note that the author declared in an interview that a large section of the novel was written during his military service during the French Algerian war of independence. Since then, Klein has devoted most of his energies to his work as editor and anthologist.

"Francis Carsac", the pseudonym of university professor and prehistorian François Bordes, bridged the gap between French science fiction of the 1930s and 1940s, and the American-influenced space operas of the 1950s. All of his works, except for his last novel, were published by the *Rayon Fantastique*, and were characterized by a profoundly humanistic, tolerant philosophy, often absent from the American works of the period. *Ceux de Nulle Part* [Those from Nowhere] (1954) featured an average Earthman volunteering to help an interstellar civilization fight a war against the Misliks, alien metallic intelligences who turn off suns. *Les Robinsons du Cosmos* [The Robinsons of the Cosmos] (1955) was a *When Worlds Collide*-like tale of men colonizing another world. *Terre en Fuite* [Fleeing Earth] (1960) described how a future scientist turns Earth into a giant ship to escape the death of our sun.

Ce Monde est Notre [This World Is Ours] (1962) took place in the same universe as *Ceux de Nulle Part*, but several centuries later. It dealt intelligently and with great sensitivity with the problem of three different cultures sharing the same planet: one is a colony of Basque humans, the second are survivors from a lost Terran ship who built a pseudo-medieval society, the third a peaceful, primitive cold-blooded reptilian race. Galactic law stating that there can only be one race per planet, a team of investigators is sent to decide who stays and who will be removed. *Pour Patrie, l'Espace* [For Homeland, Space] (1962) was a space opera about space-faring gypsies and the galactic empire from which they sprang and which they defied. Finally, Carsac's last novel, *La Vermine du Lion* [The Vermin of the Lion] (1967), published by *Anticipation*, featured Terai Laprade, an anthropologist who fights to protect an unspoiled world and its natives from a ruthless mining company. The novel was ahead of its times in terms of its political and ecological concerns.

Other notable authors published by the *Rayon Fantastique* included:

"Albert Higon", a pseudonym of writer Michel Jeury, who contributed two space operas, *Aux Étoiles du Destin* [*Destiny's Stars*] (1960), featuring a cosmic battle between the alien T'Loons and the incomprehensible Glutons, whose only communication is the wonderfully nonsensical sentence, "Sacred whirlpool matures green water", and *La Machine du Pouvoir* [The Machine of Power] (1960), which won the 1960 Jules Verne Award.

"Philippe Curval" (a pseudonym of journalist Philippe Tronche), with *Les Fleurs de Vénus* [The Flowers of Venus] (1960) and *Le Ressac de l'Espace* [The Breakers of Space] (1962), which won the 1963 Jules Verne Award, and featured the alien Txalqs who must live in symbiosis with humans to realize their ideal of beauty. These were early works and the considerable impact of both Jeury and Curval would not be felt until the 1970s.

Daniel Drode, whose only novel, *Surface de la Planète* [Surface of the Planet] (1959) proved immediately controversial because of his efforts to recreate the decadent language of a post-nuclear, underground civilization. The novel was clearly inspired by the mainstream "*Nouveau Roman*" pioneered by Françoise Sagan and Marguerite Duras, and anticipated the literary experiments of the US/UK "New Wave" of the 1970s. *Surface de la Planète* won the 1959 Jules Verne Award and exerted a considerable influence on the genre.

Serge Martel, who won the 1958 Jules Verne Award for *L'Adieu aux Astres* [Farewell to the Stars] (1958), a nostalgia-filled space opera, which was followed by *L'Aventure Alphéenne* [The Alphean Adventure] (1960).

"Jérôme Sériel" was the pseudonym of renowned scientist Jacques Vallée, better known for a number of serious books studying the UFO phenomenon. The author's first novel, *Le Sub-Espace* [Sub-Space] (1961), won the 1961 Jules Verne Award and featured an astonishing cosmic battle using what was at the time cutting edge physics. The author continued to explore the theme of alien intelligences existing in a multi-dimensional universe in his next novel, *Le Satellite Sombre* [The Dark Satellite] (1963), published by *Présence du Futur*. In 1986, another genre novel about artificial intelligence, *Alintel*, was released under Vallée's own name.

Vladimir Volkoff, the son of exiled Russians, penned the satirical, surrealist novel, *Métro pour l'Enfer* [Metro for Hell] (1963), which won the 1963 Jules Verne Award. The author then wrote the very popular *Langelot* YA series under the pseudonym of "Lieutenant X" before returning to science fiction in the 1980s with two novels, *Le Tire-Bouchon du Bon Dieu* [The Corkscrew of God] (1982), in which Earth was surrendered by the humans to an alien fungus, and *La Guerre des Pieuvres* [The War of the Octopuses] (1983). Meanwhile, he had established himself as a major writer of critically acclaimed spy thrillers such as *Le Retournement* [The Turning] (1979) and *Le Montage* [The Machination] (1982).

The *Rayon Fantastique* also published three remarkable women writers:

Françoise d'Eaubonne had already written a number of fantastic stories collected in *Démons et Merveilles* [Demons & Wonders] (1951) when she penned the ambitious future history novel, *Les Sept Fils de l'Étoile* [The Seven Sons of the Star] (1962), for the *Rayon Fantastique*. It was followed by

L'Échiquier du Temps [Time's Chessboard] (1962) and *Rêve de Feu* [Dream of Fire] (1964).

The works of Nathalie Charles Henneberg stand alone in the French SF landscape of the 1960s. Her use of the language, betraying Germanic and Russian influences, was unusually well-suited to creating larger-than-life heroic characters and epic, mythological romances. Her skills at creating intricately detailed baroque universes were second to none. Russian-born Nathalie first collaborated anonymously with her husband the German-born Charles on a flamboyant, gothic space opera featuring superhuman protagonists, <u>La Naissance des Dieux</u> [The Birth of the Gods] (1954), published by *Séries 2000*, which mixed Greek and Norse mythologies in a science fiction context. In it, a scientist, an astronaut and a poet find that they can psychically recreate life, and eventually fight for supremacy, on another planet which turns out to be Earth in the far future. In accordance with the author's philosophy, the astronaut is the hero, and the poet the misguided villain. The novel won the then-short-lived Rosny Award. That novel was followed by *Le Chant des Astronautes* [The Astronauts' Song] (1958), serialized in *Satellite*, which dealt with the battle against energy creatures from Algol; *An Premier, Ere Spatiale* [Year 1 of the Space Era] (1959), serialized in <u>Fiction</u>, about the first faster-than-light ship, and *La Rosée du Soleil* [The Dew of the Sun] (1959), published by the *Rayon Fantastique*, about the adventures of the four crewmen of a spaceship stranded on the fantastic alien world of Bellatrix.

After the death of her husband in 1959, Nathalie Henneberg began publishing under her own name, starting with *Les Dieux Verts* [The Green Gods] (1961),[229] which tells of the romance of Prince Aran and Atlena during the Emerald Age of the Earth, in the far future, when Man's Empire is on the decline and the world is ruled by the eponymous "Green Gods," powerful entities which arose from the vegetal kingdom. *Le Sang des Astres* [The Blood of the Stars] (1963) was a colorful

---

[229] Black Coat Press, ISBN 978-1-935558-47-7.

gothic fantasy in which an astronaut from the year 2700 journeys to a medieval Earth-like world ruled by kabbala, where legends live, and where he eventually falls in love with a female salamander. Her masterpiece was *La Plaie* [The Plague] (1964), a sprawling 600-page novel that told of the desperate battle by a handful of humans and angel-like mutants against a wave of pure, malevolent evil sweeping the galaxy, and which incarnates itself in the bodies of the "Nocturnes".

Christine Renard (no relation to Maurice) was another female writer who had contributed short stories to *Fiction* and wrote *À Contre-Temps* [Against Time] (1963), a love story with a time paradox, for the *Rayon Fantastique*.

Another notable female author was Marianne Andrau, whose *Les Mains du Manchot* [The Hands of the One-Armed Man] (1953), a novel about the Kafkaesque city of Parsepol which existed in another dimension, was originally published in a mainstream imprint by Denoël. The author followed it with *Le Prophète* [The Prophet] (1955), *Lumière d'Épouvante* [Light of Terror] (1956) (a collection of fantastic tales), *D.C. (Doom City)* (1957), and finally, *Les Faits d'Eiffel* [The Feats of Eiffel] (1960), another short story collection, this time published by *Présence du Futur*. Another Andrau genre novel was *L'Architecte Fou* [The Mad Architect] (1964), a dystopia telling the story of three immortals from the 20th century who discover the world of the 22nd century.

Of all the authors published by Fleuve Noir's *Anticipation* during the period, none was more remarkable than "Stefan Wul", the pseudonym of dental surgeon Pierre Pairault. His eleven novels, published between 1956 and 1959, were all classics, enlivened by their colorful, poetic imagery and their operatic stories, which took pulp clichés and turned them into powerful dramas. *Niourk* (1957) told the story of a mutant child who rediscovers civilization in the ruins of a post-cataclysmic New York (a.k.a. Niourk). Another interesting aspect of this novel was that its protagonist was black, an unusual choice for the times. *OMS en Serie* [OMS in Series] (1957) and *L'Orphelin de Perdide* [The Orphan of Perdide]

(1958) were respectively the basis for two of René Laloux' animated features, *La Planète Sauvage* [Fantastic Planet] and *Les Maîtres du Temps* [*The Time Masters*]. In the former, men have become the pets of an advanced race of alien giants. In the latter, a boy abandoned on a hostile world is linked to his rescuers through a space radio. The novel ends with a clever time paradox in which one of the rescuers turns out to be the same boy, but much older.

Other notable works by the same author included *Le Temple du Passé* [The Temple of the Past] (1958), in which spacemen who crashed on an alien world are swallowed by a giant whale-like creature and, in order to save themselves, cause it to evolve, eventually creating a new race of intelligent lizards. The lone survivor is ultimately revealed to be an Atlantean; *La Mort Vivante* [The Living Death] (1958), about a scientist who, in order to recreate a billionaire's dead daughter, creates a protoplasmic entity which ends up swallowing the world; the futuristic spy thrillers, *Piège sur Zarkass* [Trap on Zarkass] (1958) and *Odyssée Sous Contrôle* [Odyssey Under Control] (1959), which anticipated today's virtual reality sagas.

Writer André Ruellan contributed many horror novels to Fleuve Noir's *Angoisse* imprint under his pseudonym of "Kurt Steiner" and two science-fantasy novels starring the futuristic knight, Dal Ortog Dal of Galankar, *Aux Armes d'Ortog* [The Arms of Ortog] (1960) and *Ortog et les Ténèbres* [Ortog and the Darkness] (1969).[230] Knight-Navigator Dal Ortog of Galankar lives on a 50th century Earth where space travel co-exists with a medieval society. First, he is sent to the far reaches of space to find a cure for the slow death that is killing humanity after a devastating interplanetary war. But when he returns with the cure, he is too late to save his love, Kalla. In the sequel, Ortog and his friend, Zoltan Charles Henderson de

---

[230] Both in *Ortog*, Black Coat Press, ISBN 978-1-935558-28-6.

Nancy, embark on a quest through the dimensions of Death to find Kalla's soul and bring her back to Earth.

For *Anticipation*, Steiner also wrote several remarkable science fiction novels. *Salamandra* (1959) featured a love story between an Earthman and a Mercurian woman. *Le 32 Juillet* [*July 32nd*] (1959) described how a man finds himself in another dimension and explores the vast insides of a giant, living entity. *Les Improbables* (1965) is about a time war between two future cities, Babelia and Kaltarborog, and the attempts by their descendants to manipulate events to increase their probability of existence. *Les Océans du Ciel* [The Oceans of the Sky] (1967) was a colorful space opera featuring a method of birth involving cosmic exchanges between two worlds. *Les Enfants de l'Histoire* [The Children of History] (1969) was a thinly disguised allegory of the political events of May 1968 recast in the future.

In the 1970s, Steiner continued to pen well-crafted novels for *Anticipation* such as *Le Disque Rayé* [The Scratched Record] (1970) about a complex time loop; *Brebis Galeuses* [Black Sheep] (1974), a medical dystopia; and *Un Passe Temps* [A Passtime] (1979), another clever time paradox tale. More importantly, in 1974, Steiner wrote the remarkable novel *Tunnel* under his own name for *Ailleurs & Demain*. It depicted the flight of a man through a garbage jungle surrounding a bleak, futuristic Paris. The man is dragging behind him the body of his dead lover, searching for a way to resurrect her. In 1979, Ruellan write the novelization of his script for Alain Jessua's movie, *Les Chiens* [The Dogs], and, in 1984, *Mémo* for *Présence du Futur*, a novel in which a scientist's experiments with a new drug intended to stimulate memory but which ends in a nightmarish disaster.

After Wul and Steiner, one of the most interesting authors of *Anticipation* was the prolific "B.-R. Bruss" who also contributed to the *Angoisse* imprint. Bruss who also wrote pseudonym of "Roger Blondel", penned over forty novels for *Anticipation* between 1954 and 1975. His first three novels formed a trilogy about an *Earth vs. Flying Saucers* war (Nos.

33, 40, 65; 1954-56). His books were lessons about the need for mutual respect and tolerance between different species. One of his most notable earlier works was the *Cerel* trilogy (for *CERveaux ÉLectroniques*, i.e.: Electronic Brains) (1959-63), in which mankind learns to live in peace alongside the giant computers which had once enslaved it.

Men falling in love and eventually marrying alien females, often belonging to races with superior powers, were the subject of several novels such as *L'Otarie Bleue* [The Blue Otter] (1963), *L'Étrange Planète Orga* [The Mysterious Planet Orga] (1967), *L'Espionne Galactique* [The Galactic Spy] (1968) (in which the love interest is revealed to be a cyborg), and the beautiful *Les Enfants d'Alga* [The Children of Alga] (1968), in which the sterile Algans come to Earth to father children. Men coming in contact with alien entities of vast, extraordinary powers, who at first barely take notice of our existence, included *Une Mouche Nommée Drésa* [A Fly Named Dresa] (1964), *L'Énigme des Phtas* [The Enigma of the Phtas] (1965), *La Créature Éparse* [The Fragmented Creature] (1966) and *Le Mystère des Sups* [The Mystery of the Sups] (1967). Men being experimented upon by aliens and the two species ultimately gaining a form of mutual understanding included *Les Translucides* [The Transparents] (1964), in which human guinea pigs are turned into transparent giants, and *La Planète Glacée* [The Ice Planet] (1965), which featured a man whose brain has been transplanted into an alien robot.

Some of the author's best novels were *Le Grand Feu* [The Great Fire] (1964), in which the children of men and young alien sentient robots make contact on a post-cataclysmic Earth despite their elders' reluctance; later, the robots helped rescue men from giant ants; *Planètes Oubliées* [Forgotten Planets] (1965), where each planetary colony was seeded with a specific profession (surgeons, artists, psychologists, etc.), generating colorful, split cultures; *L'Astéroïde Noir* [The Black Asteroid] (1964), a harrowing exploration of the dimension of dreams; the self-explanatory *Le Trappeur Galac-*

tique [The Galactic Trapper] (1967), with its colorful alien fauna; *La Planète Introuvable* [The Unfindable Planet] (1968), in which an alien planet seems to exist simultaneously in different time zones; and *Parle, Robot!* [Speak, Robot!] (1969), a moving first-person history of a sentient robot.

Later works, however, took a more pessimistic slant, as evidenced in *La Planète aux Oasis* [The Oasis Planet] (1970), where mankind is casually exterminated by superior cosmic entities, and *Une Si Belle Planète* [Such A Beautiful Planet] (1970), where a human colony is forced to abandon a paradisial planet previously seeded by another race.

"Richard-Bessière" was another of the major writers of Fleuve Noir's *Anticipation*, writing almost one hundred novels between 1951 and 1985. Henri Richard Bessière's father was a friend and occasional writing partner of François Richard, who became the first editor of the imprint. Together, the two men had used the signature of "F. Richard-Bessière" on earlier collaborations. When *Anticipation* started in 1951, the contracts for the novels written by young Henri-Richard, and edited by François Richard, were signed by his father. The novels were therefore released under the "F. Richard-Bessière" penname. After his father's death, Henri Richard Bessière asked that the books be released under his own name, but the publishers did not want to risk losing the benefits of what they considered a valuable "house name". A compromise was reached and, starting with *Les Maîtres du Silence* [The Masters of Silence] (1965), the books were signed "Richard-Bessière", sometimes with, sometimes without, a hyphen.

Bessière's first science fiction series featured the so-called *Conquérants de l'Universe* [Conquerors of the Universe] (1951-54), a jolly band of Earthmen led by professor Bénac, the inventor of a spaceship called *Meteor*, and comprised of a young French engineer, an American journalist and a young British woman. The so-called Conquerors explored the Solar System, helping friendly aliens and thwarting evil tyrants. The novels, originally written in the mid-1940s, owed more to René-Marcel de Nizerolles than to post-World War II science fiction. The somewhat naïve adventures of these brave men were close in style to *Flash Gordon* and embodied the transition between the French science fiction of the 1920s and 1930s, and that of the 1950s and 1960s, influenced by American authors. The saga was later updated in a two-volume remake entitled *Les Pionniers du Cosmos* [The Pioneers of the Cosmos] (1965). [231]

Bessière's most popular series featured the adventures of American journalist Sydney Gordon, his ditzy wife Margaret, his catastrophe-prone son, Bud, and his scientist friends, Archie and Gloria Brent. The series began in *Création Cosmique* [Cosmic Creation] (1957) and continued through sixteen novels published between 1957 and 1980. The Sydney Gordon books were initially fairly serious tales of alien or extra-dimensional invaders, but eventually took a tongue-in-cheek turn with *Les Mages de Dereb* [The Wizards of Dereb] (1966), in which Sydney and his friends discovered the Land of Fiction where they faced the demented products of the imagination of a science fiction writer; and *Ne Touchez Pas Aux Borloks* [Don't Touch the Borloks] (1968), in which alien toys create chaos on Earth. A recurring opponent of Gordon and his friends became the "Machine", a giant, intelligent, extra-dimensional computer with god-like powers introduced in *La Machine Venue d'Ailleurs* [The Machine From Beyond] (1969), which has the power to create pocket universes in which it can run eccentric simulations. Another popular series involved the hard-boiled adventures of Dan Seymour, a futuristic *James Bond*, introduced in *Agent Spatial No. 1* [Space Agent No. 1] (1966). Seymour went on to appear in another ten novels between 1967 and 1974.

But Bessière really made his mark through a number of non-connected novels that featured an original blend of horror and science fiction. He had previously contributed to Fleuve

---

[231] A companion volume, *Météore: L'Univers Fascinant de Richard Bessière*, edited by Jean-Louis Ermine, was published by Rivière Blanche in 2016.

Noir's *Angoisse* under the pseudonym of "Dominique Keller". These were among his best novels. Monstrous aliens threatening to take over mankind were featured in *Escale chez les Vivants* [Stop-Over Among the Living] (1960); In *Les Maîtres du Silence* [The Masters of Silence] (1965),[232] Engineer Milland is summoned to a secret lab by Professor Watson, but when he arrives, Watson has just been murdered by his wife, Valerie, during what is said to be a fit of madness. Valerie had tested a machine to explore the Inner Mind invented by her husband. Milland volunteers to go into her mind-but, in so doing, unleashes creatures of darkness upon the Earth. In *Cette Lueur Qui Venait des Ténèbres* [That Light That Came Out of the Darkness] (1967),[233] a man just released from prison finds himself hired on a ghost ship that travels through time, picking up derelicts like him. He eventually ends up in a mysterious Antarctic valley, which exists outside of time, inhabited by monstrous alien parasites intent on spreading upon the rest of the Earth like an unstoppable disease.

Le Vaisseau de l'Ailleurs [The Ship from Beyond] (1972) was based on Wagnerian mythos; *Les Seigneurs de la Nuit* [The Lords of Night] (1973) described the triumph of a Nazi-like dark power. The ultimately doomed reconquest of a hellish, post-cataclysmic Earth, ruled by mutants and strange, deadly lifeforms, was the subject of *Légion Alpha* (1961). In *Les Sept Anneaux de Rhéa* [The Seven Rings of Rhea] (1962),[234] Earth is described as seven concentric spheres with Hell at its center. *Les Jardins de l'Apocalypse* [The Gardens of the Apocalypse] (1963)[235] and *Des Hommes, Des Hommes et Encore des Hommes* [Men, Men, and Always Men] (1968) and *Les Marteaux de Vulcain* [Vulcan's Hammer] (1969), all depict nightmarish worlds where survival was all but impossi-

---

[232] Black Coat Press, ISBN 978-1-61227-297-9.

[233] *They Came from the Dark* in *The Masters of Silence*, q.v.

[234] In *The Gardens of the Apocalypse*, Black Coat Press, ISBN 978-1-935558-68-2.

[235] Black Coat Press, q.v.

ble. The Coburn saga (1984) featured a spaceman constantly returned to life on yet another hellish planet. *Je m'appelle... Tous* [I'm Called... All] (1965) featured yet another lone spaceman who crashed on an alien planet and clones himself in huge numbers before eventually succumbing to madness.

Another notable writer published by *Anticipation* was "Jean-Gaston Vandel", the pseudonym of the writing team of Jean Libert and Gaston Vandenpanhuyse, who also used the alias of "Paul Kenny" to write the series *Coplan FX-18*, published by Fleuve Noir's *Espionnage* imprint. The success of *Coplan* caused the writers to abandon science fiction after only twenty novels published between 1952 and 1956. The authors' books emphasized the importance of tolerance and communication between different species: alien lifeforms in *Les Astres Morts* [The Dead Stars] (1952), where a machine called "transferator" was used; *Attentat Cosmique* [Cosmic Attack] (1953) and *Incroyable Futur* [Incredible Future] (1953), where the aliens forced a third age of enlightenment upon mankind; sentient robots in *Alerte aux Robots* [Alert: Robots] (1952), where robots revolted until men agreed to treat them more humanely, and *Territoire Robot* [Robot Territory] (1955), in which Martian robots enslaved men; and finally, mutants, such as the "Vitelians" introduced in *Fuite dans l'Inconnu* [Flight Into the Unknown] (1954) and *Raid sur Delta* [Raid Over Delta] (1955), with mutants are artificially created when mankind seemed to be doomed by incurable disease, and *Le Troisième Bocal* [The Third Jar] (1956), where it is aliens who help create mutants to save Mankind.

The survival of our species was a recurrent theme the authors' rather pessimistic fiction: the dangers of overpopulation, pollution and the evils of science unchecked were featured in *Agonie des Civilisés* [Agony of a Civilization] (1953); *Les Titans de l'Energie* [The Energy Titans] (1955), where the alien Ktongs try to save Mankind in spite of itself; *Départ pour l'Avenir* [Departure for the Future] (1955), in which thirty children are voluntarily sent into space away from a polluted Earth, and *La Foudre Anti-D* [The Anti-D Lightning]

(1956), a terrifying picture of the world running towards its doom.

Some other notable novels by Vandel included *Les Chevaliers de l'Espace* [The Space Knights] (1952) and its sequel, *Le Satellite Artificiel* [The Artificial Satellite] (1952), in which an order of space knights uses a space station to protect Earth; *Frontières du Vide* [Frontiers of the Void] (1953), which revealed that the dead still live on a distant planet; and *Bureau de l'Invisible* [Bureau of the Invisible] (1956), which was about an organization of crime-solving psychics led by the mysterious Kerrick, who uses an alien artefact to control his agents' powers. Before a villain can use the artefact for evil, an alien ship shows up and destroys it.

Michel Demuth, who in the 1970s became one of the most influential editors of OPTA, and was also a renowned translator, began publishing a series of interconnected short stories in *Fiction* in the 1960s. That series formed a 2000-year future history *à la* Heinlein, and was eventually collected in two volumes entitled *Les Galaxiales* [*The Galaxials*]. The author also penned numerous other short stories and novellas for *Satellite*, later collected in *La Clé des Étoiles* [The Key to the Stars] (1960), and for *Fiction*, sometimes using the pseudonym of "Jean-Michel Ferrer", collected in *Les Années Metalliques* [The Metal Years] (1977).

Other Notable Authors

Of all the other authors published by Fleuve Noir's *Anticipation* imprint, Jimmy Guieu was, without a doubt, the one who achieved the most surprising commercial success. His first novel, *Le Pionnier de l'Atome* [*The Pioneer of the Atom*] (1952), dealt with the classic theme of a journey into the microcosmos and used the by then old-fashioned concept of a Hindu guru's psychic powers to achieve it. With his second novel, *Au-delà de l'Infini* [Beyond Infinity] (1952), the author introduced the character of American biologist Jerry Barclay, while reversing the theme of the previous book. This time, it was our universe that was a microcosmos contained within the body of a beautiful woman from a macrocosmos. The Barclay series continued for three more books (1952-53), usually teaming Jerry up with good aliens in order to defeat evil aliens and returning him to the macrocosmos for further adventures.

With *La Dimension X* [Dimension X] (1953) and, especially, *Nous les Martiens* [We the Martians] (1954), the author introduced a new hero: archeologist Jean Kariven. In that series, Guieu began to explore his favorite themes such as UFOs and alien encounters, ancient astronauts, occult secrets and secret societies, sprinkling his novels with footnotes claiming that the various facts upon which he was basing his tales were indeed "authentic". In *Nous les Martiens*, Kariven discovers that, in the far distant past, men had emigrated from Mars to Earth. Eight more *Kariven* novels followed between 1954 and 1956, dealing with time travel, ancient civilizations, and a space war between the good Polarians and the evil reptilian Denebians, with Earth secretly caught in the middle: *La Spirale du Temps* [Time's Spiral] (1954), *Opération Aphrodite* (1955), *L'Homme de l'Espace* [The Man from Outer Space] (1955),[236] *Commandos de l'Espace* [Space Commandos] (1955), *Nos Ancêtres de l'Avenir* [*Our Ancestors From the Future*] (1956) and *Prisonniers du Passé* [*Prisoners of the Past*] (1956).[237] One of the Kariven novels, *Univers Parallèles* [Parallel Universes] (1955), even featured a crossover with Jerry Barclay, who was said to live in a parallel universe

Guieu continued to exploit the UFO and occult vein with increasing success. After Kariven, he penned a number of non-connected novels, except for two that featured two American investigative reporters, Ericksson and Wendell: *Les Monstres du Néant* [Monsters from the Void] (1956) and *Les Êtres de*

---

[236] In *The Polarian-Denebian War, Volume 1*, Black Coat Press, ISBN 978-1-61227-516-1.
[237] In *The Polarian-Denebian War, Volume 2*, Black Coat Press, ISBN 978-1-61227-555-0.

Feu [*The Beings of Fire*] (1956). He also wrote two successful non-fiction books about UFOs, *Les Soucoupes Volantes viennent d'un Autre Monde* [The Flying Saucers Come from Another World] and *Black-Out sur les Soucoupes Volantes* [Black-Out on the Flying Saucers], the latter prefaced by filmmaker Jean Cocteau. By the 1970s, he had become a major French figure in UFO circles.

Simultaneously, the author began to chronicle the exploits of two daring space traders of the future, Ronny Blade and William Baker. The series began with *Piège dans l'Espace* [A Trap in Space] (No. 224; 1959) and continued for 15 volumes published between 1963 and 1976. Two of the most notable are *Les Destructeurs* [The Destroyers] (1963), and *Joklun-N'Ghar la Maudite* [Joklun-N'Ghar The Accursed] (1968).

In 1967, with *Le Retour des Dieux* [The Return of the Gods]), Guieu revamped and updated the Kariven character into that of journalist of the occult Gilles Novak who, with the help of his girlfriend Régine Véran, and various friends and allies (often real-life friends or thinly-disguised real-life figures), fought against would-be tyrants, communists, terrorists, the drug cartel, and various alien menaces. Novak was helped in his battles by Michael Merkavim, the head of a new, powerful Knights Templar Order, equipped with futuristic weapons and based in a parallel dimension. Merkavim was introduced in the second volume, *Les Sept Sceaux du Cosmos* [The Seven Seals of the Cosmos] (1968) and returned in the best-selling *L'Ordre Vert* [The Green Order] (1969). The Gilles Novak series was comprised of 23 novels appearing regularly until *Les Fils du Serpent* [The Sons of the Serpent (1984), before being spun off as a separate, spin-off series, the *Chevaliers de Lumière* [The Knights of Light], devoted to the New Templars, consisting of ten new volumes published between 1987 and 1991.

Due to the phenomenal growth in popularity of his novels, Guieu was granted his own imprint in 1979. At first, it reprinted rewritten, updated versions of his original novels, then it began publishing new novels, featuring Gilles Novak and Blade & Baker, but written by other writers, mostly Roland C. Wagner (using the pseudonym "Richard Wolfram"), but also Philippe Randa, Nicolas Gauthier, Laurent Genefort (using the pseudonym "S. Grey"), Rémy Gallart, Arnaud Dalrune, etc. Guieu became a trademarked phenomenon, unique in the annals of science fiction, and certainly without equivalent in England or America. His success was attributable to a clever mix of occult facts, mild eroticism, ultra-conservative (even bigoted) politics and a forceful, if simple, story-telling style successfully imitated by his successors. Most of his readers were drawn from the general public rather than the science fiction audience.

The first two novels of "Pierre Barbet" (the nom-de-plume of Dr. Claude Avice), *Vers un Avenir Perdu* [Towards a Lost Future] (1962) and *Babel 3805* (1962) were published by the *Rayon Fantastique*. After the cancellation of that imprint in 1964, the author moved to Fleuve Noir's *Anticipation* in 1966, and became a steady provider of classic space operas, such as *Vikings de l'Espace* [*Space Vikings*] (1969), the tale of the conquest of the galaxy by a Viking-like warlord whose planet's sun is dying. He was amongst the first writer to introduce a blend of science fiction and fantasy into *Anticipation* with *À Quoi Songent les Psyborgs?* [*What Do Psyborgs Dream About?*] (1971), in which his Temporal Investigator Setni, the agent of a Galactic Federation ruled by preserved brains (first introduced in *L'Exilé du Temps* [The Exile of Time] (1969)) explored a planet where a trio of powerful, disembodied brains have recreated the fantasy legends of Amadis of Gaul for their own entertainment. Barbet continued to mine this vein with *La Planète Enchantée* [The Enchanted Planet] (1973) and *Vénusine* (1977), the latter written under the pseudonym "Olivier Sprigel". He also penned an alternate historical, *L'Empire du Baphomet* [The Empire of Baphomet] (1972), in which an alien attempts to manipulate the Templar Knights to take over the world during the Crusades. A sequel was *Croisade Stellaire* [Cosmic Crusade] (1974).

The Setni series continued with seven more volumes, including some alternate histories. Other series included the *Napoléons d'Eridan* [The Napoleons of Eridani] (2 volumes, 1970-84), in which a squadron of Napoleonic soldiers kidnapped by aliens end up conquering a space empire, a concept reminiscent of Poul Anderson's *High Crusade*; the adventures of the dashing Alex Courville (9 volumes, 1978-88), resembling Anderson's *Dominic Flandry*, and the saga of the *Cités de l'Espace* [Cities in Space] (6 volumes, 1979-85), reminiscent of James Blish's renowned series.

In total, Barbet wrote sixty-two novels for Fleuve Noir between 1966 and 1991; he also produced several more serious, politically oriented works, and some novels for other publishers under the pseudonyms of "David Maine" and "Olivier Sprigel".

The husband & wife writing team of Jean-Louis and Doris Le May penned numerous colorful, literary, even poetic, space operas for *Anticipation*, most of which took place in the same future Galactic Federation introduced in their first novel, *La Chasse à l'Impondérable* [The Hunt for the Weightless Element] (1966). This novel, and several others, were eventually regrouped in a loose series entitled *Enquêtes Galactiques* [Galactic Investigations], because they featured the Federation's multi-species police force, Interco. The first novel and its sequel, *L'Oenips d'Orlon* [The Oenips of Orlon] (1967), introduced the investigative team of agents Rockenret and Gerdavid, and their female partners, involved in the pursuit of drug traffickers. The trilogy ended with a huge space battle in *Les Drogfans de Gersande* [The Drogfans of Gersande] (1967). Rockenret and Gerdavid returned in *Irimanthe* (1970). As the series progressed, other novels began to depict different facets of the Federation's life, such as *La Quête du Frohle d'Esylée* [The Quest of the Frohle from Esylee] (1969); *La Plongée des Corsaires d'Hermos* [The Dive of the Corsairs of Hermos] (1970), where the point of view shifted to that of corsairs fighting Interco; *La Mission d'Eno Granger* [The Mission of Eno Granger] (1970); and *Les Créateurs d'Ulnar*

[The Creators of Ulnar] (1972), in which space explorers acquired god-like powers on the planet Ulnar, recreated a fantasy world and ended up waging an apocalyptic war.

Other, non-Federation stories—possibly myths of the Federation?—were regrouped in another series, entitled *Contes et Légendes du Futur* [Tales & Legends of the Future]. Among the best of these were *Arel d'Adamante* [Arel of Adamante] (1968), the tale of a water world where men live in harmony with a cetacean species; *Les Fruits du Métaxylia* [The Fruits of the Metaxylia] (1972); the trilogy of the *Érémides*, powerful beings who could freely roam unseen through space (1973); and the saga of a bittersweet love story between two proud contestants in a cosmic regatta across the solar system (4 volumes, 1976-77). Their forty-third novel, *L'Épaisse Fourrure des Quadricornes* [The Thick Fur of the Quadricorns] (1978), an Interco thriller about illegal poaching, was the last they wrote together.[238]

Alone, Jean-Louis Le May continued the *Contes et Légendes du Futur* series, but not the *Enquêtes Galactiques*, and added two other series, *Chroniques des Temps à Venir* [Chronicles of Times to Come], starting with *L'Ombre dans la Vallée* [The Shadow in the Valley] (1979), about the slow rebuilding of civilization in Southern France after an unspecified disaster, and the trilogy of the *Hortans* [Outside Time] (1982-85), somewhat reminiscent of the earlier *Érémides* series. He penned twenty-three more novels, until 1987.

By the time he began writing for *Anticipation* in 1959, Maurice Limat was already a veteran, having penned numerous popular adventure novels since the late 1930s. During the 1950s, he contributed a series of science fiction novels to Ferenczi's *Mon Roman d'Aventures*, such as *Les Faiseurs de Planètes* [The Planet Makers] (1951), *Comète 73* [*Comet 73*] (1953), *Courrier Interplanétaire* [Interplanetary Courrier]

---

[238] A companion volume, *Interco: La Galaxie Humaine de J. & D. Le May*, edited by Jean-Michel Archaimbault, was published by Rivière Blanche in 2013.

(1953), *Le Mal des Étoiles* [Star Sickness] (1954), *Attaque Cosmique* [Cosmic Attack] (1954), *Les Forçats de l'Espace* [The Convicts of Space] (1954), even hiding his abundant production under the pseudonyms of "Maurice Lionel", "Maurice d'Escrignelles", and "Lionel Rex". In 1955, he contributed *SOS Galaxie* [SOS Galaxy] to *Série 2000* and then, began to write for *Cosmos*. His *Monsieur Cosmos* (1956) dealt with the theme of the macrocosmic man, creator of universes. Other titles included *Planète sans Soleil* [Planet Without Sun] (1956) and *Pas de Planète pour les Terriens* [No Planets for Earthmen] (1957) and began to reflect the influence of American space operas.

His first novel for *Anticipation* was *Les Enfants du Chaos* [The Children of Chaos] (1959), in which men use psychic power to create a world, but then ask themselves whether they have earned the right to play God, a theme somewhat characteristic of his subsequent production. Limat continued to be a prolific writer, penning numerous, lyrical, sometimes even religious, space operas for *Anticipation*—one hundred and seven in total, until 1987—as well as some horror novels for the *Angoisse* imprint. His best titles included: *Moi, Un Robot* [I, Robot] (1960), which pondered if robots had souls; *Message des Vibrants* [Message from the Vibrants] (1961), about souls separated from their bodies (a recurring theme); *Lumière Qui Tremble* [Shivering Light] (1962), in which a little boy creates his own fantasy world; and *Le Sang Vert* [The Green Blood] (1963), which details the transformation of a stranded spaceman into a giant, sentient tree that eventually gives birth to new lifeforms.

Limat introduced the character of futuristic police commissioner Robin Muscat in *Les Foudroyants* [The Lightning Men] (1960), in which a hapless young man is turned into an electromagnetic force. He followed it wirth his most popular, long-running hero, the green-eyed, telepathic Chevalier Coqdor and his pet, the bat-winged pstor, Rax, introduced in *L'Étoile de Satan* [The Star of Satan] (1964). Muscat and Coqdor soon teamed up and they appeared, separately or together, in thirty or so more volumes.[239] The *Coqdor* adventures usually celebrated the power of love and tolerance, and a genuine belief in God, the Great Architect of the Universe, something unusual in science fiction. A recurring theme was that secrets that lay beyond mortal ken should not, indeed could not, be fathomed. In *Ici Finit Le Monde* [Here Ends the Universe] (1964), Coqdor reaches the literal end of the universe, but can go no further and the mystery of the white flashes that occur beyond that final border are never solved. In *Les Portes de l'Aurore* [The Gates of Dawn] (1967), Coqdor travels into the dimension of Death but is stopped before he can reach beyond the eponymous Gates. Other unfathomable cosmic secrets were the topics of *Le Treizième Signe du Zodiaque* [The Thirteenth Sign of the Zodiac] (1969) and *Flammes sur Titan* [Flames Over Titan] (1969), which featured a Prometheus-like, star-traveling scientist trying to solve the mystery of the emergence of life on another world. Two other short-lived series featured Luc Delta, a spaceship test pilot (1968), and Luxman, a man condemned to death who acquires super-powers (1984).

"Peter Randa" (the pseudonym of André Duquesne), after writing several thrillers for *Angoisse*, penned *Survie* [Survival] (1960) for *Anticipation*, the first of seventy-nine militaristic space operas, usually starring loners, soldiers or mercenaries, trapped on alien battlefields, in hopeless wars and/or missions, stranded on alien worlds, etc. His heroes ultimately succeeded against all odds in elevating themselves to positions of supreme power. Some of his best novels included *Commando de Transplantation* [Transplanted Commando] (1961), *Humains de Nulle Part* [Humans From Nowhere] (1963),

---

[239] A companion volume, *Martervenux: L'Encyclopédie du Chevalier Coqdor*, edited by Jean-Marc Lofficier, was published by Rivière Blanche in 2008. Subsequently, a new Coqdor/Muscat trilogy, written by Jean-Marc Lofficier & Jean-Michel Archaimbault, was published by Rivière Blanche in 2006-09.

Zone de Rupture [Breaking Zone] (1964), *La Grande Dérive* [The Great Drift] (1967), *Les Ides de Mars* [The Ides of Mars] (1967), *L'Héritier des Sars* [The Heir of the Sars] (1968), *L'Homme Éparpillé* [The Scattered Man] (1969) and *L'Univers des Torgaux* [The Universe of the Torgaux] (1970). His major series was that of *Les Ancêtres* [The Ancestors] (4 volumes, 1963-72), about the unique society formed by the crews of light-speed starships which were the sole links between the human planets of a star-spanning civilization; their name was due to the fact that, to planet-bound humans, they appeared to age far more slowly. They also controlled a greater variety of technology. Another series was the trilogy devoted to a star conqueror, *Elteor* (1976-77).

After his last novel, *Escale à Hango* [Stop-Over at Hango] (1980), in a phenomenon unique in the annals of science fiction, his son, Philippe" continued his career in the same style and inspiration. His first novel was *Les Fusils d'Ekaistos* [The Guns of Ekaistos] (1981). Philippe wrote a total of twenty-two space operas, ending with in 1988 with *Le Mal d'Ibrator* [The Disease of Ibrator]. His best series included those of the *Empire Terrien* [*The Terran Empire*] (5 volumes, 1981-83); *Les Voyageurs de Vestera* [The Travelers of Vestera] (3 volumes, 1983-87) and *Les Pirates de l'Espace* [The Space Pirates] (3 volumes, 1985-87).

Another regular contributor to *Anticipation* in the 1950s and 1960s (but not the least) was the equally prolific "Max-André Rayjean" (a pseudonym of Jean Lombard), whose novels often dealt with alien contacts and strange biological mutations. His first novel was *Attaque Sub-Terrestre* [Subterranean Attack] (1956), about a microscosmic invasion. He went on to write 77 novels for *Anticipation* until 1987, and eight more for Rivière Blanche in the 2000s. His *Le Péril des Hommes* [The Peril of Men] (1960), was about human sterility; *Le Quatrième Futur* [The Fourth Future] (1967) and *L'An Un des Kreols* [Year One of the Kreols] (1969), featured, in the former, the artificial creation, in the latter, the natural emergence, of new races of men. Unlike most other *Anticipation* novels, some of the author's books had bleak endings, often featuring the end of the human race. Among these were *Ere Cinquième* [Fifth Era] (1959); *Les Magiciens d'Andromède* [The Wizards of Andromeda] (1961); and *Terrom, Âge "Un"* [Terrom Age One] (1963). Some depicted humans being experimented upon by exceedingly bizarre alien lifeforms, such as *Round Végétal* [Vegetal Battle] (1964), *Le Zoo des Astors* [The Zoo of the Astors] (1966) and *Relais Kéra* [The Kera Relay] (1969). A notable work was *Les Forçats de l'Energie* [The Energy Convicts] (1965), which depicted microbes as intelligent aliens and told the story of their desperate travel from body to body from the viewpoints of both the microbes and their infected human host. His regular series included the adventures of investigative reporter Joe Maubry, introduced in *La Folie Verte* [The Green Madness] (1958) (7 more volumes, 1960-77); and space security agent Jé Mox, introduced in *L'Arbre de Cristal* [The Crystal Tree] (1972) (5 more volumes, 1975-79).

"André Caroff" (a pseudonym of André Carpouzis) wrote seventeen science fiction horror thrillers for *Angoisse* novels, starting in 1964, with an 18th novel being published much later in the *Anticipation* imprint.[240] These starred the *Sinistre Mme Atomos* [The Sinister Mrs. Atomos], a deadly, brilliant, but twisted female Japanese scientist out to revenge herself against the United States for the bombings of Hiroshima and Nagasaki. A sample plot had the evil title character unleash a deadly new threat, such as radioactive zombies, only to be stopped in the nick of time by the heroes, Smith Beffort of the FBI, Dr. Alan Soblen and Yosho Akamatsu of the Japanese Secret Police. With the help of former criminal Owen Bernitz, Beffort also organized the "Green Dragon" squad to fight Madame Atomos. An interesting development was the creation by Madame Atomos of a younger version of herself, Mie Azusa, dubbed "Miss Atomos", groomed to continue the fight should she die. Mie eventually fell in love with Beffort,

---

[240] Three authorized sequels, written by Michel and Sylvie Stéphan, were published in 2013-15.

married him and joined forces with him to fight her evil progenitrix. Madame Atomos herself regenerated into a younger self in the thirteenth novel, but remained as revenge-bent as ever. Starting in 1968, the series was adapted into black and white, digest-sized comics by French publisher Aredit. [241]

Paul Berato (who used the pseudonyms of "Yves Dermèze" and Paul Béra), was an experienced writer who had

---

[241] The *Madame Atomos* series in available from Black Coat Press in 11 volumes: 1. *The Terror of Madame Atomos* (includes *La Sinistre Mme Atomos* (1964) & *Mme Atomos Sème la Terreur* (1965)), ISBN 978-1-935558-41-5; 2. *Miss Atomos* (includes *Mme Atomos Frappe à la Tête* (1965) & Miss Atomos (1965)), ISBN 978-1-61227-018-0; 3. *The Return of Madame Atomos* (includes *Miss Atomos contre KKK* (1966) & *Le Retour de Mme Atomos* (1966)), ISBN 978-1-61227-030-2; 4. *The Mistake of Madame Atomos* (includes *L'Erreur de Mme Atomos* (1966) & *Mme Atomos Prolonge la Vie* (1967)), ISBN 978-1-61227-069-2; 5. *The Monsters of Madame Atomos* (includes *Les Monstres de Mme Atomos* (1967) & *Madame Atomos Crache des Flammes* (1967)), ISBN 978-1-61227-087-6; 6. *The Revenge of Madame Atomos* (includes *Mme Atomos Croque le Marmot* (1967) & *La Ténébreuse Mme Atomos* (1968)), ISBN 978-1-61227-119-4; 7. *The Resurrection of Madame Atomos* (includes *Mme Atomos Change de Peau* (1968) & *Mme Atomos Fait Du Charme* (1969)), ISBN 978-1-61227-157-6; 8. *The Mark of Madame Atomos* (includes *L'Empreinte de Mme Atomos* (1969) & *Mme Atomos Jette Un Froid* (1969)), ISBN 978-1-61227-223-8; 9. *The Spheres of Madame Atomos* (includes *Mme Atomos Cherche la Petite Bête* (1970) & *Les Sphères de Mme Atomos* (1979)), ISBN 978-1-61227-259-7 ; as well as the Stéphan authorized sequels: 10. *The Wrath of Madame Atomos* (includes *Mme Atomos Sème la Tempête* (2013) & *Mme Atomos Parie sur la Mort* (2014)), ISBN 978-1-61227-330-3 ; and 11. *The Sins of Madame Atomos* [*Mme Atomos joue sur les maux*] (2015), ISBN 978-1-61227-672-4.

been producing popular adventure and juvenile genre novels since the early 1940s, also using several other pseudonyms such as "Jean Vier", "Michel Avril", "Jean Mars", "Paul Mystère", etc. (making his bibliography a nightmare to research). In the 1950s, as Dermèze, he wrote *La Folie Rouge* [The Red Madness] (1954) for *Arabesque*. Then for *Série 2000*, he penned *Le Titan de l'Espace* [*The Space Titan*] (1954), about the conflict between two energy beings on Earth, a novel which was, at the time, deemed to have been influenced by A. E. Van Vogt's *Black Destroyer*, even though Berato had written it prior to the latter's translation. He also penned *Via Velpa* (1955), a wonderful space opera ahead of its times, in which an Altairian rebel uses time travel and passages between universes to defeat the terrifying threat of the alien, sand-like Mobiks. Other works of the period included *La Pierre Vivante* [The Living Stone] (1958) and *Les Envoyés du Paradis* [The Envoys from Paradise] (1963). In 1970, the author, now signing "Paul Béra", began writing for both the *Anticipation* and *Angoisse* imprints of Fleuve Noir—titles to be reviewed in our next chapter.

Série 2000 also published several space operas by renowned genre historian "Pierre Versins" (a pseudonym of Jacques Chamson), who published and edited the fanzine *Ailleurs* [*Elsewhere*]. A Swiss resident, the author produced the genre radio series *Passeport pour l'Inconnu* [Passport Towards the Unknown]. His novels included *Les Étoiles ne s'en foutent pas* [The Stars Do Care] (1954), *En Avant Mars!* [Towards Mars] (1955) and *Feu d'Artifice* [Fireworks] (1956) and offered a radical—In the political sense—brand of space opera, something unusual at the time.

Among the other notable French genre authors published during this period were:

"Arcadius" (a pseudonym of Alain Hilleret) wrote several well-received, literary science fiction stories for *Fiction* in the 1960s as well as two novels for *Le Rayon Fantastique*: In *La Terre Endormie* [The Sleeping Earth] (1961), mankind was placed in a coma by the "green bomb" and the world was taken over by plants. His next and last novel was *Planète d'Exil* [Planet of Exile] (1963).

"Lieutenant Kijé" (a pseudonym of Alain Yawache), penned three militaristic space operas for *Le Rayon Fantastique*, such as *La Guerre des Machines* [The War of the Machines] (1959), *Celten Taurogh* (1961), *L'Épée de l'Archange* [The Sword of the Archangel] (1963) and, later, *Les Cendres de la Terre* [The Ashes of Earth] (1976). As "Alain Yaouanc", Yawache was also famous for his espionage thrillers.

In John Amila's *Le Neuf de Pique* [The Nine of Hearts] (1956), space travelers discover that we lived in a microcosmos contained inside a card player's eye in a macrocosmos.

Finally, in Yvon Hecht's striking *La Fin du Quaternaire* [The End of the Quaternary] (1962), humans gave birth to the insect-like race that was fated to replace them.

The writing team of Henri Keller and Grégoire Brainin provided a number of easy-to-read if somewhat unoriginal space operas to *Visions Futures* [Future Visions], *Grands Romans-Sciences-Anticipations* [Great Novels of Science & Anticipation], Cosmos and *Série 2000*. These included *Planète Atlante* [Atlantean Planet] (1953), *L'Attaque des Vénusiens* [The Venusians Attack] (1953), *La Machine à Explorer le Rêve* [The Dream Machine] (1955), *Le Tour du Soleil en 80 Jours* [Around the Sun in 80 Days] (1955), *Au Centre de l'Univers* [At the Center of the Universe] (1956) and *Et le Temps s'arrêtera* [And Time Shall Stop] (1956).

Léopold Massiéra was one of the regular contributors to Ferenczi's *Mon Roman d'Aventures*, for which he penned a variety of genre titles such as *L'Énigme des Soucoupes Volantes* [The Mystery of the Flying Saucers] (1953), *Le Monde des Abîmes* [The World of the Abyss] (1954), *Les Troupeaux de la Lune* [Cattle on the Moon] (1955) and *Le Guide de l'Avenir* [The Guide from the Future] (1956).

Another regular contributor was Gil Roc, with *L'Univers des Gouffres* [The World of the Pits] (1955) and *L'Horrible Planète* [The Awful Planet] (1956).

Belgian author R. Kulavik wrote *Terre contre Mars, La Bataille des Hommes de Fer* [Earth vs. Mars, The Battle of the Iron Men] (1948).

Robert Teldy-Naïm wrote *Paradis Atomiques* [Atomic Paradises] (1949) and *Cela Arrivera Hier* [It Will Happen Yesterday] (1954).

Lucien Bornert wrote *Le Péril Vient du Ciel* [The Danger Comes from the Sky] (1953) and *Robots Sous-Marins* [Underwater Robots] (1953).

Denis Gabriel Guignard wrote *Pyramidopolis* (1953).

Jean Lec wrote *L'Être Multiple* [The Multiple Being] (1954) and *La Machine à Franchir la Mort* [The Machine to Thwart Death] (1955).

Claude Yelnick wrote *L'Homme, Cette Maladie* [Man, This Disease] (1954), in which a man finds access to another world through a lighthouse.

Y.F.J. Long wrote *Les Atlantes du Ciel* [The Atlanteans from the Sky] (1955).

Belgian authors Albert & Jean Crémieux wrote *Chute Libre* [Freefall] (1955) and its sequel, *La Parole Perdue* [The Lost Word] (1956), about the exploration of Earth by an alien from planet "54".

Jacques-Henri Juillet wrote *Atomes à Vendre* [Atoms For Sale] (1955) and *Les Visiteurs de l'An 2000* [The Visitors from the Year 2000] (1956).

The notorious horror writer "Marc Agapit" (whom we reviewed at length in our companion volume) penned a science fiction novel under his real name of Adrien Sobra, *Portes sur l'Inconnu* [Doors into the Unknown] (1956).

The founder and editor of *Satellite*, Michel Benâtre, used the pseudonym of "Jean Cap" to pen *Nurma* (1956) and *La Brigade du Temps* [The Time Brigade] (1960).

Serge Alkine wrote two space operas, *La Révolte de la Terre* [The Revolt of Earth] (1956) and *L'Or de la Lune* [Gold on the Moon] (1957).

François Lourbet wrote *Les Bagnes de l'Espace* [The Space Penitentiaries] (1960) and *Sortilège Temporel* [Time Spell] (1960).

René Cambon wrote *L'Homme Double* [The Double Man] (1960).

D.A.C. Danio wrote *Les Cuirs Bouillis* [The Boiled Leathers] (1961).

P.-A. Hourey wrote *Vuzz* (1955).

M. & T. Tavera wrote *L'Ogive du Monde* [The World Cone] (1959).

Jean Bommart, the author of a popular series of mysteries starring the "Poisson Chinois", used the pseudonym of "Kemmel" to pen *Je Reviens De...* [I Come Back From...] (1957) and *Au Bout du Ciel* [At the End of the Sky] (1962).

Finally, from 1945 to 1948, the Éditions & Revues Françaises published a pulp series of *Fu-Manchu*-like adventure novels featuring the dreaded Pao Tcheou, nicknamed "Master of the Invisible". The series was massive in its scope, spanning all of Earth and beyond, including a journey to Mars. The evil Asian mastermind was opposed by the heroic team of Lapertot, a stalwart adventurer, and Professor Faustulus, a learned doctor, who assists with the scientific aspects of the adventures. Pao Tcheou's efforts to take control of the world are many and varied, including robots, atomic bombs, and giant monsters. Episodes 1 to 20 were attributed to "Edward Brooker" and episodes 21 to 36 to "Sam P. Norwood", both being pseudonyms for the same writer, Edouard Ostermann. Bound volumes collecting installments of the series were issued in the 1950s under different titles.

Mainstream Authors

Because science fiction was perceived as a new genre, one coming from far-off, exotic America, it immediately attracted the attention of a few stellar mainstream literary personalities such as Boris Vian, Jean Cocteau, André Maurois, Michel Butor, and Raymond Quéneau.

The editorial policies of Robert Kanters at *Présence du Futur* were to attract to mainstream writers who normally would not have contributed to the genre. The results were excellent, with works of high literary quality and, often, genuinely new ideas, including:

Jean-Louis Curtis' *Un Saint au Néon* [A Neon Saint] (1956), a collection of five satirical short stories about the future.

Jean Paulhac's *Un Bruit de Guêpes* [The Sound of Wasps] (1957), another collection of biting, satirical stories.

Jean Hougron's *Le Signe du Chien* [The Sign of the Dog] (1960), a remarkable novel on the difficulties of communication between alien species. In 1980, Hougron returned to the genre and penned another epic novel on a similar theme, *Le Naguen*.

René Sussan (a.k.a. René Réouven) with *Les Confluents* [The Confluence] (1960), a novel about a future when the human race produces children through artificial means and, upon discovery that these children eventually become sexless, tries to modify key moments in history to alter the future. The author also penned *L'Anneau de Fumée* [The Smoke Ring] in 1974.

Finally, Edward de Capoulet-Junac penned *Pallas ou la Tribulation* [Pallas, or The Tribulations] (1967), in which human beings were abducted by bizarre aliens.

Kanters also reprinted René Barjavel's *Le Voyageur Imprudent* and *Le Diable l'Emporte* before publishing *Colomb de la Lune* [Colombus of the Moon] (1962), which took place in the same universe, but earlier, and featured Mr. Gé and the first, doomed Moon expedition.

Neo-surrealist Belgian author Jacques Sternberg published a notorious essay, *Une Succursale du Fantastique nommée Science-Fiction* [A Branch of the Fantastic Called Science Fiction] (1958) before embarking on a career as a dark comedian. His genre tales displayed the same biting, absurdist humor, and were collected in *La Géométrie dans l'Impossible* [The Impossible Geometry] (1953); *Entre Deux Mondes Incertains* [Between Two Uncertain Worlds] (1957); *Univers Zéro* [Universe Zero] (1970); and *Futurs sans Avenir* [Future Without Future] (1971). His themes included aliens misguidedly posing as African-Americans to invade the U.S., the 533rd crucifixion of Jesus Christ, the casual destruction of Earth by aliens who cannot understand humans, etc. The author anticipated the more experimental texts of the New Wave, or the humor of Douglas Adams. His novels had the same dark, nihilistic, misanthropic characteristics, minus the humor. In *La Sortie est au Fond de l'Espace* [The Exit is at the End of Space] (1956), aliens who despise mankind cause microbes to grow and, ultimately, use euthanasia to kill the few survivors who have found refuge on their world. *Attention, Planète Habitée* [Beware, Inhabited Planet] (1969) followed the same, merciless logic.

Existentialist author Boris Vian also blended elements borrowed from surrealism and traditional *fantastique* with science fiction. One of the main literary personalities of the 1950s, he translated American authors such as A. E. Van Vogt and Ray Bradbury. The author was himself a writer of "new wave"-like speculative fiction, well ahead of his times. His *L'Herbe Rouge* [The Red Grass] (1950), adapted for television in 1985 by Pierre Kast, blended time travel with nostalgia. *L'Automne à Pékin* [Autumn in Beijing] (1947) was a desert utopia set in an alternate universe. He skillfully used the imagery of science fiction to create hostile environments which assaulted his protagonists' sense of individuality, in a style anticipating that of Philip K. Dick.

Of all the mainstream authors who penned works that could easily be labeled science fiction, none was as important as Pierre Boulle, whose 1963 classic *La Planète des Singes* [Planet of the Apes] became one of the world's best-known science fiction film & TV franchise. In addition to being the author of the non-genre best-seller *The Bridge on the River Kwai*, the author used science fiction themes to tell moral fables sprinkled with heavy doses of satire. His short stories were collected in *Les Contes de l'Absurde* [Absurd Tales] (1953) and $E = MC2$ (1957). In the latter's title story, Einstein's formula reverses itself, energy becomes matter again, and the citizens of Hiroshima find themselves buried under uranium flowers. The short story "*Une Nuit Interminable*" [An Endless Night] (1957) told the story of an endless time war between the Badarian from the far past and the Pergolians from the far future, in which each side paradoxically ends up becoming its own opponent. Other notable works include *Le Jardin de Kanashima* [Kanashima's Garden] (1964), which deals with the conquest of the Moon, *Quia Absurdum* (1970) and the dystopia, *Les Jeux de l'Esprit* [Mind Games] (1971).

Just as interesting was the renowned Romain Gary, a former diplomat turned writer and winner of the Goncourt Award. He, too, used genre elements to morally dissect situations that were rarely (if ever) brought up in ordinary science fiction. In *Tulipe* [Tulip] (1946), the blacks inherit the Earth. *Gloire à nos Illustres Pionniers* [Glory to Our Illustrious Pioneers] (1962) is a collection that includes several genre tales. In *La Danse de Gengis Cohn* (1967), the ghost of a Jewish comedian possesses the body of his Nazi assassin. Finally, in *Charge d'Âme* [*Soul Power*] (1978), men's souls are used for fuel and energy, and even war.

Of almost equal importance was Jacques Audiberti, a prolific mainstream writer and playwright who also used genre themes in his works. *La Nâ* (1944) (snow in Savoyard patois) and *Les Tombeaux Ferment Mal* [Tombs Don't Close Properly] (1963) reveal that survivors of Atlantis live in underground cities and control the Earth's crust. (*Les Tombeaux* also include time travel.) *L'Opéra du Monde* [The Opera of the World] (1947) postulated the existence of an ancient, precataclysmic Lemurian civilization. *Marie Dubois* (1952) and *Infanticide Préconisé* [Recommended Infanticide] (1958) were, respectively, stories about a superman, and mutant children, who all live among us. *Les Naturels du Bordelais* [The

Naturals of Bordeaux] (1953) was a play in which intelligent crickets eventually replace man.

In Yves Gandon's *Le Dernier Blanc* [The Last White Man] (1945), a virus kills all white men. His *La Ville Invisible* [The Invisible City] (1953) was a daring novel in which men use advanced mental manipulation techniques to reinvent a new past for themselves. *Après les Hommes* [After Men] (1963) featured an intelligent, ethical race of ferromagnetic creatures, not unlike those depicted in Rosny's *La Mort de la Terre*. The author's genre stories were collected in *En Pays Singulier* [In a Singular Country] (1949) and *Pour un Bourbon Collins* [For A Bourbon Collins] (1967).

Other notable mainstream writers who wrote genre works during this period included:

Henri d'Amfreville was a surrealist writer who penned *La Terre est Chaude* [Earth Is Hot] (1946), a novel in which animals threaten to replace man, and *L'Homme Nu* [The Naked Man] (1951), about a man of the future who has acquired god-like powers.

Raymond Asso in *Les Hors-La-Vie* [The Out-Lifers] (1946) theorized that it is possible to travel between dimensions by assembling sophisticated puzzles.

Romain Rolland, a writer better known for his masterpiece *Jean-Christophe*, wrote *La Révolte des Machines ou La Pensée Déchaînée* [The Revolt of the Machines, or Thought Unbound] (1947).

Swiss writer Dominique André's *Conquête de l'Éternel* [Conquest of the Eternal] (1947) was yet one more sequel to Poe's *Adventures of Arthur Gordon Pym*. In it, he described a secret Antarctic civilization of perfect, immortal beings. Eventually, its protagonist, a female mad scientist, destroys the Earth after having plunged all its inhabitants into a coma.

Gustave Thibon wrote the apocalyptic *Face à la Peur - La Fin du Monde est pour Demain* [Facing our Fear - The End of the World Is for Tomorrow] (1947). In his *Vous Serez Comme des Dieux* [You Will Be Like Gods] (1954), public and private transportation were relegated to the rooftops of Paris.

Raymond Abellio's *Les Yeux d'Ézéchiel Sont Ouverts* [The Eyes of Ezekiel Are Open] (1949) was an esoteric novel in which we learned that supermen are hidden among us and have secretly been controlling the events of World War II. His *La Fosse de Babel* [The Pit of Babel] (1962) showed the future decadence of the western society.

Raymond Caen's *Les Stas, ou Le Journal d'un Dieu* [The Stas, or The Diary of a God] (1950) was about a race of indestructible men whose lives had been "stabilized".

Claude Saint-Yves, who had already penned an Atlantis novel in 1932, returned to the theme with two romantic fantasies, *Les Aventures du Dernier Atlante* [The Adventures of the Last Atlantean] (1950) and *La Fiancée du Dernier Atlante* [The Fiancée of the Last Atlantean] (1953).

In *Le Serpent* [The Serpent] (1957) and *Tes Yeux m'ont vu* [Your Eyes Saw Me] (1957), Maryse Choisy-Clouzet wrote about cyberneticists who were the descendants of Atlantis and created golem-like creatures.

Jules Romains penned the pessimistic anticipations, *Violation de Frontières* [Border Violation] (1951) and *Passagers de cette Planète, Où allons-nous?* [Passengers of this Planet, Where Are We Going?] (1955).

Roger Ikor's *Les Grands Moyens* [Powerful Means] (1951) depicted a bleak post-nuclear, communist Europe, where everything of importance was buried under tons of rubble. New, powerful and, ironically, even more destructive means were used to move the Earth's crust. His six-volume saga, *Si Le Temps...* [If Time...] (1960-69), was a series of novels attempting to map out man's future progress, beginning with a mystic who wished to rid the world of money, the root of all evil.

Writer/artist "Vercors" (a pseudonym of Jean Bruller) wrote several allegorical genre stories, including *Les Animaux Dénaturés* [The Unnatural Animals] (1952), in which a new race of primates, discovered in New Guinea, challenged the differences that exist between man and ape. His *Colères* [Wrath] (1956) dealt with the quest for immortality, and in *Sylva* (1961), a female fox was turned into a woman, before reverting to type.

Louis Velle's *Ma Petite Femme* [My Little Woman] (1953) was a novel about the miniaturization of a woman.

Michel Carrouges' *Les Portes Dauphines* [The Dauphine Gates] (1954) featured a slot-machine which turned out to be a gate leading onto another world. His *Les Grands-Pères Prodiges* [The Prodigal Grandfathers] (1957) illustrated the social problems that could be caused by the introduction of techniques of rejuvenation into our society. The author was also the first in France (with Jimmy Guieu) to pen a serious book about UFO, the luridly mistitled *Apparitions de Martiens* [Martian Apparitions] (1954).

René Albérès was another mainstream writer who produced two collections of short stories centered around science fiction themes: *L'Autre Planète* [The Other Planet] (1958) and *Manuscrit Enterré dans le Jardin d'Éden* [Ms. Buried in the Garden of Eden] (1967).

In Georges Blond's *Les Naufragés de Paris* [The Castaways of Paris] (1959), the disintegration of paper provoked a social collapse.

Coincidentally, in the earlier *2 Morts... 20 Milliards* [2 Dead... 20 Billion] (1949), Robert Collard had imagined a paper-destroying ray!

Jean de Patmos penned *Anthropthéose* [Anthropotheosis] (1958), a novel about supermen.

La Fusée [The Rocket] was a 1958 stage play written by Roger Gadeyne and Adelin Tilman about a dozen couples who left Earth to colonize another planet.

Another genre play was *Chroniques d'une Planète Provisoire* [Chronicles of a Temporary Planet] (1962), by Armand Gatti, in which Earth astronauts observe the evolution of an alien planet not unlike ours, but are unable to intervene to change the course of events.

In Henri Gillet's *Le Voleur d'Instants* [The Thief of Moments] (1959), a scientist finds a way to record and preserve the best moments of a man's life.

In *Les Grenouilles* [The Frogs] (1962), Belgian writer Raymond Duesberg penned the description of a weird post-nuclear society.

In *Le Sud* [The South] (1962), Yves Berger depicted an alternate Virginia before the Civil War.

In 1967, Robert Escarpit penned *Honorius, Pape* [*Pope Honorius*], a satirical novel in which Earth has been reduced to a handful of islands inhabited by the descendants of a scientific congress.

The same year, Jean Rignac penned *Le Réveil des Titans* [The Titans Awake], an occult novel that mixed esoteric elements with science fiction concepts.

A genre which became increasingly popular in the late 1950s and throughout the 1960s was that of thrillers and espionage novels, many of which dabbled with science fiction.

In 1957, journalist and espionage author Georges Langelaan wrote his famous short story "*La Mouche*" [The Fly], later reprinted in his remarkable collection, *Nouvelles de l'Anti-Monde* [Stories from the Anti-World] (1962). This well-known horror story was filmed twice, in 1958 with Vincent Price, and later by David Cronenberg in 1986. Other notable works with genre elements included *Le Dauphin Parle Trop* [The Dolphin Spoke Too Much] (1964), *Le Zombie Express* [Zombie Express] (1964) and *Le Vol de l'Anti-G* [The Flight of the Anti-G] (1967).

Another thriller writer, Henry Ward (a pseudonym of Henri Viard) penned *Les Soleils Verts* [The Green Suns] (1956), in which a parallel universe intersected with ours, neutralizing all atom bombs and making the West and the East believe the other has found a new weapon. His other genre novel was *L'Enfer est dans le Ciel* [Hell Is in the Sky] (1958).

Also in 1956, George-Marie Bernanose wrote *La Porte Interdite* [The Forbidden Door], a detective novel taking place in 1975 pitting a policeman against a mad scientist.

The cold war and the ever-present threat of World War III were the themes of *La Troisième Guerre Mondiale Durera Six Heures* [WWIII Will Last Six Hours] (1950) by Hector Ghilini.

In *La Guerre est pour Demain* [War Is for Tomorrow] (1956), Henry Clérisse detailed a hypothetical invasion of Europe by the Soviets.

Marcel Guichard in *Feu Paris* [The Late Paris] (1958) also showed the destruction of the French capital.

Science fiction made further inroads in the espionage genre through specialized imprints such as *Espions de Demain* [*Tomorrow's Spies*] by Arabesque, which published ten genre novels in 1960:

Michel Rosel's *Trafic de Cerveaux* [Brain Traffic] (1960).

Franck Erboy's *Mat aux Automates* [The Automatons in Check] (1960).

Éric Cartier's *Les Inhumains* [The Inhumans] (1960).

"Ex-Agent SR 27"'s *Ici, Base Spatiale 15* [Space Base 15 Calling] (1960).

Another author of science fiction espionage was Luc Barsac, who wrote at least two genre thrillers for Arabesque's *Espionnage* imprint, such as *Duel chez les Jaunes* [Duel with the Chinese] (1958) and *Évadé de l'Espace* [Escape in Space] (1963).

Even popular spy heroes in the tradition of *James Bond* often engaged in sci-fi adventures. Among the most notable characters were:

OSS 117, the hero of over a hundred thrillers written by "Jean Bruce" (a pseudonym of Jean Brochet), the after his death, his wife, Josette (née Przybyl). A number of novels featured genre elements, such as *Arizona Zone A* (1959), in which OSS 117 unmasked alien invaders, and *Magie Blanche pour OSS 117* [White Magic for OSS 117] (1969).

Coplan FX-18 by "Paul Kenny" (see above). Some books, such as *Bataillon Fantôme* [Ghostly Battalion] (1959), also featured genre elements; *H* by Bruno Bax with a dozen novels between 1956 and 1960. *Lecomte* by "F.-H. Ribes" (a pseudonym of Richard-Bessière); *Luc Ferran* and *Le Commander* by G.-J. Arnaud; *Mr. Suzuki* by Jean-Pierre Conty with such genre novels such as *Horizons Fantastiques pour Mr. Suzuki* [Fantastic Horizons for Mr. Suzuki] (1975), *Project Cyclope* [Project Cyclops] (1976) and *Dr. Suzuki et Mr. Hyde* (1978); *Bonder* by André Caroff; *Face d'Ange* [Angel Face] by Adam Saint-Moore; and many more.

Finally, for something completely different, the 1950s saw the novelization of the riotously funny radio serial *Signé Furax* by Pierre Dac and Francis Blanche, in which a colorful cast of characters fought an international crime cartel of bearded villains. Furax' incredible adventures included traveling back in time to change history during the Crimean War, journeying through space on a flying atoll to the far-off planet Asterix, and fighting a horde of parasitic, alien invaders, the last and best saga entitled *Le Gruyère qui Tue* [The Gruyere That Kills].

In the same vein, Robert Beauvais' *Quand Les Chinois...* [When The Chinese...] (1966), about a hypothetical Chinese invasion of France, was adapted into a comedy, *Les Chinois à Paris*, a 1974 film by Jean Yanne.

The YAs

After World War II, science fiction themes found a welcoming home in the field of juvenile or "young adult" novels which picked up the slack from the pulpish adventure magazines of the 1920s and 1930s.

Pierre Devaux founded the YA imprint *Sciences & Aventures* for publisher Magnard, which released twelve novels between 1946 and 1962, including detailed postfaces to provide the readers with scientific explanations of what was possible, and what was not.

Among the original French novels written and/or published by Devaux in his imprint were *XP 15 en Feu!* [XP15 On Fire!] (1946) and its sequel, *L'Exilé de l'Espace* [Exiled in Space] (1947), both about the conquest of space. His writing partner, Henri-Georges Viot, penned *La Cité Fantastique* [The Fantastic City] (1947) and *Chronastro* (1953), a time travel story. Together, the two co-wrote *L'Écolier Invisible* [The Invisible Schoolboy] (1950), *La Minute Dérobée* [The Purloined Minute] (1952), a sequel to *Chronastro*, *La Conquête d'Almériade* [The Conquest of Almeriade] (1954), and *Explorations dans le Micro-monde* [Explorations in the Microworld] (1957).

Another publisher, Mame, followed suit with *Succès Anticipation*, which, between 1955 and 1958, published five volumes, among which were translations of the so-called "juveniles" by Robert Heinlein.

In 1952, Belgian publisher Marabout launched a new YA imprint, entitled *Marabout Junior*, which released a steady flow of adventure novels, including some space operas, such as Jacques Pierroux' *Pilotes pour Demain* [Pilots for Tomorrow] (1956) and *Police Spatiale* [Space Police] (1961); J.-J. Mézière's *Satellite Lune* [Moon Satellite] (1955) and Paul Vallène's *Aller-Simple pour l'Anadyr* [One-Way Ticket for Anadyr] (1964).

Marabout also released several novels by Jimmy Guieu (who had been in a dispute with Fleuve Noir) under the pseudonym of "Claude Vauzière", such as *Traffic Interstellaire* [Interstellar Trafic] (1960) and *Échec aux Végans* [The Vegans in Check] (1962).

But by far the most popular series launched by *Marabout Junior* were an espionage hero created by André Fernez, *Nick Jordan*, whose adventures, such as *Virus H-84* (1960), occasionally contained genre elements; and *Bob Morane*, by Henri Vernes (a pseudonym of Charles-Heneri Dewisme), which began in 1963 and has continued to this day, even after the death of its creator in 2021, totaling about 200 volumes!

Bob is a retired air force major, with the help of his friend, a tough, burly Scotsman, Bill Ballantine, fand the beautiful journalist Sophia Paramount, ought evil throughout the world, sometimes in space, and even through time itself. One of the longest and most popular juvenile adventure series in the world, *Bob Morane* has also the subject of one live action and one animated television series and an ongoing series of graphic novels.

Bob Morane's colorful rogues' gallery included the diabolical Monsieur Ming, a.k.a. the "Yellow Shadow", a fiendish Asian mastermind bent on universal domination; SMOG, an international crime cartel led by the beautiful but deadly Miss Ylang-Ylang and Roman Orgonetz, her ruthless henchman, a professional assassin with teeth of gold; the megalomaniacal Dr. Xhatan, "master of light", served by an artificially-created green-skinned men; the Toad-Men, descendants of an alien race stranded on our world long ago; the Tiger, an ordinary tramp whose intelligence was boosted with the memories of several brilliant scientists and that of a deadly man-eating tiger; etc.

One sub-set of *Bob Morane* adventures was *Le Cycle du Temps* [The Time Saga], which pitted Morane and the Time Patrol (previously encountered twice in the series) against the Yellow Shadow who was always trying to change the course of history to conquer the world. Another notable sub-set was *Le Cycle d'Ananké* [The Ananke Saga], in which Bob and Bill tried to escape from a nightmarish, other-dimensional world.

In 1967, *Marabout Junior* changed its name to *Marabout Pocket*, and added several new series including translations of *Doc Savage*, and *Kim Carnot*, another spy by Jacques Legray (one of his novels, *Destination Espace* [Destination Space] (1967), featured plans to settle another planet); but throughout, the focus remained on *Bob Morane*, the undisputed star of the imprint.

Another popular YA series of the 1960s and 1970s was *Langelot*, published by publisher Hachette's long-standing, popular imprint, *Bibliothèque Verte* [Green Library]. Written under the pseudonym of "Lieutenant X" by Vladimir Volkoff, it began in 1965 and went on for about forty volumes, the last released in 1986. The series starred the eponymous young French secret agent, member of S.N.I.F., a secret French intelligence service. Several of the novels pitted Langelot against megalomaniacal villains, such as Mister T, an obese and crippled mad scientist whose lair was a satellite orbiting the Earth; the international crime cartel SPHINX; the B.I.D.I., a spy ring led by an indomitable, evil old woman; etc. A spin-off series included two volumes about *Corinne*, a young female agent and Langelot's occasional girlfriend.

Another popular YA genre was about a group of fearless time travelers called *Investigations Spatio-Temporelles* [Spatio-Temporal Investigations]. It was written by Swiss author Jean-Claude Froelich for Magnard, and was comprised of *Voyage au Pays de la Pierre Ancienne* [Voyage to the Land of Old Stones] (1962), *Naufrage dans le Temps* [Castaways in Time] (1965), *La Horde de Gor* [The Horde of Gor] (1969), *Le Masque du Taureau* [The Mask of the Bull] (1969) and *La Gaule Appelle IST* [Gaul Is Calling IST] (1971).

Other notable authors of YA science fiction during the 1950s and 1960s included:

Guy Séverac, with *Les Conquérants de l'Infini* [The Conquerors of Infinity] (1945).

Roger Trubert, with *L'Astre Rouge* [The Red Star] (1945).

Lucien Prioly, with *Nous Étions Sept Astronautes* [We Were Seven Astronauts] (1946), *L'Île des Hommes de Fer* [The Island of the Iron Men] (1948) and *Alerte aux Martiens* [Martian Alert] (1954).

André Baruc, with *Gobe-Lune* [Moon Swallower] (1948), *Contes de la Zérozième* [Tales from the Zeroth Grade] (1949) and *Les Pantins de Cristal* [The Crystal Puppets] (1957).

Fanny Clar, with *Dix-Sept et Un* [17 and 1] (1950), in which Earth, under pressure from underground gas, might explode.

Belgian writer Jean-Claude Alain, with *Demain il fera jour* [Tomorrow the Sun Will Rise] (1952), an Wellsian novel in which one race toils underground while another one lives in a Golden City in the world above.

Speleologist Norbert Casteret, with two novels about underground explorations conducted with a giant mole machine, *La Montagne Creuse* [The Hollow Mountain] (1962) and *Mission Centre Terre* [Mission Center of the Earth] (1964). The author also penned *Muta, Fille des Cavernes* [Muta, Daughter of the Caves] (1965), a prehistoric novel.

In the same vein, Jean Darrau had previously written *À la Conquête du Mammouth* [The Conquest of the Mastodon] (1947).

Georges Duhamel, with *Les Voyageurs de l'Espérance* [The Voyagers of Hope] (1953), about the flight of men trying to escape Earth's destruction by the deadly Z bombs.

Paul Berna, with a series of books about the conquest of the Moon, such as *Nous Irons à Lunaterra* [We Shall Go to Lunaterra] (1954), *La Porte des Étoiles* [The Gate of Stars] (1954), *Le Continent du Ciel* [The Continent of the Sky] (1955) and *Le Jardinier de la Lune* [The Gardener of the Moon] (1955).

Emil Anton, with *Les Robots du Mont Maudit* [The Robots of the Accursed Mountain] (1954) and *On se Bat sur la Lune* [Battle on the Moon] (1956).

Renowned science fiction scholar Jacques Van Herp used a variety of pseudonyms, such as "Michel Jansen", "André Jouly" and "Michel Goissert", to pen a number of young adult novels such as *Les Raiders de l'Espace* [Space Raiders] (1955) (co-written with Jean Erland) about a gang of space pirates, *La Porte sous les Eaux* [The Underwater Gate] (1960) (based on a story by Jean Ray) and *Rona sur l'Amazone* [Rona on the Amazon] (1963), a novel about antigravity.

Pierre de Sarcus, with *La Ville Souterraine* [The Underground City] (1957).

Jacques Chabar, with *L'Étoile au Fond des Mers* [The Star at the Bottom of the Sea] (1958), in which a rocket travels undersea before going into space.

Françoise d'Eaubonne teamed up with Jacques Bergier and L. Jean-Charles to pen a juvenile space opera describing the exploration of the asteroid Icarus, *Le Sous-Marin de l'Espace* [The Space Submarine] (1959).

Paul Cogan followed in the same vein with *Les Pionniers de l'Espace* [The Space Pioneers] (1959).

Henriette Robitaillie penned two poetic science fiction novels, Algue [*Algae*] (1959) and *Les Sept Portes d'Ebène* [The Seven Ebony Doors] (1959).

André Massepain wrote several novels in which young heroes thwarted villainous plots involving science fiction elements, such as *La Fusée Mystérieuse* [The Mysterious Rocket] (1959), *Une Affaire Atomique* [An Atomic Affair] (1961) and *Les Flibustiers de l'Uranium* [The Uranium Pirates] (1974). He also penned two novels with prehistoric elements, *La Grotte aux Ours* [The Bear Cave] (1966) and *L'Île aux Fossiles Vivants* [The Island of the Living Fossils] (1967).

Marcelle Manceau, with a prehistoric novel, *Le Talisman du Soleil* [The Talisman of the Sun] (1966).

Christian Pineau, with *La Planète aux Enfants Perdus* [The Planet of Lost Children] (1960), which featured cosmonauts landing on Venus and finding an Eden-like world ruled by a good fairy and inhabited by lost children and their pets.

Christian Fontugne and Mary Carey, with *Disparus dans l'Espace* [Vanished in Space] (1961).

Another "Lost in Space" novel was *Le Chant des Abîmes* [*Songs of the Abyss*] (1962) by X. B. Leprince, who also wrote *Dans le Sillage de l'Altaïr* [In the Wake of the Altair] (1970).

Georges Bayard, with *Les Pionniers du Déluge* [The Pioneers of the Flood] (1961), in which a mad scientist threatens to drown the Earth in a new flood. The author was also the author of the popular YA series *Michel*, about the adventures of a clever and spunky teenager, with over 20 volumes published by *Bibliothèque Verte* between 1958 and 1980. Two books contained marginal genre elements: *Michel et la Soucoupe Flottante* [Michel & The Underwater Saucer] (1963) and *Michel et les Maléfices* [Michel & The Evil Spells] (1979).

In the same vein, Paul-Jacques Bonzon wrote a dozen, popular YA novels in the 1960s and 1970s, featuring the *Six Compagnons*, a band of teenagers from Lyon who solved crimes and fought a variety of evildoers. *Les Six Compagnons et L'Homme des Neiges* [The Six Companions & The Yeti] and *Les Six Compagnons et la Pile Atomique* [The Six Companions & The Nuclear Pile] contained genre elements.

Marie-Louise Vert took her readers across a cosmic tour of various planets in *Le Bal des Étoiles* [The Ballroom of the Stars] (1962), and entertained younger children with *Un Grillon dans la Lune* [A Cricket on the Moon] (1973).

Suzanne Pulicani's *Monsieur Touminou Cosmonaute* [Mr. Pussycat Cosmonaut] (1964) was also a charming space adventure for young children.

Claude Cénac, with several, excellent genre novels, such as *La Planète Bonheur* [Planet Happiness] (1963), *La Citadelle de l'Espoir* [The Citadel of Hope] (1964), *Le Robot Sauvage* [The Savage Robot] (1966) and *Des Milliards de Soleils* [Billions of Suns] (1971).

Jean-Luc Beno, with *1990, ou Les Moins de 15 Ans à l'Assaut du Cosmos* [1990, or The Under-15s Going for the Cosmos] (1963).

A minor genre classic was René Guillot's *La Planète Ignorée* [The Unknown Planet] (1963), published by *Bibliothèque Verte*, in which a student came in contact with humanoid aliens who lived hidden among us and came from a dying planet located on the other side of the sun. A genre children's book by Guillot was *Un Petit Chien va dans la Lune* [A Little Dog Goes to the Moon] (1970).

Another remarkable YA novel as Henry Thilliez' *La Planète sans Rivage* [Planet Without Shores] (1964), in which explorers of Venus discover an underground civilization.

Maurice Vauthier, with *La Planète Kalgar* [The Planet Kalgar] (1966), in which two races fight a war on an alien planet in the 24th century. The author had also penned *La Terrible Bombe X* [The Dreaded X Bomb] (1964).

RICHARD-BESSIERE

LES MARTEAUX DE VULCAIN

FLEUVE NOIR

BIBLIOTHÈQUE
MARABOUT

GERARD KLEIN

le gambit des étoiles

Sur l'échiquier des tourbillons interstellaires
un homme joue sa dernière chance

The 1970s

The 1970s was a decade of expansion for French science fiction, marked by a politization of the genre as well as "new wave" stylistic experiments, the emergence of major new authors, and a commercial boom that lasted until the middle of the next decade.

The famous events of May 1968 shook French political and cultural life, and their consequences were naturally felt in the field of science fiction. French science fiction became increasingly political, leaning towards the radical left, bringing together a variety of causes such as opposition to the Vietnam war, nuclear power, industrial pollution, capitalism, imperialism, etc. into a style that became known as "New Science Fiction". The translations of "new wave" American and British authors such as Harlan Ellison, Norman Spinrad, etc., as well as the emergence of younger, radical French authors of "new science fiction" in the pages of *Fiction*, such as Jean-Pierre Andrevon, provoked irate letters from older readers.

As a new generation came of age, science fiction exploded commercially and a plethora of new imprints were started all throughout the 1970s, reaching a peak in 1977 where virtually every French publisher had at least one genre imprint, if not more, creating a boom that lasted until the early 1980s. And as fans turned pro, these imprints were edited by new talent as well.

The Publishers

The major publishing event of the decade was the creation in 1969 of the *Ailleurs & Demain* [*Elsewhere & Tomorrow*] imprint by Gérard Klein at publisher Robert Laffont.

This silver-foiled, trade paperback line published some of the best American works of the period (including Frank Herbert's *Dune*), as well as providing a forum for French authors such as Michel Jeury, Philippe Curval and André Ruellan. Klein also edited the short-lived YA imprint, *L'Âge des Étoiles* [The Age of the Stars] (1977-79), *Ailleurs & Demain Classiques*, a reprint imprint, and a short-lived series of non-fiction essays.

Denoël's *Présence du Futur* also began to publish a new generation of French writers, including Jean-Pierre Andrevon, Philip Goy and Philippe Curval. In 1976, editor Robert Kanters was replaced by Elisabeth Gille, who continued and expanded her roster with names like Daniel Walther, Pierre Pelot, Patrice Duvic, Serge Brussolo and Emmanuel Jouanne.

Fleuve Noir's monolithic *Anticipation* started attracting some new blood in 1968 with Louis Thirion, then in 1970 came Robert Clauzel, in 1971 Jean-Pierre Andrevon (under the pseudonym of "Alphonse Brutsche") and G.-J. Arnaud, in 1972 Pierre Pelot (also under a pseudonym. That of "Pierre Suragne") and in 1976 Julia Verlanger (also under a pseudonym, that of "Gilles Thomas"). The previously independent Fleuve Noir was taken over by the giant publishing group, Presses de la Cité, in 1966 and increased its number of releases from two to six titles a month! In 1974, control of the editorship passed into the hands of Patrick Siry, who also supervised a reprint program of older titles.

Two imprints were started during the decade, which concentrated on publishing French authors:

Nebula, launched in 1975 by OPTA, and edited by Alain Dorémieux, alternated between American, British and French "new wave" authors and published the first novels of Dominique Douay, Joël Houssin and Jean-Pierre Hubert. It was cancelled in 1977.

Ici & Maintenant [*Here & Now*], launched in 1977 by Swiss publisher Rolf Kesselring, and edited by Bernard Blanc, published radical political "new science fiction" titles by Yves Frémion and Maxime Benoit-Jeannin, as well as a magazine called *Alerte*.

Other genre imprints (many simply called *Science-Fiction*) created during this prolific decade included:

Science-Fiction, launched in 1970 by publisher J'ai Lu, and edited by Jacques Sadoul, became one of the most important paperback lines of the decade, making science fiction classics accessible to a large public. During the 1970s, J'ai Lu published a few selected French authors such as Michel Jeury, Dominique Douay and Pierre Pelot, but concentrated mostly on classic American science fiction. It also put out a quarterly magazine, *Univers*, started in 1975, edited by Yves Frémion.

Science-Fiction, launched in 1969 by publisher Marabout, and edited by Jean-Baptiste Baronian, also put out some new titles by Jean-Pierre Fontana (under the pseudonym of "Guy Scovel"), Daniel Walther, Bernard Villaret and Landry Merillac and two noted French anthologies edited by Henry-Luc Planchat.

Science-Fiction, launched tentatively in 1968 by Albin Michel, then relaunched in 1972, was a line of silver-foiled paperbacks edited by Georges H. Gallet and Jacques Bergier. A separate line of trade paperbacks was added in 1977 under the name *Super+Fiction*. It published mostly classic American authors, with a few French reprints and some new works by Nathalie Henneberg and Pierre Barbet (under the pseudonym of "David Maine").

Anti-Mondes [*Anti-Worlds*], launched in 1972 by OPTA, and edited by Michel Demuth, published mostly contemporary American science fiction. It was cancelled in 1977.

Dimensions, launched in 1973 by Calmann-Levy, and edited by Robert Louit, published mostly contemporary American and British authors, plus a few French writers such as Dominique Douay and Philippe Curval.

Le Masque-Science-Fiction, launched in 1974 by the Librairie des Champs-Élysées, and edited successively by Jacques Van Herp, then Michel Demuth, published mostly works by classic American authors, with a few reprints of Nathalie Henneberg and Yves Dermèze.

Science-Fiction, launched in 1974 by the Livre de Poche-Hachette, and edited by Michel Demuth and Gérard Klein, published mostly reprints of classic genre novels, with no French authors.

Science-Fiction, launched in 1977 by Presses Pocket, and edited by Jacques Goimard, also published mostly reprints of classic genre novels, but added new French works by Michel Jeury, Pierre Pelot, Vladimir Volkoff and Philippe Curval.

Autres Temps, Autres Mondes [*Other Times, Other Worlds*] (1966-1983), by Belgian publisher Casterman, released a series of hardcover anthologies edited by Alain Dorémieux.

Science-Fiction (1972-77), soon followed by *Titres SF* (1979-83), by publisher Jean-Claude Lattès, put out a large number of Edgar Rice Burroughs and Robert E. Howard's *Conan* translations, edited by Marianne Leconte.

Other, often short-lived imprints included:

Champ Libre (1974-78), by Chute Libre; *Futurama* (1974-82), by Presses de la Cité, edited by Jean-Patrick Manchette & Jean-Pierre Bouyxou; *Constellation* (1975-77), by Seghers, edited by Gérard Klein; *Marginalia* (1975-79), by comic book publisher Jacques Glénat, followed by *Train d'Enfer-SF* [(1980); *Autrepart* (1977), by Presses de la Renaissance; *Bibliothèque des Utopies* (1977-78), by Adel-Balland, edited by Pierre Versins; Bibliothèque *Aérienne* (1977-78) and *Horizons Illimités* (1977), by comic-book publisher Les Humanoïdes Associés; *Changez de Fiction* (1977-78), by Le Dernier Terrain Vague, edited by Lionel Hoebke; *Travelling sur le Futur* (1977-81), by Duculot; *Écrits Possibles* (1978-80) and *Espaces Mondes* (1979-80), by Ponte Mirone; *L'Utopie Tout de Suite* (1979-80), by Encre, edited by Bernard Blanc; *Mémoires d'Outre-Ciel* (1979-82), by Garry; *Fantastique/Science-Fiction* (1979-88) by Nouvelles Éditions Oswald; and *S.F.* (1980-81) by Fernand Nathan.

On the magazine front, in addition to *Fiction* and *Galaxie* (which was cancelled in 1977), OPTA launched *Marginal*

(1973-77). Editors included Alain Dorémieux until 1974, Michel Demuth, then Daniel Riche from 1977 to 1980.

Horizons du Fantastique [Horizons of the Fantastic] was published between 1967-76, co-created with Alain Schlockoff, (who went on to create the film magazine *L'Ecran Fantastique*) and edited by Dominique Besse, which covered science fiction, fantasy and esoterism in books, films and comics, and published Joëlle Wintrebert.

Other notable but short-lived magazines included *Imagine* (1975), *Mouvance* (1977), *SF Magazine* (1976-77), a translation of the British *SF Monthly*, and two versions of *Futurs* (1978).

Major Authors

The first of the French "new wave" writers was Jean-Pierre Andrevon, whose career began in the pages of *Fiction*, coincidentally in the May 1968 issue. The author was then at the forefront of an informal movement of left-wing political science fiction authors whose themes included socialist ideology, ecology, anti-nuclear power and anti-militaristic concepts. His first novels were published by *Présence du Futur*. These included the delightful science fantasy *Les Hommes-Machines contre Gandahar* [The Machine Men vs. Gandahar] (1969) and four collections of political short stories, *Aujourd'hui, Demain et Après* [Today, Tomorrow and After] (1970), *Cela Se Produira Bientôt* [It Will Happen Soon] (1971), *Repères dans l'Infini* [Markings in Infinity] (1975), and *Dans les Décors Truqués* [Behind the Fake Decors] (1979) and novels like *Le Temps des Grandes Chasses* [The Time of the Great Hunts] (1973) as well as the remarkable *Le Désert du Monde* [The Desert of the World] (1977), an evocative tale of the last days of man on Earth. Also at *Présence du Futur*, Andrevon launched and edited a three-volume series of ecological science fiction anthologies, *Retour à la Terre* [Back to Earth] (1974-77).

Simultaneously, from 1971 to 1975, the author used the pseudonym of "Alphonse Brutsche" to pen three non-political space operas for Fleuve Noir's *Anticipation* imprint and four horror novels for *Angoisse*. Surprisingly, some were among his best works of the period. *La Guerre des Gruulls* [The War Against the Gruulls] (1971) featured a space war between Earth and the alien Gruulls which was the result of a simple misunderstanding. In *Le Dieu de Lumière* [The God of Light] (1973), a star probe discovered an Earth-like world in the Orion system. In 1984, the author returned to Fleuve Noir having abandoned his pseudonym, and contributed four more science fiction novels, plus three horror novels, under his own name. *Soupçons sur Hydra* [Suspicions over Hydra] (1984) and *Le Premier Hybride* [*The First Hybrid*] (1985) dealt with a colonial conflict between Earthmen and the native inhabitants of Hydra. His previous works were also revised and reissued under his own name.

During the 1980s, Andrevon continued to produce novels and short story collections that were still imbued with his political slant, but with less dogmatism than before and featuring greater emotional nuances and richer characters. Among these were *Neutron* (1981), *Il Faudra Bien Se Résoudre à Mourir Seul* [We Must Accept to Die Alone] (1983), *C'est Arrivé mais on n'en a rien su* [It Happened But We Never Found Out] (1984) and *Sukran* (1989) for *Présence du Futur*. The latter described a Europe where the sea level was rising and an anti-islamic crusade was raging. At J'ai Lu, the author published *Cauchemar... Cauchemars!* [Nightmare... Nightmares!] (1982), the tale of an identity search, and Le Travail du Furet à l'Intérieur du Poulailler [The Weasel's Work Inside the Chicken Coop] (1983). The latter described a *Logan's Run*-like world where the government used hired killers nicknamed "weasels" to "retire" people whose economic usefulness has come to an end. This moving love story between such a "weasel" and his intended victim was adapted into an eponymous 1994 television movie. *La Trace des Rêves* [The Trace of Dreams] (1988), also written for J'ai Lu, described a pseudo-fantasy world in which the human survivors of a nuclear conflict have been reduced to five inches in order to survive and eventually reclaim Earth.

Through the 1980s and 1990s, the author diversified his career further, producing crime thrillers, adventure novels and YA novels, as well as horror, fantasy and science fiction.

Michel Jeury burst upon the French science fiction scene with the Philip K. Dick-inspired *Le Temps Incertain* [*The Uncertain Time*] (1973),[242] published by *Ailleurs & Demain*. Prior to it, the author had previously written two space operas for the *Rayon Fantastique* under the pseudonym of "Albert Higon". It was this novel, and its loosely connected sequel, *Les Singes du Temps* [*The Time Monkeys*] (1974), that made him one of the most important writers of the 1970s. Both novels dealt with time and its manipulation through the use of "chronolytic" drugs. Their protagonists were "psychronauts", helpless explorers of a confusing, multidimensional universe, facing threats from alternate realities, such as Harry Krupp Hitler 1st, Emperor of the Undetermined, or the mysterious "Phords" from the future world of Garichankar. They always searched, and often found, secret paradises, such as the tropical realm of the "Divers of Ruaba", hidden within the folds of space and time, away from the bleak realities. In his next book, *Soleil Chaud, Poisson des Profondeurs* [Warm Sun, Deep Fish] (1976), the author returned to the same jumble of alternate realities. This time, the novel took place in 2039, when the world was torn between two warring mega-corporations and their rival computer systems which permeated every facet of reality. Meanwhile, psychiatric patients escaped through fugues that seemed to carry them either to a peaceful tropical island, or to the serenity of an underwater world.

Throughout the 1970s and 1980s, Jeury continued to produce a series of remarkably original novels for *Ailleurs & Demain*, always of the highest literary quality. While he was

---

[242] Once available from Black Coat Press as *Chronolysis*, but now out of print.

certainly representative of a certain style of French science fiction popular in the 1970s and 1980s, he was nevertheless not a part of the political "new wave" movement. *Le Territoire Humain* [The Human Territory] (1979) featured yet another oasis of humanity existing on the borders of a dehumanized megastate. *Les Yeux Géants* [The Giant Eyes] (1980) theorized that modern-day UFOs were projections of mankind's collective unconscious in the late 20th century and imagined what the next century's manifestations would be like. The remarkable *L'Orbe et la Roue* [The Orb and the Wheel] (1982) featured a twenty-thousand-year-old rebel brought back to life in a far future, when the entire solar system had become a giant Dyson's Sphere, controlled by the rival powers of the Orb (its Lords) and the Wheel (its engineers). Finally, *Le Jeu du Monde* [The World-Game] (1985) returned to the universe of the first three volumes, featuring an Earth which had become a giant gaming arena, and a conflict between two organizations, one representing chance, the other the eponymous World-Game. Its hero eventually found refuge on space islands orbiting the planet.

Throughout the 1970s, the prolific Jeury also managed to write genre novels for virtually every other publisher. He resurrected the pseudonym of "Albert Higon" for J'ai Lu, for which he wrote *Les Animaux de Justice* [The Justice Animals] (1976), about aliens who used humans to tell right from wrong; *Le Jour des Voies* [The Day of the Ways] (1977), about a false prophet whose predictions of a new and better universe surprisingly come true; and *La Croix et la Lionne* [The Cross and the She-Lion] (1986), about the adventures of an Earthwoman on an alien world inhabited by a race of Lion-people. During this period, he also contributed two novels to Gérard Klein's short-lived YA imprint *Le Sablier Vert* [The Green Hourglass] (1977) and *Le Monde du Lignus* [The World of the Lignus] (1978); one political genre novel, *Poney-Dragon* (1978) to *Ici & Maintenant*; and two more elaborate novels, *L'Univers-Ombre* [The Shadow Universe] (1979) and

Les Enfants de Mord [The Children of Mord] (1979), to Presses-Pocket.

In 1979, Jeury also became a regular contributor to Fleuve Noir's *Anticipation* imprint, for which he wrote a total of nineteen novels between 1980 and 1992. The first, *Les Îles de la Lune* [The Islands of the Moon] (1979), started a series of six interconnected books (1979-81) that developed elements that had already been hinted at in the *Ailleurs & Demain* novels, progressively building the notion of a coherent Uuniverse that included "chronolysis", space islands, history being manipulated by the "geoprogrammers", etc. Other series included the future history of the alien Hebrew-like *Goer* race, a saga that began with *La Planète du Jugement* [The Planet of Judgment] (1982) and continued for three more books (1982-85); and *Le Dernier Paradis* [The Last Paradise] (1985), two books about the survivors of Paradise 5, the last city of men on Earth after the planet was abandoned. Other notable, non-series titles included *Les Tours Divines* [The Divine Towers] (1983), *L'Anaphase du Diable* [The Devil's Anaphase] (1984) and *Aux Yeux la Lune* [The Eyes of the Moon] (1988) (originally intended for *Ailleurs & Demain*).

In parallel with his production for *Anticipation*, Jeury created the saga of the *Colmateurs* [The Pluggers] for Presses-Pocket, starting in 1981 with *Cette Terre* [That Earth], and continuing with *Le Vol du Serpent* [The Flight of the Serpent] (1982) and *Les Démons de Jerusalem* [The Demons of Jerusalem] (1985). This ambitious trilogy told the story of a pan-dimensional corps of monitors set up by the mysterious geoprogrammers to "plug" holes between alternate Earths. Their enemies were the equally mysterious "Brownians" who attempted to open such holes and facilitate interworld travel. The *Colmateurs* series was arguably the author's masterpiece, combining strong, dramatic characters, tightly paced narration, cutting-edge science and epic conflicts on a truly mind-boggling scope. Unfortunately, the series was left unfinished when, in the late 1980s, the author turned to writing a stream of mainstream best-selling novels about life in his native southwestern France at the turn of the century. In order to keep his two literary careers separate, he then reused the "Albert Higon" pseudonym when Fleuve Noir published his last two genre novels, *La Chimère Infernale* [The Infernal Chimera] and *Le Vaisseau-Démon* [The Demon-Ship], in 1992. Jeury recently returned to writing science fiction, penning a 1998 YA novel with his daughter, Dany, for the *Vertige* imprint.

"Philippe Curval" (a pseudonym of Philippe Tronche) also published his first space operas in the *Rayon Fantastique* in the 1960s. He then contributed another, *Les Sables de Falun* [*The Sands of Falun*], to *Fiction* in 1970. Simultaneously, he published two literary works, *La Forteresse de Coton* [*The Fortress of Cotton*] (1967) and a collection of short stories, *Attention, Les Yeux* [Watch Out for the Eyes] (1973). His first "new wave" novel was *L'Homme à Rebours* [The Backwards Man] (1974), published by *Ailleurs & Demain*, a complex work on the theme of parallel universes, and the ability to choose one's reality. *Cette Chère Humanité* [That Darling Humanity] (1976), also published by *Ailleurs & Demain*, became an instant classic. It took place in a near-future Europe dubbed "Marcom" [Common Market], closed off from the rest of the planet. An oniromancer from the Marcom sends a mysterious SOS towards the "Payvoides" [Developing Countries], who then send an agent to investigate. What he finds is a strange dystopia where space and time have been dilated by the experiments of a mad genius. Another *Marcom* novel, which dealt with time travel, was *En Souvenir du Futur* [In Remembrance of the Future] (1983), also published by *Ailleurs & Demain*.

Curval's novels were poignant, often bitterly dark, character-driven social satires. *Le Dormeur s'éveillera-t-il?* [Shall The Sleeper Awake?] (1979), published by *Présence du Futur*, was another major work presenting a mutating world that had fallen apart, where new myths were perhaps tools implanted by the old masters to prepare their return. In many of his novels, space and time seemed to obey biological rather than physical laws. Even in his old-fashioned, satirical space opera,

Rut aux Étoiles [Rutting Stars] (1979), hyperspace was portrayed as an artery crisscrossing the body of the galaxy. Alternate universes interpenetrated like living amoebas in *Un Soupçon de Néant* [A Touch of Nothingness] (1977), which takes place in the "Solar Social System" and features a protagonist who has acquired the power to materialize beings created by his own subconscious. In *Y-a-quelqu'un?* [Anyone There?] (1979), a man searches for his girlfriend, the victim of merging parallel Earths. Aliens live on separate mental planes in *La Face Cachée du Désir* [The Hidden Face of Desire] (1980), where ethnological communication between Earthmen and the blue-furred Chulies who inhabit the strategically important hyperspatial world of Standard is all but impossible. The same feeling of true alienness pervaded *L'Odeur de la Bête* [The Scent of the Beast] (1981), in which a Russian investigator attempts to discover the connection between two decadent races of natives on a Russian space colony.

Curval also edited two remarkable anthologies of new French authors for *Présence du Futur*, *Futurs au Présent* [*Present-Day Futures*] (1978) and *Superfuturs* [Superfutures] (1986), in which he featured most of the major names of the 1980s and 1990s, including Serge Brussolo, Jean-Marc Ligny, etc. *Présence du Futur* also gathered his short stories in several collections, such as *Regarde, Fiston, s'il n'y a pas un Extra-Terrestre Derrière la Bouteille de Vin* [Sonny, Look and See If There Isn't an E.T. Hiding Behind the Wine Bottle] (1980), *Debout les Morts, le Train Fantôme Entre en Gare* [Get Up, Dead Men, the Ghost Train Is Entering the Station!] (1984), *Comment Jouer à l'Homme Invisible en Trois Leçons* [How To Play Invisible Man in Three Lessons] (1986) and *Habite-t-on Réellement Quelque Part?* [Do We Really Live Anywhere?] (1989). Like Jeury, Curval shifted towards mainstream literature in the 1990s.

Pierre Pelot was already a prolific author of YA novels, such as the popular *Dylan Stark* western series for *Marabout Pocket* and two genre novels, *Les Étoiles Ensevelies* [The Buried Stars] (1972) and *Une Autre Terre* [Another Earth] (1972), when he began publishing a series of remarkably mature space operas for Fleuve Noir's *Anticipation* (as well as modern-day horror thrillers for *Angoisse*) under the pseudonym of "Pierre Suragne". Between 1972 and 1980, the author contributed fourteen science fiction novels and seven horror novels to Fleuve Noir. His *Anticipation* novels were notable for their bleak endings, which was unusual at the time, as well as their new concepts, often incorporating post-1968 political ideas. They were written in a hard-hitting style borrowed from thrillers rather than space operas and included an occasional sex scene. *La Septième Saison* [The Seventh Season] (1972) saw Men fail to settle on another world after having hopelessly polluted the Earth. *Mal Iergo le Dernier* [Mal Iergo the Last] (1972) was the story of a doomed quest. The poetic *L'Enfant qui Marchait sur le Ciel* [The Child Who Walked on the Sky] (1972)[243] featured a maladjusted eight-year-old forced to flee the strange, artificial world of Zod, but his search for truth and a better life will take him to an entirely new world, beyond even his imagination. *Et puis les Loups Viendront* [And Then the Wolves Came] (1973) was a violent *Mad Max*-like tale of survival. *Ballade pour Presqu'un Homme* [Ballad for Almost a Man] (1974) was another tale of man reverting to savagery. The best novel of the period was *Mais si les Papillons Trichent?* [*But What If the Butterflies Cheat?*] (1974),[244] taking place in a bizarre, dystopic future America where a wave of mental illnesses may be attempts at communication by entities beyond that reality. Later novels, such as *Virgules Téléguidées* [Remote-Controlled Commas] (1980) and *Dérapages* [Out of Control] (1980) were increasingly political in tone.

Starting in 1977, and throughout the 1980s, Pelot produced a huge number of novels for virtually every genre publisher. Most, if not all, carried the same message, vilifying the evils of the modern, capitalistic, military-industrial world. They all described dystopic police states cohabiting with ei-

---

[243] Black Coat Press, ISBN 978-1-61227-107-1.
[244] In *The Child Who Walked on the Sky*, q.v.

ther savage no man's lands or peaceful utopias and featured doomed rebels who tried to see behind the veil of their protected lives.

For *Ailleurs & Demain*, the author penned *Transit* (1977), one of his most accomplished novels, which returned to the concepts of *Mais si les Papillons Trichent?* In it, an experimental hypnotic journey leads a researcher to a peaceful utopia. For *Ici & Maintenant*, he wrote *Le Sommeil du Chien* [The Sleep of the Dog] (1978), an ecological novel. For *Dimensions*, he penned *Les Pieds dans la Tête* [The Feet in the Head] (1982), where the new technology of "Bifurcated Paradoxal Sleep" enables the government to beam dreams directly into one's brain.

For J'ai Lu, he wrote six novels between 1977 and 1983, including *Les Barreaux de l'Éden* [The Bars of Eden] (1977), about a religious dystopia; *Delirium Circus* (1977), about a future actor who rebels against his simulacrum existence; other dystopias were depicted in *Parabellum Tango* (1980), *Kid Jesus* (1981) and *La Foudre au Ralenti* [The Slow-Motion Lightning] (1983).

For *Présence du Futur*, he wrote four novels between 1977 and 1982, including *Foetus-Party* (1977), depicting a world based on euthanasia and ruled by the "Holy Management"; *Canyon Street* (1978), about a planet-wide city; *La Guerre Olympique* [The Olympic War] (1980), where future sports are used as an alternative to war; and *Mourir au Hasard* [To Die Randomly] (1982), depicting a world where everyone's death is programmed from birth.

The author's major stream of dystopic novels during the 1980s, however, were produced for Presses-Pocket, for which he wrote twelve novels between 1977 and 1990, starting with *Le Sourire des Crabes* [The Smile of the Crabs] (1977). Most fit loosely in a series entitled *Les Hommes sans Futurs* [Men Without Future], which began with *Les Mangeurs d'Argile* [The Clay Eaters] (1981) and continued in five more books portraying the desperate and often futile wanderings of the last men and women on an Earth now inhabited by unfathomable mutants. Other notable stand-alone novels included *La Rage dans le Troupeau* [The Rage in the Flock] (1979), *Le Ciel Bleu d'Irockee* [The Blue Sky of Irockee] (1980) and *Les Îles du Vacarme* [The Islands of Clamor] (1981).

In 1985, Pelot returned to *Anticipation*, using his real name, writing another eighteen science fiction novels until 1991. Some of these were regrouped in series, such as *Chromagnon Z* (4 volumes, 1985-86), about a future ruled by merciless multinational corporations; *Tony Burden* (5 volumes, 1986-87), about a future war veteran who carries a psychic virus; *Les Raconteurs de Nulle Part* [The Story Tellers from Nowhere] (4 volumes, 1990); and finally, a *Conan* parody, *Konnar* (5 volumes, 1990-91).

In the 1990s, he further diversified his career further, producing crime thrillers, adventure novels, and a few more science fiction works, such as *Messager des Tempêtes Lointaines* [Messenger of the Far Storms] (1996) for *Présence du Futur*.

The first author to herald a real change at *Anticipation* was Louis Thirion, who had previously written the surreal *La Résidence de Psycartown* [The Psycartown Residence] for Losfeld (1968). For *Anticipation*, the author wrote a total of twenty-one literary space operas, starting with *Les Stols* (1968) until *Requiem pour une Idole de Cristal* [Requiem for a Crystal Idol] (1991). Several of these starred a semi-existentialist spaceman, Jord Maogan who has first beemn introduced in *Les Stols* (6 more volumes, 1968-73). His role in these colorful, poetic novels, was often that of a mediator between mankind and various alien lifeforms. The best in the series were *Les Whums se vengent* [The Whums' Revenge] (1969) and *Ysée-A* (1970), in which two powerful space entities are themselves hunted by an even more awesome one. Another series featured the temporal adventures of Gern Enez Sanders (6 volumes, 1985-89). One of these, *Que l'Eternité Soit avec Vous!* [May Eternity Be With You!] (1986) was a clever Holmesian pastiche. Thirion also wrote several radio scripts for scripts for *Le Théâtre de l'Étrange* [Theater of the Weird].

Georges-Jean Arnaud made his first appearance in *Anticipation* in 1971 with *Les Croisés de Mara* [The Crusaders of Mara] (1971), the first volume of a trilogy entitled *Chroniques de la Longue Séparation* [Chronicles of the Long Separation] (1971-72), in which a group of characters from the lost human colony of Mara, which had reverted to feudalism, rediscover their origins and then embark on a quest through space to find Earth. Arnaud was a prolific writer, the author of well over three hundred novels in different genres, including espionage thrillers, mysteries, horror (for *Angoisse*), erotic fiction and mainstream literature. His espionage novels included two series: *Luc Ferran* (16 novels written under the pseudonym of "Gil Darcy" for L'Arabesque from 1963 to 1969; and *Le Commander* for Fleuve Noir's *Espionnage*, with about fifty-odd novels written between 1967 and 1980. The author also used the pseudonyms of "Saint-Gilles" and "Georges Murey" Some of these featured science fiction elements. Arnaud made a lasting mark in the genre with his series *La Compagnie des Glaces* [The Ice Company], which will be reviewed in our next chapter.

Yann Menez wrote six novels for *Anticipation* between 1974 and 1980, all remarkable for their well-constructed plots that eventually culminated in clever climaxes, such as *Un Monde de Héros* [A World of Heroes] (1975), in which androids were implanted with the personalities of great artists of the past. *Appelez-moi Dieu* [Call Me God] (1976) was a complex futuristic battle between good and evil involving scientific astrology, religion, messianic power, reincarnation and time travel. In *Demandez le Programme* [Ask for the Program] (1980), gifted children hacked into computers.

Julia Verlanger used the pseudonym of "Gilles Thomas" to pen a dozen science fiction novels for *Anticipation* between 1976 and 1980. Notable science fiction titles included *L'Autoroute Sauvage* [The Savage Highway] (1976-79), the first in a trilogy that followed the adventures of a young survivor in a post-cataclysmic France; *Les Voies d'Almagiel* [The Ways of Almagiel] (1978), the fascinating study of an alien society divided between masters and slaves; *La Légende des Niveaux Fermés* [The Legend of the Closed Levels] (1978) and *L'Ange aux Ailes de Lumière* [The Angel with Wings of Light] (1978), about the colorful planet Malvie; and *Horlemonde* [Worldbeyond] (1980), about a deadly space penitentiary.

At OPTA, under the editorship of Alain Dorémieux, "new wave" authors were given room to express themselves in the pages of *Fiction* and the *Nebula* imprint. Two anthologies were published that tried to imitate Michael Moorcock's *New Worlds* or Harlan Ellison's *Dangerous Visions*: *Les Soleils Noirs d'Arcadie* [The Black Suns of Arcadia] (1975), edited by Daniel Walther, and *Banlieues Rouges* [Red Suburbs] (1976), edited by Joël Houssin and Christian Vilà.

Daniel Walther had been publishing stories in *Fiction* since the 1960s. In 1972, he self-published his first novel, a "new wave" space opera entitled *Mais l'Espace, Mais le Temps...* [But Space, But Time...]. After *Les Soleils Noirs d'Arcadie*, he published a collection of short stories, *Requiem pour Demain* [Requiem for Tomorrow] (1976) at Marabout; then *Krysnak, ou le Complot* [Krysnak, or the Conspiracy] (1978), a "new wave" apocalyptic story at *Présence du Futur*; and finally, what may be his best work, *L'Épouvante* [The Terror] (1979) at J'ai Lu. Influenced by Richard McKenna's *The Sand Pebbles*, Dino Buzzati's *The Desert of the Tartars* and Joseph Conrad's *Into the Heart of Darkness*, *L'Épouvante* described the harrowing odyssey of a Lieutenant of the Earth forces as his gunboat traveled on a nightmarish planet.

In 1982, the author began contributing to *Anticipation* for which he wrote another half-a-dozen novels such as *Embuscade sur Ornella* [Ambush on Ornella] (1983), in which powerful aliens end a long-standing space war; *Apollo XXV* (1983), an interesting speculation on the role of God in space travel; *La Pugnace Revolution de Phagor* [The Pugnacious Revolution of Phagor] (1984), about an alien revolution; *Le*

Veilleur à la Lisière du Monde [The Watcher on the Edge of the World] (1985) and *La Planète Jaja* [Planet Jaja] (1989). During this period, he also wrote *Happy End* (1982), a picaresque variation on the classic utopia *City of the Sun*, and several collections of short stories, such as *L'Hôpital* [The Hospital] (1982), *Coeur Moite* [Moist Heart] (1984) and *Sept Femmes de mes Autres Vies* [Seven Women of my Other Lives] (1985) for NéO.

Joël Houssin's first "new wave" novel, *Locomotive Rictus*, was published by *Nebula* in 1975. The author then contributed several science-fiction thrillers to *Anticipation*, included *Le Champion des Mondes* [The Champion of Worlds] (1982), the description of a frightening world revolving entirely around games; *Blue* (1982), which takes place in a claustrophobic city full of mutant gangs who are kept prisoner there by unseen forces; (*Phantom*, an original comic-book sequel, was written by Houssin and drawn by Philippe Gauckler in 1987). *City* (1983) was the story of a duel between a policeman and a mad motorcyclist in a crumbling futuristic city; *Game Over* (1983) was a *Damnation Alley*-like odyssey in a *Mad Max*-type world. The success of the *Dobermann* thriller series and of the author's television writing career eventually took him in a different literary direction, but he returned to science fiction in 1989 to pen two remarkable, award-winning novels: the surreal *Argentine* (1989), which takes place in a desertic prison world where naked men fight under the shadows of huge, black zeppelins; and the cyberpunk, rock-themed *Le Temps du Twist* [The Time of Twist] (1990), both for *Présence du Futur*.

Dominique Douay's first novel was *Éclipse* (1975), the story of the fall of a futuristic military dictatorship, published by *Nebula*. It was followed by several Dickian novels, such as *L'Échiquier de la Creation* [The Chessboard of Creation] (1976), published by J'ai Lu, in which two entities, the white king Galaad and the black king Aumaire, play a game of planetary chess; *Strates* [Strata] (1978), published by *Présence du Futur*, in which a mental illness dubbed "losttime" enables people to escape a politically harsh world by fleeing into the past; *La Vie Comme une Course de Chars a Voile* [Life as a Sailcar Race] (1978), published by *Dimensions*, a novel following the narrative pattern of a race in which a man discovers that his universe is not real; and *Le Principe de l'Oeuf* [The Principle of the Egg] (1980), also at *Dimensions*, in which the eponymous fetus-like entity recreates a uchronic history. A collection of his short stories was *Cinq Solutions pour en Finir* [Five Solutions to End It All] (1978).

With *L'Impasse-Temps* [Dead End Time] (1980), published by *Présence du Futur*, Douay struck a more personal note. The novel featured a man who finds a mysterious "lighter" which enables him to freeze time; at first, he uses it to commit petty crimes, but then realizes to his horror that the device is slowly turning him into a grey-skinned, carnivorous, reptilian monster. *Rhino* (1985), published by *Anticipation*, takes place in a galactic future where the mysterious alien Qalaqs are the only ones who can guide spaceships through hyperspace. Order is maintained by three super-beasts, a rhinoceros, a unicorn and a mastodon, psychically connected a human handler. Rhino, the rhinoceros handler, eventually realizes that they, too, can do what the Qalaqs do, and fights Licorice, the unicorn handler, for the future of mankind. Other notable works included the collection *Le Monde est un Théâtre* [The World Is a Stage] (1982) and *La Fin des Temps et Après* [The End of Time and Afterward] (1991), a novel featuring the unexpected appearance of time bubbles from the past, both published by *Présence du Futur*.

Jean-Pierre Hubert's first novel was *Planète à Trois Temps* [Three Times Planet] (1975), published by *Nebula*, the story of three artists from a decadent Earth on a galactic tour. It was followed by two political science-fiction novels published by *Ici & Maintenant*, *Mort à l'Etouffée* [Death by Suffocation] (1977) and *Couple de Scorpions* [Couple of Scorpions] (1980). Throughout the 1980s, the author wrote a series of grim, colorful and powerful novels for *Presence du Futur*: In *Le Champ du Rêveur* [The Dreamer's Field] (1983), an alien civilization becomes contaminated by the dreams of an Earth child; *Les Faiseurs d'Orage* [The Storm Makers] (1984) featured an Earthman subjected to the capricious whims of five powerful, god-like figures who had once been created by Mankind to explore the cosmos; *Ombromanies* [Shadowmania] (1986); and finally, *Roulette Mousse* [Soft Roulette] (1987), a collection of short stories. The author returned to science fiction in 1997 with a YA novel, *Le Bleu des Mondes* [The Blue of the Worlds] (1997).

At *Présence du Futur*, Philip Goy wrote *Le Père Eternel* [The Eternal Father] (1974), a satirical novel in which a megalomaniacal biologist, Jerome Stereod, tries to perpetuate himself through a dynasty. It was followed by the "new wave" *Le Livre-Machine* [The Machine-Book] (1975), a caricatural utopia; a collection of short stories, *Vers la Révolution* [Towards the Revolution] (1977); and finally, *Faire le Mur* [To Jump the Wall] (1980). His works were either too political or too *avant-garde* to be widely appreciated, but they became representative of a period of literary experimentation.

Jean-Pierre Fontana had already edited the fanzine *Mercury* and contributed numerous genre stories to *Fiction* when *Présence du Futur* published <u>Shéol</u> (1976), about a "bubble-city" and its cortege of nomads searching for energy on a devastated Earth. Ther author went on to pen *La Femme Truquée* [The Fake Woman] (1980) for NéO, about a parallel universe where Paris is divided into two blocs, like Berlin. Then, in 1984, he embarked on a long series of fantasy collaborations with Alain Paris for *Anticipation*. His stand-alone science fiction novels included *La Jaune* [The Yellow] (1986), about a military experiment gone wrong; and *La Colonne d'Émeraude* [The Emerald Column] (1992).

During the 1970s, J'ai Lu published two remarkable novels by journalist and thriller writer Claude Veillot. In *Misandra* (1974), the author depicted a strikingly memorable, savage world ruled by amazon-like women who hunt men. *La Machine de Balmer* [Balmer's Machine] (1978) was an original time travel romance in which a man oscillates between 1925 and the present, searching for the beautiful Cassandra.

In 1978, *Ailleurs & Demain* published *La Maison du Cygne* [The House of the Swan] by two renowned authors of fantasy, Yves and Ada Rémy; it told the story of two warring cosmic entities, the Swan and the Eagle, who fight on Earth through human agents.

"New wave" science fiction blossomed towards the end of the 1970s with the appearance of Kesselring's *Ici & Maintenant* imprint, thus labeled as a manifesto-like challenge to Klein's classic *Ailleurs & Demain*, and *L'Utopie Tout de Suite*, put out by small publisher Encre. Both were edited by Bernard Blanc, the author of a much-publicized essay entitled "Why I killed Jules Verne" which read as a virulent manifesto in favor of "new wave" science fiction.

Kesselring put out several political anthologies with eloquent titles such as *Ciel Lourd, Béton Froid* [Heavy Sky, Cold Concrete], *Planète Socialiste* [Socialist Planet], *Quatre Milliards de Soldats* [Four Billion Soldiers] (all 1977). He also published a variety of titles by established writers such as Michel Jeury, Pierre Pelot, Jean-Pierre Hubert, as well as new authors such as Yves Frémion, Maxime Benoit-Jeannin, Philippe Cousin and Pierre Marlson. Blanc also published Joëlle Wintrebert's first novel, *Les Olympiades Truquées* [*The Fake Olympics*] (1980), which she revised in 1987 and won the Rosny Award in 1988

Journalist Yves Frémion, also the editor of *Universe* for J'ai Lu, was the first author published by *Ici & Maintenant* with a collection of stories entitled *Octobre, Octobres* [October, Octobers] (1977). The author then edited two notable anthologies, *La Planète Larzac* [Planet Larzac] (1980) and *Territoires du Tendre* [Territories of Tenderness] (1982), and published *Rêves de Sable, Châteaux de Sang* [Dreams of Sand, Castles of Blood] (1986) at J'ai Lu. His YA novel, *Tongre* (1986), told the sentimental story of the life of a centaur-like creature of the alien world of Soline; it received a mainstream award. Frémion then wrote *Ronge* [Gnaw] (1988) for *Antici-*

pation and the award-winning *L'Hétéradelphe de Gane* [The Heteradelph of Gane] (1989), before being elected on a Green Party platform to the European Parliament.

Maxime Benoit-Jeannin penned two novels for *Ici & Maintenant*: *La Terre était ici* [Earth Was Here] (1978) and *L'Adieu des Industriels* [Farewell to the Industrials] (1980); he also wrote a more traditional space opera for OPTA's *Galaxie-Bis*, *L'Ami des Ambrosiens* [The Ambrosians' Friend] (1981).

Philippe Cousin's first short story collection for *Ici & Maintenant* was *Le Retour du Boomerang* [The Return of the Boomerang] (1980), also the last title published by the imprint. He went on to collaborate with Jean-Pierre Andrevon on several notable anthologies with ecological/urban themes for *Présence du Futur*, such as *L'Immeuble d'En Face* [The Building Across the Street] (1982), *Hôpital Nord* [North Hospital] (1984) and *Gare Centrale* [Central Station] (1985). He also published the collection *Mange ma Mort* [Eat My Death] (1983) and *La Solution du Fou* [The Madman's Solution] (1989) at *Présence du Futur*.

"Pierre Marlson" (a pseudonym of Martial-Pierre Colson) had collaborated with Michel Jeury on *L'Empire du Peuple* [The People's Empire] (1977) for Albin Michel and written "new wave" works for publisher Ponte Mirone, *Hyménophage* (1978) and the anhology *Des Métiers d'Avenir* [Future Jobs] (1979). For *Ici & Maintenant*, he wrote *Désert* (1979), and penned *Les Compagnons de la Marciliague* [The Companions of Marciliague] (1979) for Encre.

For Encre, Michel Jeury wrote *L'Univers-Ombre* [The Shadow Universe] (1979) and Jacques Boireau's *Les Années de Sable* [The Years of Sand] (1979).

"New wave" science fiction ultimately proved to be an experiment that remained commercially unsuccessful, but was nevertheless important and influential. Some of that influence was positive in that these works opened new vistas and made the field more relevant; but it also had a negative side, alienating casual readers who did not find them entertaining enough.

Other Notable Authors

Yves Dermèze finally made his appearance at *Anticipation*, using the pseudonym of Paul Béra, with *Planète Maudite* [Accursed Planet] (1970). It was the first in a series of adventures of a friendly, self-aware robot with three brains named *Robi*, which continued for three more volumes (1970-72). In total, the author penned twenty-one novels for *Anticipation* between 1970 and 1983. Another of his series was that of the parallel world of the *Oeus* (two volumes, 1972-78). Other notable novels included *Le Vieux et son Implant* [The Old Man and his Implant] (1975), in which a disease kills young people, forcing them to become attached to old people; *Jar-Qui-Tue* [Jar-Who-Kills] (1978), in which three men from different eras become aware of each other's existence; *Ceux d'Ailleurs* [Those From Beyond] (1979), a colorful journey beyond death; *La Horde Infâme* [The Awful Horde] (1980), a prehistoric novel; *Changez de Bocal* [Change of Jars] (1981), featuring a society where people can change their ages at will; and *L'Ombre du Tueur* [The Shadow of the Killer] (1983), a *Tenth Victim*-like story. During that period, the author used the "Dermèze" pseudonym for two well-crafted science fiction novels published by *Le Masque-Science-Fiction*, *L'Image de l'Autre* [The Image of the Other] (1974) and *Les Lumières* [The Lights] (1976), about an Earth inhabited by savage mutants with deadly powers; as well as one juvenile novel, *Le Sharoun de Gallicad* [The Sharoun of Gallicad] (1974), published by Marabout.

Robert Clauzel began the series of the cosmic adventures of *Claude Éridan* with *La Tâche Noire* [The Black Spot] at Anticipation in 1970. Eridan was a galactic trouble-shooter from the advanced planet of Gremchka who, with the help of his Earth friends, Gus and Arièle Béranger, uncovered awesome secrets about the "true" nature of the universe, and the indescribable forces who inhabit it. The series went on for another fifteen volumes until 1979. The author's other novels tended to be straightforward science fiction horror creating a sense of utter powerlessness at the hands of incomprehensibly powerful alien entities. In total, he penned thirty-one novels for *Anticipation*, until *Les Survivants de la Mer Morte* [The Survivors of the Dead Sea] (1984)

Jan de Fast made his entrance at *Anticipation* in 1972 with *L'Envoyé d'Alpha* [The Envoy from Alpha] (No. 495), the first of the adventures of *Dr. Alan*. Alan traveled across the galaxy on his ship the "Blastula", acting as a trouble-shooter for a peace-loving human civilization based on planet Alpha, led by the seductive Artificial Intelligence, Nora. Being a medical doctor, many of the author's plots were based on, or made use of, his knowledge of biology. The *Alan* series went on for twenty-four more volumes until 1980. In total, the author wrote forty-three novels between 1972 and 1981, his last one being *Il Fera Si Bon Mourir...* [It Will Be So Good to Die...] (1981), about a galactic rebellion.

Jean-Pierre Garen (a pseudonym of Jean-Pierre Goiran) was another prolific author of space operas for *Anticipation*. He made his debut with *Le Bagne d'Edenia* [The Edenia Penitentiary] (1974) but soon became very popular with the adventures of a series about the *Surveillance Service of Primitive Planets*, the galactic troubleshooting arm of the Terrestrial Union, most starring an agent called Marc Stone. It was introduced in *Le Dernier des Zwors* [The Last of the Zwors] (1982) and totaled forty-two novels. Its considerable commercial success (not unlike that of Germany's *Perry Rhodan*) got it its own imprint.

Jacques Hoven's (a pseudonym of Jacques Conia) first novel, *Adieu, Cered* [Farewell to Cered] (1972), was a moving novel about a space convict fraternizing with powerful aliens. The author wrote only nine novels for *Anticipation*, but they were all imbued with the same humanistic ideals and often relied on strange time paradoxes. In *Sombre est l'Espace* [Dark is Space] (1973), men go searching for their cosmic roots; *Les Intemporels* [The Intemporals] (1974) featured three characters from three different futures; *La Porte des Enfers* [The Gates of Hell] (1978) described an endless journey through terrifying parallel universes. Also notable were *Robinson du Cosmos* [Cosmic Robinson] (1980) and his last novel, *Les Non-Humains* [The Non-Humans] (1981).

When Fleuve Noir cancelled its *Angoisse* horror imprint, André Caroff, the creator of the popular *Madame Atomos* series, swiftly moved to *Anticipation* with *Le Rideau de Brume* [The Curtain of Mist] (1971). The author produced thirty-four more novels between 1971 and 1989. His series included the adventures of a futuristic space trooper named *Rod* (4 volumes, 1980); and *Abel 6666* (8 volumes, 1983-85), which takes place in a computerized future. Several of the author's *Bonder* espionage novels also contained genre elements, such as *Bonder Super-Tueur* [Bonder Super-Killer] (1974), *Bonderscopie* (1975), *Bonder contre Dr. Astro* [Bonder vs. Dr. Astro] (1976), *Bonder Opération Magie* [Bonder Operation Magic] (1976), *Bonder Mach 3* (1977), *Bonder Connexion 12* (1978), *Bonder Stade Zombi 4* (1979), etc.

Gabriel Jan (a pseudonym of Jean Demont) had previously contributed two horror novels to Fleuve Noir's *Angoisse* when he published *La Planète aux Deux Soleils* [The Planet with Two Suns] (1974) at *Anticipation*. The author wrote thirty-five science fiction novels for the imprint between 1974 and 1987, his last being *Les Elus de Tôh* [The Elects of Toh] (1987). The most notable included a series about a future polluted Earth where humans lived in domed cities (2 volumes, 1978); and the trilogy *Surmonde des Gofans* [Overworld of the Gofans] (1981-82), in which bisexual entities can be split into two separate individuals.

Paul-Jean Hérault's (a pseudonym of Michel Rigault) first novel for *Anticipation*, *Le Rescapé de la Terre* [The Survivor from Terra] (1975) featured the character of *Cal* (or Cal from Ter), a spaceman from Earth's future who finds himself stranded on Vaha, a prehistoric world. Using suspended animation and advanced technology, Cal returns periodically to check on his adopted world's progress, helping it evolve across the centuries. The series was comprised of six volumes and appeared until 1984. Two other notable series were *Durée des Équipages: 61 Missions* [Crews Duration: 61 Missions], featuring the adventures of space pilot Gurvan in a warlike, overpopulated future (3 volumes, 1987-88); and *La Treizième Génération* [The Thirteenth Generation] (2 volumes, 1990). In total, the author wrote twenty-two novels until *Ceux qui ne voulaient pas Mourir* [Those Who Refused to Die] (1996).

"Jean Mazarin" (a pseudonym of René-Charles Rey, an author known for his police thrillers under the pseudonym of "Emmanuel Errer" and his horror novels under the pseudonym of "Charles Nécrorian") contributed *Pas Même un Dieu* [*Not Even A God*] (1976), a sad novel about a young savage who believes himself to be the son of a god, to *Anticipation*. The author published twenty novels in that imprint until 1986, before switching to horror fiction. His best works included a trilogy about a star-spanning Terran Empire (1977) and a remarkable uchronia, *L'Histoire Détournée* [The Hijacked History] (1984), which takes place in a universe where, ten days after Hitler's suicide in 1945, V-6 atomic weapons destroy London, Washington and Moscow. The story is about a coup attempt in Burgundy that threatens to start a new world war between the Great Reich and Japan. The author also penned two novels about *Face*, a murderous female android, *Poupée Tueuse* [Killer Doll] (1985) and *Poupée Cassée* [Broken Doll] (1986), his last novel.

Gérard Marcy began a short-lived career at *Anticipation* with a space opera thriller, *La Neige Bleue* [The Blue Snow] (1969), before a trilogy featuring the heroic investigator Captain Glenn who is looking for vanished startships in the year 2230 (1970-72).

"Georges Murcie" (a pseudonym of Pierre Gérome) wrote thirty-one novels for *Anticipation*, starting with *Garadania* (1970), including *La Folie du Capitaine Sangor* [The Madness of Captain Sangor] (1975), *La Courte Eternité d'Hervé Girard* [The Short Eternity of Hervé Girard] (1977) and *Tetras* (1980), his last novel.

"Pierre Courcel" (a pseudonym of Roger Tribot) contributed three novels to *Anticipation*: *Equipages en Péril* [Crews in Danger] (1970), *Bases d'Invasion* [Invasion Bases] (1971) and *Escales Forcées* [Forced Stopover] (1972).

"Dan Dastier" was a pseudonym created shared by at least two writers, Marc Bréhal and Yves Chantepie, who was also the author of another genre novel published by Albin Michel under the pseudonym of "Jean-Yves Chanbert", *Les Sirènes de Lusinia* [The Sirens of Lusinia] (1974). As Dastier, their first novel for *Anticipation* was *Les Déracinés d'Humania* [Uprooted from Humania] (1972). Chantepie reportedly took over from Bréhal around 1975. In total, the author penned thirty-four novels, the last being *Le Sixième Symbiote* [The Sixth Symbiote] (1987), most taking place in the samer Galactic Empoire. The best of them featured the daring space explorer, *Julian de Cerny*, who first appeared in *La Planète aux Diamants* [The Diamond Planet] (1973) and returned for three more adventures (1974-80).

Daniel Piret also began his *Anticipation* career in 1972 with Année 500.000 [Year 500,000] (1972). The author wrote thirty-four novels for the imprint, the last being *La Parole* [The Spoken Word] (1984). He also contributed five more genre novels to the short-lived *Mémoires d'Outre-Ciel* [Memoirs from Beyond the Sky] imprint from publisher Garry under the pseudonym of "Red Ilan". *Prométhée* [Prometheus] (1982) and *Le Fils de Prométhée* [The Son of Prometheus] (1983) formed an ambitious time travel novel sub-titled *Les Ellipses Temporelles* [Temporal Ellipses].

Christian Mantey began to write for *Anticipation* in 1976 with *Transit pour l'Infini* [Transit for Infinity] (1976). He wrote six novels between 1976 and 1984, including the *Mel Titcht* series (4 volumes, 1981-84), about a detective of the future working for the *Bureau of Parallel Cases*, who investigates extra-dimensional entities. With Jean-Philippe Berger, the author used the pseudonym of "Jean-Christian Bergman" to pen three more novels in 1979-80. And with Pierre Dubois, he used the pseudonym of "Budy Matieson" to pen two more novels, the post-apocalyptic *Chroniques du Retour Sauvage* [Chronicles of the Savage Return] (1980).

"Frank Dartal" (a pseudonym of Gilbert Bucher)'s first novel for *Anticipation* was *Les Brumes du Sagittaire* [The Mists of Sagittarius] (1977). The author wrote fifteen novels, until *L'Épopée du Draco* [The Draco's Odyssey] (1988). Notable titles were *Le Règne du Serpent* [The Reign of the Serpent] (1979), *Civilisations Galactiques - Providence* [Galactic Civilisations - Providence] (1980), *Et Un Temps Pour Mourir* [And a Time to Die] (1982) and *Eridan VII* (1986).

Chris Burger had already contributed two *Angoisse* novels prior to penning *Quand Elles Viendront* [When They Will Come] (1977) and *Le Temps des Autres* [The Time of Others] (1977) for *Anticipation*.

Finally, Vincent Gallaix (a pseudonym of Jacques Acar) only wrote two novels for *Anticipation*, *Orbite d'Attente* [Waiting Orbit] (1977) and *Zoomby* (1977), about a perfect android, rejected by the human race.

Other notable authors of the period published by other imprints included:

Bernard Villaret made his debut at Marabout with a grim space opera, *Mort au Champ d'Étoiles* [Death on a Field of Stars] (1970). He then moved to *Présence du Futur* where he published two novels, *Deux Soleils pour Artuby* [Two Suns for Artuby] (1971) and *Le Chant de la Coquille Kalasai* [The Song of the Kalasai Shell] (1976), which illustrated the dangers of introducing Earth culture to a Polynesian-like planet. Having spent time in French Polynesia, the author knew how to give his novel a strong ring of authenticity and feeling. He also published one collection of stories, *Visa pour l'Outre-Temps* [Visa for Beyond Time] (1976), two juvenile genre novels, *Pas d'Avenir pour les Sapiens* [No Future for Homo Sapiens] (1980) and *L'Infini Plus Un Mètre* [Infinity Plus One Meter] (1981), and one more novel, *Quand Reviendra l'Oiseau-Nuage* [When the Cloud Bird Returns] (1983), for Albin Michel.

Landry Merillac published an ambitious space opera, *Les Sept Soleils de l'Archipel Humain* [The Seven Suns of the Human Archipelago] (1973) at Marabout.

Marabout also published two Belgian authors: Vincent Goffart published a romantic time travel story, *Jonathan à Perte de Temps* [Jonathan Losing Time] (1975); and Paul Hanost, with a space opera, *Le Livre des Étoiles* [The Book of Stars] (1977).

Albin Michel published Patrick Ravignant with *Les Mutants de la Voie* [*The Mutants of the Way*] (1972) and Belgian writer Yves Varende with *Le Gadget de l'Apocalypse* [The Apocalypse Gadget] (1978). The author went on to pen a trilogy of novels for comic-book publisher Jacques Glénat, *Tamaru*, *Les Tueurs de l'Ordre* [The Killers of Order] and *Tuez-les Tous!* [Kill Them All!] (1980).

Ailleurs & Demain published a number of outstanding books by various authors:

Tellur (1975), a collection of genre stories by Pierre-Jean Brouillaud.

Les Prédateurs Enjolivés [The Beautified Predators] (1976), another collection by Pierre Christin, better known for being the writer of the popular comic-book space opera *Valérian*. The author went on to pen *Le Futur est en Marche Arrière* [The Future Is in Reverse] for Encre in 1979.

L'Hippocampe [The Sea-Horse] (1981) by Lorris Murail, who had already penned two surreal novels for publisher Lattès, *Omnyle* (1975) and *La Secte* [The Sect] (1977).

And, finally, *Tous ces Pas vers le Jaune* [All These Steps Towards Yellow] (1979), the first novel by Christian-Yves Lhostis, the surreal tale of people living their lives in a completely green-colored environment.

Other notable works included:

Georges Soria's *La Grande Quincaillerie* [The Great Hardware Store] (1975), published by *Présence du Futur*.

Jean Le Clerc de la Herverie's *Ergad le Composite* (1976), published by *Nebula*.

Pierre Giuliani's *Séquences pour le Chaos* [Sequences for Chaos] (1977), published by Lattès and *Les Frontières d'Oulan-Bator* [The Borders of Ulan-Bator] (1979), published by *Dimensions*.

Pierre Bameul's *Je Paye Donc Je Suis* [I Pay Therefore I Am] (1977) and *Écrit dans le Passé* [Written in the Past] (1978), published by OPTA.

Cyrille Kaszuk's *L'Épreuve de Judith* [Judith's Test] (1978), published by J'ai Lu.

Finally, one should note Louis Bayle's two-volume collection *Aièr e Deman* (1970), "Elsewhere and Tomorrow" in the Provencal language, a collection of fourteen fantastic tales telling the history of Mankind from 200,000 BC to the far future, written in that language.

Mainstream Authors

The most interesting mainstream writer to have contributed to science fiction in the 1970s was Robert Merle, a Goncourt Award winner, who in 1968 penned *Un Animal Doué de Raison* [An Animal Gifted with Reason], a fascinating examination of the political and scientific consequences of communication with dolphins, translated and better known as *The Day of the Dolphin*, and made into an eponymous 1973 film. The author's 1972 novel, *Malevil*, was a starkly realistic description of the rebuilding of civilization after a nuclear conflict. It, too, became a best-seller and was also adapted into a feature film in 1980. *Les Hommes Protégés* [The Protected Men] (1974) was an elaborate social satire that featured the pandemic destruction of the male population of the United States, with the resulting consequence of women taking over. Other notable works included *Madrapour* (1976), *Homme Invisible, Pour qui chantes-tu?* [Invisible Man, For Whom Do You Sing?] (1984) and *L'Enfant-Roi* [The Child-King] (1993).

The other best-selling mainstream genre writer of the decade was (again) René Barjavel who made a startling return to science fiction with *La Nuit des Temps* [The Dawn of Time] (1968), which became an immediate commercial success, tapping into the spirit of the youthful rebellion of the times. In it, a man and a woman, the survivors of a pre-cataclysmic civilization that destroyed itself, are found frozen in a giant sphere at the South Pole. Their revival, and the tale of their doomed love, ignite social upheavals *à la* May 1968. The author followed it with *Le Grand Secret* [The Great Secret] (1973), a novel that begins as a political thriller with the discovery by an Indian scientist in the 1950s of the secret of a contagious form of immortality which could destroy the world and ends up describing a doomed island utopia *à la Odd John*. *Le Grand Secret* was adapted as a television movie. *Une Rose au Paradis* [A Rose in Paradise] (1981) was a touching love story taking place in the same universe as *Le Diable l'Emporte* and *Colomb de la Lune*, featuring the return of Mr. Gé, the builder of the Last Ark. Finally, *La Tempête* [The Tempest] (1982) was a panorama of various ills perpetrated by mankind upon itself in the near future.

Other notable mainstream authors who penned genre works during the period included:

Emmanuelle Arsan, the author of the renowned erotica classic *Emmanuelle*, with *Nouvelles de l'Érosphere* [Stories from the Erosphere] (1969), a collection of short, erotic fiction, many containing genre elements.

Michel Butor, with *La Rose des Vents* [The Rose of the Winds] (1970), another collection of short, poetic stories about the future of mankind.

Jean-Marie Fonteneau, with *Les Champignons* [The Mushrooms] (1970), an allegorical novel in which the world is taken over by mushrooms.

Gilbert Beau de Loménie, with *Le Monde Sans Grand-Mères* [The World Without Grandmothers] (1970), in which a nuclear fall-out turns women into men when they reach the age of forty.

Swiss author Jérôme Deshusses, with a striking anarchist utopia, *Le Grand Soir* [The Big Night] (1971); other notable works in this vein included *Sodome-Ouest* (1966) and *Délivrez Prométhée* [Free Prometheus] (1979).

Jean Marabini, with *Les Enfants Fous - An 2021* [The Mad Children - Year 2021] (1971), and *Les Hommes du Futur* [Future Men] (1965).

Claude Ollier, with *La Vie sur Epsilon* [Life on Epsilon] (1972), a surreal novel in which four astronauts, stranded on the eponymous planet, experience psychological attacks, not unlike what happens in *Solaris*.

Jean Raspail, with *Le Camp des Saints* [The Camp of the Saints] (1973), about an overpopulated world in which Europe succumbed to a Third World invasion; other notable works included *Le Jeu du Roi* [The King's Game] (1976) and *Septentrion* (1979).

Jean-Michel Barrault with the self-explanatory *...Et Les Bisons Brouteront à Manhattan* [...And the Buffalos Will Graze in Manhattan] (1973).

Renowned humorist Pierre Daninos, better known for his satire, *Les Carnets du Major Thompson* [Major Thompson's Notebooks], penned *La Première Planète à Droite en sortant par la Voie Lactée* [The First Planet to the Right When You Exit at the Milky Way] (1975), a satirical science-fantasy.

Frantz-André Burguet, with *Vanessa* (1977), a fictional future biography of the author's daughter, written as if it were the year 2004, when she has grown up to become a famous concert pianist.

Laurence Korb, with *Paris-Lézarde* [Paris-Lizard] (1977), about the destruction of Paris.

Philippe d'André, with *Les Ruses de l'Assaillant* [The Ruses of the Attacker] (1978), a collection of genre stories.

Marius-Pierre Guibert, with *Étranges Retours* [Strange Returns] (1978), in which a spaceman returns to a post-nuclear Earth.

Willy de Spens, with *La Nuit des Long Museaux* [The Night of the Long Snouts] (1978), featuring a revolt of domesticated animals.

Jacques Massacrier, with *Outre-Temps* [Beyond Time] (1978), where the survivors of a global ice melt create a utopian society.

Michel Polac, with *Le Q.I. ou le Roman d'un Surdoué* [The I.Q. or A Novel of the Gifted] (1978), a shocking novel where mankind, after discovering that intelligence can be increased by eating brains, fall prey to a cannibal holocaust and a genetic apocalypse.

Hugo Verlomme, with *Mermère* (1978), the tale of a conflict between mankind and an underwater civilization.

Florence Vidal, with *L'Aolès Férox* (1978), an African political satire with science fiction elements.

Finally, in the futuristic espionage category, in 1971, Fleuve Noir launched a dedicated imprint called *Espiomatic Infra-Rouge*, featuring the adventures of super-agent Vic Saint-Val, written by one of their *Espionnage*'s authors, Gilles Morris. The *Vic Saint-Val* adventures totaled sixty novels, published until 1979. Most included science-fiction elements in the form of advanced technology. The author later continued Vic Saint-Val's adventures in the *Kamikaze* trilogy published in *Anticipation* imprint in 1984, in which Saint-Val defeats an evil organization that was trying to forcibly bring peace to the world through the use of deadly, miniature flying saucers.

The YAs

The 1970s saw the blossoming of true science fiction in the field of YA and children's books, with a slate of new authors, who also occasionally contributed to regular adult imprints. In spite of the failure of the short-lived imprint *L'Âge des Étoiles*, which published eleven volumes between 1977 and 1979), with works by Michel Jeury and Christian Léourier, sporting covers by renowned French artists such as Jean-Claude Mézières and Moebius, science fiction was healthily represented in the catalogs of publishers such as Magnard, Hatier, and Hachette in its *Bibliothèque Verte* imprint.

Christian Léourier was probably the best and most famous author to have continually crossed the fence between

YA and adult science fiction. The author's first novel was *Les Montagnes du Soleil* [The Mountains of the Sun], featuring the adventures of a savage warrior rediscovering the secrets of ancient Earth after a cataclysmic flood. It was published in the prestigious *Ailleurs & Demain* imprint in 1972. The author later contributed one more novel to that imprint, *La Planète Inquiète* [The Worried Planet] (1979), about an Earth colony mysteriously falling prey to chaos, and one novel to *L'Âge des Étoiles*, *L'Arbre-Miroir* [The Mirror-Tree] (1977), a coming-of-age tale on a planet torn between the human colonists and the natives. With *Le Messager de la Grande Île* [The Messenger from the Great Island] (1974) the author embarked on his most famous series, the cosmic adventures of a group of colorful characters from the water world of Thalassa who, led by Jarvis of Helan, search the galaxy for the legendary Mother Earth. Eight *Jarvis* novels were published between 1974 and 1980.

In the 1980s, Léourier continued to alternate between adult genre novels and YA books. The former were published at J'ai Lu, and included *Ti-Harnog* (1984), in which a human observer challenges the rigid caste system of an alien society; *L'Homme qui tua l'Hiver* [The Man Who Killed Winter] (1986), in which a female archeologist and a native search for a mythical lost city; *Mille Fois Mille Fleuves* [A Thousand Times a Thousand Rivers] (1987), a love story between an alien woman and an Earthman on a water world; *Les Racines de l'Oubli* [The Roots of Oblivion] (1988), *La Loi du Monde* [The Law of the World] (1990), *Les Masques du Réel* [The Masks of Reality] (1991) and *La Terre de Promesse* [The Earth of the Promise] (1994), all novels which featured intricate alien cultures.

The latter included *Petit Dragon* [Little Dragon] (1986), *Eli le Rêveur* [Eli the Dreamer] (1988) and *E.V.A. ou l'Été de la Lune* [EVA or The Summer of the Moon] (1991).

Christian Grenier was by far the most prolific provider of young adult science fiction throughout the 1970s and 1980s. In 1972, the author penned a remarkable non-fiction book,

Jeunesse et Science-Fiction [Youth & Science Fiction], one of the first essays on the topic. His first novel was *Sabotage sur la Planète Rouge* [Sabotage on the Red Planet] (1972), which was followed by *Aïo, Terre Invisible* [Aio, Invisible Land] (1973), *Messier 51, ou l'Impossible Retour* [Messier 51, or The Impossible Return] (1975), and Le Secret des Mangeurs d'Étoiles [The Secret of the Star Eaters] (1978), all well crafted space operas for publisher Hatier. More notable was the intricate *La Machination* [The Machination] (1973), which won a literary prize awarded by French television, the first volume in a series of YA novels written for publisher GP and featuring remarkable characterizations, sophisticated concepts worthy of any adult novel, with strong narratives worthy of Robert Heinlein. These included a two-volume saga co-written with William Camus devoted to a planet colonized by Native Americans, *Cheyenne 6112* (1974) and *Une Squaw dans les Étoiles* [A Squaw Among The Stars] (1975), as well as stand-alone novels like *Le Satellite Venu d'Ailleurs* [The Satelite From Beyond] (1975), *Les Fleurs de l'Espace* [The Space Flowers] (1976) and *Le Soleil va Mourir* [The Sun Will Die] (1977). His *Les Cascadeurs du Temps* [The Time Stuntmen] (1977) won another major award. He also contributed *Le Montreur d'Étincelles* [The Spark Performer] (1978), about an alien world resisting colonization, to *L'Âge des Étoiles*.

In the 1980s and 1990s, Grenier continued his career with novels like *L'Habitant des Étoiles* [The Star Dweller] (1985) and the award-winning *Le Coeur en Abîme* [The Heart in the Abyss] (1985). In 1995, he launched the YA series of *Aina, Fille des Étoiles* [Aina, Daughter of the Stars] for publisher Nathan (six volumes), yet another award-winning series, and the saga of the *Multimonde* [Multiworld], a mysterious gateway leading into other universes that seemed to be patterned after the novels written by the uncle of one of its young heroes. It was comprised of *La Musicienne de l'Aube* [The Musician of Dawn] (1996); *Les Lagunes du Temps* [The Lagoon of Time] (1997), which took place in an alternate future Venice; *Cyberpark* (1997), featuring a devastated future Earth crawling with killer robots; and *Mission en Mémoire Morte* [Mission in a Dead Memory] (1997), the last three published by Denis Guiot in his new imprint *Vertige*.

The writing team using the pseudonym of "Michel Grimaud" (a pseudonym of Marcelle Perriod & Jean-Louis Fraysse) alternated between YA and regular science fiction and fantasy. They began their genre career with two volumes featuring the adventures of the young savage *Rhôor l'Invincible* [Rhoor the Invincible] published by Alsatia in 1971. It was followed by a series of literary YA novels, such as *La Ville sans Soleil* [The City Without Sun] (1973), *Soleil à Crédit* [Sun on Credit] (1975) and the remarkable *L'Île sur l'Ocean Nuit* [The Island on the Ocean of Night], published in *L'Âge des Étoiles* in 1978. The authors also contributed two of the bext YA novels published by Duculot's short-lived *Travelling sur le Futur* imprint, *Les Esclaves de la Joie* [Slaves of Joy] (1977) and *Le Temps des Gueux* [The Time of the Poor] (1980).

In the 1980s, Grimaud penned three notable adult novels for *Présence du Futur*, including two science fiction works, *La Dame de Cuir* [The Leather Lady] (1981), a love story between a man and an alien woman, who was purposefully treated as an animal in order to render the colonization of her world legally possible; and *L'Arbre d'Or* [The Gold Tree] (1983), a humorous romp through a colorful, anachronistic universe. In the YA field, the authors continued to produce such notable novels as *Le Passe-Monde* [The Passwrord] (1982) and *Le Tyran d'Axilane* [The Tyrant of Axilane] (1982), as well as many fantasies and, more recently, horror thrillers.

Another major contributor of young adult genre novels was the prolific Philippe Ébly who, throughout the 1970s and 1980s, penned several major series. The best known was *Les Conquérants de l'Impossible* [The Conquerors of the Impossible], published by *Bibliothèque Verte*, which began in 1971 with *Destination Uruapan* and totaled 21 volumes. The series featured the adventures of Serge, Thibaut, the beautiful Souhi and their teenage companions, in the present, involving aliens, robots, time travel to the past and the future, to an era when oceans have expanded and civilization collapsed. The author's other series included *Les Évadés du Temps* [*Escape in Time*], comprised of nine novels also published by *Bibliothèque Verte* between 1977 and 1988; and the short-lived *Les Patrouilleurs de l'An 4003* [The Patrollers of the Year 4003], comprised of five novels published in 1984 and 1986.

Huguette Carrière created the spunky character of *Tony* in 1971 with *Tony et l'Homme Invisible* [Tony and the Invisible Man] (1972) for the *Bibliothèque Rose*, a children's imprint. Its adventures were comprised of six novels, many featuring genre elements. The author also penned a remarkable young adult series, *L'Envoyé* [The Envoy] for Alsatia in 1977.

Robert Alexandre's series, *Mykir*, was also published by Alsatia and began with *Le Survivant* [*The Survivor*] (1973) and continued through five more volumes, until *Les Orphelins d'Almeray* [The Orphans of Almeray] (1981). For Alsatia, the author also penned *Sandrihar* (1975), *Tiguir* (1977) and *Les Héritiers des Sept Mondes* [The Inheritors of the Seven Worlds] (1982); he also wrote one adult novel for *Anticipation*, *Yriel* (1989).

William Camus penned *Opération Clik-Clak* (1975), *Un Bonheur Électronique* [An Electronic Happiness] (1977) and *Une Drôle de Planète* [A Funny Planet] (1978) for GP. He also collaborated with Christian Grenier, Pierre Pelot & Jean Coué for *Le Canard à Trois Pattes* [The Three-Legged Duck] (1978), and Jacky Soulier for *Le Péril Vient de la Terre* [The Danger Comes from Earth] (1981).

Claude & Jacqueline Held wrote *Le Chat de Simulombula* [The Cat from Simulombula] (1971), *Expédition Imprévue sur la Planète Éras* [Unforeseen Expedition to Planet Eras] (1978), *L'Antre de Starros* [The Lair of Starros] (1979), *Trois Enfants dans les Étoiles* [Three Children Among the Stars] (1980) and *La Poudre des Sept Planètes* [The Powder of Seven Planets] (1990).

François Celier penned the adventures of *Éric Matras*, published by *Bibliothèque Verte*, including *Les Chevaliers de l'Océan* [The Knight of the Ocean] (1969) and *La Vallée Fantastique* [Fantastic Valley] (1970), which featured giant anthropoids.

Adrien Martel penned the adventures of *Gil*, in *Gil dans le Cosmos* [Gil in the Cosmos] (1971) and *Gil Revient sur Terre* [Gil Returns to Earth] (1971).

Jean Cernaut wrote *Zone Interdite* [Forbidden Zone] (1972).

Yvonne Meynier wrote *Delphine, Reine de la Lumière* [Delphine, Queen of Light] (1972).

Geoffrey X. Passover wrote *Joar de l'Espace* [Joar from Space] (1972) and *Les Survivants de l'An 2000* [The Survivors of the Year 2000] (1977).

Philippe V. Rivages wrote *La Planète de l'Eau Bleue* [The Planet of the Blue Water] (1973).

Jacqueline Monsigny wrote the adventures of a super-agent *Freddy Ravage*, a series that comprised several volumes published between 1975 and 1977. Of genre interest were *Freddy Ravage et les Diplodocus* [Freddy Ravage & The Diplodocus] (1975) and *Freddy Ravage Prisonnier des Pharaons* [Freddy Ravage Prisoner of the Pharaohs] (1976).

Daniel Valiant wrote *La Légende du Goëland Blanc* [The Legend of the White Seagull], comprised of *Ciel des Sables* [Sky of the Sands] (1976) and *La Caverne du Temps* [The Cavern of Time] (1977).

Finally, Pierre Probst, who, in 1965, had taken his intrepid heroine, *Caroline*, to the Moon in *Caroline sur la Lune* [Caroline on the Moon] (1965), continued her fantastic adventures through the 1970s and 1980s with *Caroline et la Petite Sirène* [Caroline & The Little Mermaid] (1977), *Caroline chez les Lilliputiens* [Caroline in Lilliput] (1984), *Caroline à travers les Âges* [Caroline Throughout the Ages] (1985) and *Caroline et le Robot* [Caroline & The Robot] (1986).

SCIENCE-FICTION
Pierre Pelot

LES MANGEURS D'ARGILE

LES HOMMES SANS FUTUR

The 1980s

The 1980s saw the end of the boom of the 1970s and a retrenchment of science fiction. It was also a decade of transition.

The political experimentations of the "new wave" science fiction of the 1970s eventually ended, for the most part because of its lack of commercial success. The election of a socialist president, François Mitterand, in 1981 demonstrated that left-wing ideology was not the *panacea* for France's ills and put to rest the overwhelming utopian influence of May 1968. Also, the overly political books were ultimately rejected by all readers, except for a small circle of fans. As the commercial boom ended, publishers were forced to refocus on what actually sold in the marketplace.

Another generation of new writers emerged; these were more likely to follow their own voices, and less encumbered by the baggage of previous generations, who had had to stick together to face a hostile literary world. The success of *Star Wars* and other big-budget sci-fi pictures meant that science fiction had now become part of the cultural mainstream. It was easier than ever for a number of writers to leave the confining economic restrictions of the dedicated imprints and turn to more general and financially rewarding outlets.

Indeed, one of the most notable experiments of the decade was the *Limites* group, comprised of authors such as Emmanuel Jouanne and Antoine Volodine. *Limites* attempted to merge science fiction with highly stylized general literature, as a reaction against both traditional space opera and the political "new wave" of the 1970s. By cutting itself off from the genre's popular roots, however, *Limites* ultimately failed to enlist enough readers to become a commercially viable proposition.

The Publishers

The 1980s saw the progressive disappearance of most of the imprints that had been launched, often too quickly, in the 1970s:

The emblematic imprint of the post-1968 generation, Kesselring's *Ici & Maintenant*, was cancelled in 1980.

Marabout's *Science-Fiction* and the Librairie des Champs-Élysées's *Le Masque-Science-Fiction* were cancelled in 1981.

Garry's *Mémoires d'Outre-Ciel* and the Presses de la Cité's *Futurama* were cancelled in 1982.

Lattès' *Titres SF* and Casterman's *Autres Temps, Autres Mondes* were cancelled in 1983.

Calmann-Levy's *Dimensions* and Albin Michel's *Science-Fiction* were cancelled in 1984.

OPTA's *Galaxie-Bis* was cancelled in 1988.

Fiction, the one magazine that had been the most dominant voice of the French science fiction community since 1953, was cancelled in February 1990.

The most active imprint remained Fleuve Noir's *Anticipation*, which, under the editorship of Patrick Siry, managed to attract authors like Michel Jeury in 1980, Joël Houssin and Daniel Walther in 1981, Serge Brussolo in 1982, Jacques Mondoloni and Jean-Pierre Andrevon in 1984, and Jean-Marc Ligny in 1988. It also fostered new talents such as Michel Pagel, Alain Paris, Roland C. Wagner and Michel Honaker.

Under Elisabeth Gille's editorship, *Présence du Futur* continued to publish some of the best French science fiction of the decade: Jean-Pierre Andrevon, Pierre Pelot, Jean-Pierre Hubert and new authors such as Serge Brussolo and Jean-Marc Ligny. *Présence du Futur* championed the efforts of *Limites*, publishing the works of Emmanuel Jouanne, Antoine Volodine, Francis Berthelot and the group's anthology, *Malgré le Monde* [In Spite of the World] (1987). Gille left the editorship of *Présence du Futur* in 1986 and was replaced by Jacques Chambon.

The other three major imprints, Gérard Klein's *Ailleurs & Demain*, Jacques Sadoul's *Science Fiction* at J'ai Lu and Jacques Goimard's *Science Fiction* at Presses-Pocket, published some French authors, such as Emmanuel Jouanne, Michel Jeury, Pierre Pelot and Vladimir Volkoff, but on a more occasional basis.

Major Authors

One of the most important genre writers to come out of the 1980s was the prolific Serge Brussolo. He relied on powerful visual imagery rather than on conventionally structured plots, disturbing images rather than original characters, strikingly original and bizarre ideas rather than standard concepts. His strength lay in the accumulation of dark, sometimes obscene, often disgusting, details. The author constantly straddled the line between horror and science fiction, thrillers and fantasy. He received the French Science Fiction Grand Prize for his short story "*Funnyway*" in 1978, published in Philippe Curval's anthology, *Futurs au Présent* [Present-Day Futures], about a surreal prison-maze, and for his first collection of short stories, *Vue en Coupe d'une Ville Malade* [Cut-Out View of a Sick City] (1980), published by *Présence du Futur*. There, he followed it with *Aussi Lourd que le Vent* [Heavy as the Wind] (1981), *Sommeil de Sang* [Sleep of Blood] (1982), featuring a decadent society of carnivores who eat the flesh of fabulous animals frozen inside mountains; *Portrait du Diable en Chapeau Melon* [Portrait of the Devil Wearing a Bowler Hat] (1982), another striking novel exploring the world of *Funnyway*; and *Le Carnaval de Fer* [The Iron Carnival] (1983), the tale of a grim pilgrimage in a dark fantasy world.

During the same period, the author penned a juvenile genre novel, *Les Sentinelles d'Almoha* [The Sentinels of Almoha] (1981) for Nathan, revised in 1994 for publication in *Anticipation*, and *Traque-La-Mort* [Death Tracker] (1982) for *Titres SF*, also taking place in the Almohan universe and featuring men functioning as living bombs. He then embarked on a series of very dark thrillers, but simultaneously began producing a steady flow of genre novels—twenty-seven in total until 1989—for *Anticipation*. He began with *Les Mangeurs de Murailles* [The Eaters of Walls] (1982), about a bunker-like cubic city threatened by giant termites, Other notable titles include *Territoire de Fièvre* [Fever Land] (1983), taking place in the Almohan universe, featuring a planet-sized beast floating in space; *Les Lutteurs Immobiles* [The Motionless Fighters] (1983); taking the concept of the protection of inanimate objects to its limits, i.e.: if someone breaks an object, one of his bones is broken as punishment. Monstrous worlds where men are the victims of ghastly plagues, mutations and inexplicably hostile environment were featured in *Les Bêtes Enracinées* [The Rooted Beasts] (1984); *Ce Qui Mordait Le Ciel...* [What Bit the Sky...] (1984) and its sequel, *Crache-Béton* [Spit-Concrete] (1984), in which a disease causes people to literally spit gravel; and the trilogy of the *Cycle des Ouragans* [Saga of the Storms] (1985-86), taking place in the Almohan universe, on the planet Santal, plagued by terribly destructive winds. There, a teenage girl, Nathalie, and her Dobermann, Cedric, encounter slaughterhouse concerts and are pursued by from mad priests. Novels about mercilessly hostile futures included the award-winning series *Les Soldats de Goudron* [The Tar Soldiers] (4 volumes; 1984-87), with its underwater subway, cannibal ambulances and inextinguishable fires; *Enfer Vertical en Approche Rapide* [Vertical Hell Rapidly Approaching] (1986), with its tower-like prison of Shaka-Kandarec where convicts can be set free if they win twenty ghastly trials, one for each floor of the tower; and *Danger Parking Miné!* [Danger: Mined Parking!] (1986), where concrete is poured inside buildings to kill the homeless.

In the late 1980s, Brussolo returned to *Présence du Futur* with a new series of brilliant novels, just as horrific as ever, and always exploring biological themes, such as *Procédure d'Évacuation Immédiate des Musées Fantômes* [Procedure for the Immediate Evacuation of the Phantom Museums] (1987), in which the souls of the departed are used as an energy source; *Le Château d'Encre* [The Ink Castle] (1988), featuring shadows serving as medical symbiotes; *L'Homme aux Yeux de Napalm* [The Man With Napalm Eyes] (1989), a grim, hallucinatory Christmas tale; *Le Syndrome du Scaphandrier* [The Deep Sea Diver's Syndrome] (1992); and *Mange-Monde* [World-Eater] (1993), a collection of short stories.

In the 1990s, Brussolo diversified his production even further: more thrillers, including the *Conan Lord* series a the Librairie des Champs-Élysées; more horror novels, and some dark fantasies under the pseudonym of "Kitty Doom" at *Présence du Futur*; as well as some mainstream and historical fiction. He returned to *Anticipation* in 1992 with a few genre novels, such as *Rinocérox*, about berseker-like robot tanks; and *Capitaine Suicide* [Captain Suicide] (1992), about a living planet.

One of the major genre achievements of the 1980s was G.-J. Arnaud's prodigious, award-winning series, *La Compagnie des Glaces* [The Ice Company] published at *Anticipation*, starting with *La Compagnie des Glaces* [The Ice Company] (1980).[245] *The Ice Company* is the sprawling saga of a future Earth under a new Ice Age. Mankind lives in domed cities, connected by extended rail networks, controlled by powerful companies which effectively rule the world. This new Ice Age was created when the Moon exploded and the resulting debris blocked all of the Sun's light. Civilization collapsed, and, after several centuries of barbarism, the age of the Ice Companies eventually arose. Their rail networks carry power as well as trains. That world is ruled by a variety of powerful organizations, such as the sect-like Dispatchers' Guild, the Church of the Neo-Catholics, and others. On the ice shelf live tribes of mysterious, red-furred humanoids who can stand the freezing cold, and whose origins are a baffling mystery. A scientist, Lien Rag, embarks on an odyssey to discover the secret origins of his world. As the series progresses, other

---

[245] Black Coat Press, ISBN 978-1-935558-31-6.

major characters are established: the Gnome, a circus dwarf who goes on to set up the powerful Ice Shelf Company on top of the frozen Pacific; Lady Diana, the head of the Transamerican Company and one of the few persons to know the secrets origins of the world; Yeuse, the beautiful cabaret singer who eventually reaches a position of power; Kurts the pirate, a mutant with a powerful computerized rogue locomotive; etc. Lien's quest eventually takes him into space, where all the secrets of his world are at last revealed. Reclaiming Earth from its frozen state then became the focus of his adventures. For its sheer scope and ambition, and unrivalled craftsmanship, *The Ice Company* ranks with such established masterpieces as *Foundation* and *Dune*. It quickly became a bestseller, won the 1982 French science fiction Grand Prize, spawned a popular role-playing game, and was awarded its own dedicated imprint in 1988. The author reached a conclusion of sorts with Volume 62, *Il Était Une Fois La Compagnie Des Glaces* [Once Upon a Time, The Ice Company] (1992), but then went on to write new stories taking place several centuries earlier in a new series entitled *Chroniques Glaciaires* [Ice Chronicles] (11 volumes, 1996-2000), as well as continuing the original saga after a fictional break of fifteen years in *La Compagnie des Glaces – Nouvelle Époque* (24 volumes, 2001-05).

During the 1980s, *Présence du Futur* introduced several major new authors of the decade.

The most notable of these was Jean-Marc Ligny, who had also appeared in Curval's anthology, *Futurs au Présent* [*Present-Day Futures*]. His first novel, *Temps Blancs* [*White Times*], was published in 1979 and featured a city governed by powerful computers which also regulated time itself. Outside was a white, icy wilderness inhabited by mutants and telepathic wolves. The author continued to pen a series of dark, pessimistic novels throughout the 1980s. *Biofeedback* (1979) was about a near-future world caught in the madness of a giant computer; *Furia!* (1982) was the first in a series of novels influenced by rock music; *Yurlunggur* (1987) showed the Australian Aborigenes' eponymous dream-snake invading the grim reality of the modern Paris suburbs; *D.A.R.K.* (1988) was a nihilistic vision of World War III.

In 1988, Ligny began to write novels for *Anticipation*, starting with two collaborations with filmmaker Dominique Goult, *Kriegspiel* and *Dreamworld* (1988), followed by his series *Les Voleurs de Rêves* [*The Stealers of Dreams*] (6 volumes; 1989-90); the trilogy of *Op Tao* (1990), which continued in the series, *Chroniques des Nouveaux Mondes* [Chronicles of the New Worlds] (4 more volumes, 1991), taking place in a galactic civilization where mankind cohabits with two other alien species. Other notable novels included *Aqua* (1993) and *Cyberkiller* (1993) for *Anticipation*; the award-winning *Inner City* (1996), a cyberpunk novel for J'ai Lu; and *Slum City* (1996), a YA/RPG novelization for *Vertige*.

Emmanuel Jouanne was one of the founders of *Limites*. He tried to bring science fiction and mainstream literature closer together by writing several highly literary, poetic works that emphasized style over content. His first novel, *Damiers Imaginaires* [Imaginary Squares] (1982), published by *Présence du Futur*, featured a future mankind living in vast, floating palaces which moved like chess pieces on an invisible board in an unfathomable game. His next novel, *Nuage* [Cloud] (1983), published by *Ailleurs & Demain*, was a variation on *Solaris*, i.e.: a world materializing people's unconscious desires; in this case, only Prune, a little girl, was able to adapt and survive. The author then returned to *Présence du Futur* for a series of stylistically striking novels and short story collections, such as *Ici Bas* [*Down here*] (1984); *Dites-le avec des Mots* [Say It With Words] (1985), co-written with Jean-Pierre Vernay; *Cruautés* [Cruelties] (1987), *Terre* [Earth] (1988), *Le Rêveur de Chats* [The Dreamer of Cats] (1988) and *La Trajectoire de la Taupe* [The Mole's Trajectory] (1989).

The major female writer of the decade was Joëlle Wintrebert, whose first novel, *Les Olympiades Truquées* [The Fake Olympics], had originally been published in 1980 in *Ici & Maintenant* (see above), and which won an award in its revised version, published in 1987 by *Anticipation*. The author followed it with *Les Maîtres-Feu* [The Fire Masters] (1982) for J'ai Lu, which featured the adventures of Jordane, a young human linguist, and Beni, a young sentient native dinosaur, on the volcanic planet of Dante. Her next novel, *Chromoville* (1983), also at J'ai Lu, told how various exotic characters were reluctantly forced to foment a revolution in a futuristic city. *Le Créateur Chimérique* [The Chimerical Creator] (1988), still at J'ai Lu, won another award. It takes place on the water world of Farkis, among the native Ouqdars, who worship the goddess Khimer. But nothing is as it seems, and Farkis is ultimately revealed to be an artificial eco-system manipulated by men. Other notable works included *Bébé-Miroir* [Mirror Baby] (1988) for *Anticipation*, a collection of short stories, *Hurlegriffe* [Screamclaw] (1996) and many excellent YA novels.

Amongst the other notable authors of the 1980s were:

Francis Berthelot whose first novel, *La Lune Noire d'Orion* [The Black Moon of Orion] (1980), was a gay-themed space opera for *Dimensions*. The author went on to write two award-winning novels for *Présence du Futur*, the allegorical *La Ville au Fond de l'Oeil* [The City at the Bottom of the Eye] (1986); and *Rivage des Intouchables* [Shore of the Untouchables] (1990), which takes place on the planet Erda-Rann where the sea is a living entity acting as the natives' collective unconscious.

Jacques Barbéri wrote five novels for *Présence du Futur*, starting with *Kosmokrim* (1985), and continuing with *Une Soirée à la Plage* [An Evening at the Beach] (1988), *Narcose* (1989), *Guerre de Rien* [War of Nothing] (1990) and *La Mémoire du Crime* [The Memory of the Crime] (1992). The author also collaborated with Yves Ramonet under the pseudonym of "Oscar Valetti" to pen three space operas for *Anticipation*: *Labyrinth-Jungle*, *L'Ombre et le fléau* [The Shadow and the Scourge] and *Chair inconnue* [Unknown Flesh] (1992-93).

Belgian author Alain Dartevelle made a notable debut in 1984 with *Borg, ou l'Anatomie d'un Monstre* [Borg, or The

Anatomy of a Monster], which was then followed by *Script* (1989), both published at *Présence du Futur*; then an experimental, Kafkaesque novel taking place in the city of Newgorod. *Imago* (1994), published at J'ai Lu, yet another surreal journey through an imaginary city, organized according to the laws of Freudian theories.

Antoine Volodine debuted in 1985 with *Biographie Comparée de Jorian Murgrave* [Comparative Biography of Jorian Murgrave], published at *Présence du Futur*. The book was a mosaic of fragments of texts composing the biography of the eponymous character, who came to Earth after his native world had been destroyed by war, but did not find peace on our planet. Other novels published at *Présence du Futur* included *Un Navire de Nulle Part* [A Ship from Nowhere] (1986), which painted a striking image of Russia submerged under a luxuriant jungle; the award-winning *Rituel du Mépris, Variante Moldscher* [Ritual of Contempt, Moldscher Variation] (1987) and *Des Enfers Fabuleux* [Fabulous Hells] (1987), all of which fit within the *Limites* school. In the 1990s, the author turned his back on science fiction and committed himself entirely to mainstream literature, producing a string of critically acclaimed novels for publisher Minuit. Nevertheless, a few of these, such as *Le Nom des Singes* [The Name of the Apes] (1994), *Le Port Intérieur* [The Inner Harbor] (1996) and *Nuit Banche en Balkhyrie* [White Night in Balkiria] (1997), still contained genre elements.

Michel Pagel's first *Anticipation* novel was *Demain Matin au Chant du Tueur!* [Tomorrow Morning When the Killer Sings] (1984), a post-cataclysmic tale of survival in a France destroyed by earthquakes. The author wrote twenty-two novels for *Anticipation* until *Orages en Terre de France* [Storms Over the Land of France] (1991). Some of these titles were fantasy series, written under both his name and the pseudonym of "Félix Chapel", as well as a vampire novel. Among his more notable science fiction works were *La Taverne de l'Espoir* [The Inn of Hope] (1984), a moving portrayal of a dystopian world; *Le Viêt-Nam au Futur Simple* [Future Tense

Vietnam] (1984), a tale of World War III; *Pour Une Poignée d'Helix Pomatias* [For a Fistful of Helix Pomatias] (1988), a hard-boiled parody; and *Le Cimetière des Astronefs* [The Graveyard of Spaceships] (1991).

Alain Paris wrote thirty-three novels for *Anticipation*, including nine in collaboration with Jean-Pierre Fontana, starting with *Les Bannières de Persh* [The Banners of Persh] (1984), in which an Earth astronaut stranded on an alien world becomes a pawn in a game played by intelligent insects. Their other collaborations included the trilogy of *Les Ravisseurs d'Éternité* [The Ravishers of Eternity] (1984-86), a tale about a post-cataclysmic world where men live in closed cities such as New Jericho; and *Le Désert des Cendres* [The Desert of Ashes] (1992). Alone, Paris penned several other fantasy series, but his more notable science fiction works included *Soldat-Chien* [Dog Soldier] (2 volumes, 1986-87) about a mercenary operating in a dark future; *Reich* (1986), based on the idea that the Nazis had discovered time travel in 1945; and *AWACS* (1993). In 1988, he also penned *Achéron* for publisher Aurore, and *Daïren* for J'ai Lu.

Jacques Mondoloni's first novel was *Je Suis Une Herbe* [I Am an Herb] (1982) for J'ai Lu and featured a mutant vegetable. It was followed by *Papa 1er* [Daddy the 1st.] (1983) for *Présence du Futur*; and the *Goulags Mous* [Soft Gulags] for Anticipation (4 volumes, 1984-87) in which the world was a semi-communist state monitored by telepaths.

Finally, Pierre Stolze enjoyed a cult following for *Le Serpent d'Éternité* [The Serpent of Eternity] (1979) and *Kamtchatka* (1980), both published by OPTA in their *Galaxie-Bis* imprint. Later the author penned the humorous *Marilyn Monroe et les Samourais du Père Noël* [Marilyn Monroe and Santa Claus' Samurais] (1986) for J'ai Lu; and *Intrusions* (1990), a collection of strong, imaginative short stories. Other notable works included *Theophano 960* (1995) for *Anticipation* and *La Maison Usher ne chutera pas* [The House of Usher Shall Not Fall] (1996).

Other Notable Authors

At the very end of the 1970s, as science fiction became more popular, a number of Fleuve Noir authors who had previously been writing espionage and detective thrillers switched to *Anticipation* and began writing genre novels.

The first of these was "Piet Legay" (a pseudonym of Baudoin Chailley) who had acquired a well-deserved reputation writing crisp spy and war thrillers. His first genre novel was *Demonia, Planète Maudite* [Demonia, Cursed Planet] (1977). In total, the author penned fifty-five novels until *Shaan!* (1994). Some of the most notable included *Vega IV* (1978), the story of a forbidden romance between an Earthwoman and an alien, a theme reversed in *Le Défi Génétique* [The Genetic Challenge] (1980). *L'Ultime Test* [The Ultimate Test] (1980) was a clever murder mystery on a planetoid; *Un Monde Si Noir* [Such a Dark World] (1982) and *Elle s'appelait Loan* [Her Name Was Loan] (1982) both featured a beautiful alien woman whose job it was to find human bodies for her people; *Dimension Quatre* [Dimension Four] (1983) was about secret Illuminati living among us who can access another dimension; *Viol Génétique* [Genetic Rape] (1985) has mankind attempt to force a race of alien merfolk into slavery. Later novels were loosely connected through the series *Dossiers Maudits* [Accursed Files], which started with *Mortel Contact* [Deadly Contact] (1987), in which the entire personnel of a space outpost have inexplicably vanished; another notable title in the series is *Les Portes de l'Enfer* [The Gates of Hell] (1987), in which a man is found to be both alive and dead. The series continued for a total of 14 volumes until 1990. Another series was the *Chronos* trilogy (1991) about Earth settlers trying to colonize a new planet.

"Gilles Morris" (a pseudonym of Gilles Dumoulin) had been writing the *Vic Saint-Val* series for Fleuve Noir since 1973 (see above). When it was discontinued in 1979, he naturally switched to Anticipation with *Facteur Vie* [Life Factor] (1979). The author penned a total of fifty-seven genre novels, until *Psychosphère* (1992). Several of these were comprised of trilogies, often published years apart. The most notable included the post-nuclear world of the *Villes-Corolles* [Corolla Cities] (3 vol;umes, 1979-82); *La Nappe Verte* [The Green Slick], in which a living organism attacks planets (3 volumes, 1980-81); *Les Cervoboules* [The Ball-Brains], in which the crew of a spaceship fights living brain creatures (3 volumes, 1981-82); *Les Calins* [The Kitties], about cute alien felines which use their mental powers to take over the world (3 volumes, 1982-83); *Hellium*, about the colonization of an alien world (3 volumes, 1984); *Apocalypse* (3 volumes, 1984-85); *Le Talion*, about an ultra-violent future (3 volumes, 1985-86); *La Medicarchie*, about a future world ruled by doctors (3 volumes, 1986); *Les Oumladrs*, in which Earth is threatened by extra-dimensional beings (3 volumes, 1986); *Les Mitochondres*, about an alien intelligence who tests then gives superpowers to men (3 volumes, 1987).

"Christopher Stork" (a pseudonym of Stéphane Jourat) also made his debut at *Anticipation* in 1979 with *L'Ordre Établi* [The Established Order]. In total, the author wrote forty-seven novels for the imprint until *Alter Ego* (1988). Some of his more notable works included *Achetez Dieu!* [Buy God!] (1980), the description of a world-wide theocracy; *L'Usage de l'Ascenseur est Interdit aux Enfants de Moins de Quatorze Ans Non Accompagnés* [The Use of the Elevator Is Forbidden to Unaccompanied Children Under 14] (1980), which featured a race of alien children who considered adulthood as a disease; *Les Derniers Anges* [The Last Angels] (1981), which showed how Earth's religions were manipulated by aliens; *L'An II de la Mafia* [Year II of the Mafia] (1982), which described a post-cataclysmic USA ruled by the Mafia; *Pièces Détachées* [Spare Parts] (1984), a frightening look at organ smuggling; *Les Lunatiques* [The Lunatics] (1985), a thriller taking place inside a Lunar hospital; and *Billevesées et Calembredaines* [Nonsense and Gobbledygook] (1985), of which the author himself is the hero, against two intelligent insects who have shrunk him to their size. From 1973 to 1988, he also used the pseudonym "Marc Avril" to pen a series of espionage novels written in the first person, about a team of four gifted freelance spies. The series was comprised of over thirty titles, several of which included genre elements: super-weapons, space stations, Nazi conspiracies, devil worshippers, parapsychologists and mediums working for the CIA and KGB, love potion, etc.

Finally, the last prolific author of Fleuve Noir who switched to writing for *Anticipation* in 1979 was "Adam Saint-Moore (a pseudonym of Jacques Douyau), who penned eight novels belonging to a series entitled *Chroniques de l'Ère du Verseau* [Chronicles of the Age of Aquarius] between 1979 and 1985. These depicted the history of a post-nuclear future where Earth was under the domination of a matriarchal society. The author also wrote numerous espionage novels featuring the character *Face d'Ange* [Angel Face]. Some of these included marginal genre elements such as *Face d'Ange, la Dame et l'Ogre* [Angel Face, The Lady & The Ogre] (1976), *Face d'Ange dans le Cercle Magique* [Angel Face in the Magic Circle] (1977) and *Face d'Ange et le Dinosaure* [Angel Face & The Dinosaur] (1979).

Michel Honaker's first *Anticipation* novel was *Planeta Non Grata* (1983), featuring alien vampire birds holding a world in thrall. The author wrote nineteen novels blending horror and science fiction, until *L'Oreille Absolue* [The Absolute Ear] (1992). Notable titles included *Le Semeur d'Ombres* [The Sower of Shadows] (1985), in which a space outpost is invaded by an alien plant; *Lumière d'Abîme* [Light from the Abyss] (1985), in which regulators hunt missing clones; *Building* (1987), about a planet-wide city; and the *Vorkul* trilogy (1986-87), about mysterious aliens with strange powers. In 1989, with *Bronx Ceremonial,* the author brought to *Anticipation* his character of *Commander Ebenezer Graymes*, a grim devil-hunter initially created for *Media 1000* and continued the series there.

Hugues Douriaux was one of *Anticipation*'s steady providers of fantasy novels, his first being *Les Démoniaques de*

Kallioh [The Demons of Kallioh] (2 volumes, 1984-85), in which an alien princess and her Terran lover fight demon-like beings. The author's science fiction titles included the aptly-entitled *Galax-Western* (1985); *P.L.U.M. 66-50* (2 volumes, 1986), about a female android from Vega-II on the run on Earth; *Tragédie Musicale* [Musical Tragedy] (1986), a sci-fi rock tale of murder and revenge; *Vermine* [Vermin] (1987); *Syndrome Apocalypse* (1989), *Roche-Lalheue* (1991), *Malterre* (1992), *Symphonie Pastorale* [Pastoral Symphony] (1993), *Warrior* (1994) and *Interférences* (1996). In total, he produced thirty-eight novels for Fleuve Noir.

Th. Cryde (a pseudonym of Cédric Debarbieux) wrote five novels for *Anticipation* between 1984 and 1993, including the *Insects* trilogy (1984-85) about mutated insects which end up creating a third race, half-insect, half human.

Thierry Lassalle wrote *Nord* [North] (1984) and *La Piste du Sud* [Trail of the South] (1986) for *Anticipation*, which make up a single novel in which the son of a Southern King escapes from the frigid North.

Gilbert Picard contributed four novels to *Anticipation* in 1985 and 1986, including *Le Miroir du Passé* [The Mirror of the Past] (1985), about a mirror showing images from the past; and *Le Volcan des Sirènes* [The Mermaids' Volcano] (1985) and *Les Combattants des Abysses* [The Fighters of the Abyss] (1986) which take place in the post-cataclysmic world of the 26th century when survivors try to build a new, underwater society

Claude Ecken (a pseudonym of Claude Eckenschwiller) wrote six novels for *Anticipation*, including *La Mémoire Totale* [The Total Memory] (1986), about an amnesia plague; the *Chroniques Télématiques* [Telematic Chronicles], about a hyper-computerized future (1987); *L'Ère du Pyroson* [The Pyroson Era] (2 volumes, 1989); and *Le Cri du Corps* [The Body Scream] (1990).

Gérard Delteil (a pseudonym of Gérard Folio), who had already written many detective novels for Fleuve Noir, penned four futuristic thrillers, including *Transfert* [Transfer] (1986), about body transfer; *Hors-Jeu* [Out of the Game] (1987) and *Tchernobagne* [Chernocamp] (1989).

Guy Charmasson, whose previous genre credits included *Le Crépuscule des Surhommes* [The Twilight of the Supermen] published by Marabout in 1978, began writing for *Anticipation* in 1986 with *L'Heure Perdue* [The Lost Hour]. He penned four novels, including *Les Tueurs d'Elmendorf* [The Killers of Elmendorf] (2 volumes, 1988).

Patrice Duvic, whose first novel was *Poisson-Pilote* [Pilot Fish] published by *Présence du Futur* in 1979, wrote *Naissez, Nous Ferons le Reste* [Be Born, We'll Take Care of the Rest] for Presses-Pocket in 1979 and novelized his script for the motion picture *Terminus* for J'ai Lu in 1982.

The eclectic Jean-Pierre Vernay published *L'Enfer en ce Monde* [Hell in This World] (1980) at Ponte Mirone; and *Fragments du Rêve* [Dream Fragments] (1989) for *Présence du Futur*.

The twin hosts of the popular television show, *Temps X*, Igor & Grichka Bogdanoff, penned *La Machine Fantôme* [The Ghost Machine] (1985) for J'ai Lu, and *La Mémoire Double* [The Double Memory] (1989), as well as a study on the perception and definition of science fiction by mainstream personalities, *L'Effet Science-Fiction* [The Science Fiction Effect] (1979).

Titres SF published two striking genre novels by guitarist and film director Marc Bourgeois, *Altiplano* (1980), about a baroque future Earth, and *Vautours* [Vultures] (1982), which took on a space colony threatened by native flying creatures.

Titres SF also published Michel Calonne's *Hurleville* [Screamcity] (1981), about a future Europe threatened by a new ice age. The author had previously published a collection, *Le Plus Jeune Fils de l'Écureuil* [The Squirrel's Youngest Son] (1958), which included several genre stories, and a novel, *Une Folie au Bord de la Mer* [A Folly at the Sea Shore] (1960), in which a new construction material was used to build a futuristic, sixteen-story residence.

Garry's short-lived *Mémoires d'Outre-Ciel* imprint published works by "Yves Dermèze" (a.k.a. Paul Béra), "Red Ilan" (a.k.a. Daniel Piret), "Lionel Rex" (a.k.a. Maurice Limat), "Roy Morrisson" (a.k.a. Robert Clauzel), plus Maurice Merault, with *Meurtres Transtemporels* [Transtemporal Murders] (1980) and *L'Être de la Grande Spirale* [The Being From the Great Spiral] (1982); Janine Renaud, with *La Base Interdite* [The Forbidden Base] (1979) and *Les Suppliciés d'Iryknos* [The Tortured Men of Iryknos] (1982); and Guadalcazar, with *Le Dernier Combat* [The Last Battle] (1979) and *Xirlo* (1980).

Franchised paperback series such as *The Executioner*, *The Destroyer*, and their French counterparts, Malko Linge a.k.a. *S.A.S.*, sold in huge numbers through newstands and paperback bookstores. This extended to science-fiction with dedicated imprints devoted to *Perry Rhodan*, *Blade*, E.C. Tubb's *Dumarest* and Jimmy Guieu's characters. Three new genre imprints were added:

Jag le Félin [Jag the Feline], published under the house name of "Zeb Chillicothe", was started in 1985 by Christian Mantey, and included thirty-four volumes as of 1994. While the author wrote and/or plotted the majority of the series, some were written in collaboration with Serge Brussolo, Pierre Dubois, Joël Houssin and Jacques Barbéri. Jag was a fierce warrior in a futuristic, post-cataclysmic Earth, devastated by the realisation that the universe was no longer expanding but contracting.

Russ Norton, published under the house name of "Terence Corman" and "Don A. Seabury", was started in 1987 by Richard D. Nolane (a pseudonym of Olivier Raynaud). Only six volumes were published. It was a post-nuclear saga taking place in world plagued by mutants and monsters.

Other notable works were *Adonai* (2 volumes; 1984-85) by "Michaël Clifden" (a pseudonym of Hervé Jaouen); *Quand Souvenirs Revenir, Nous Souffrir et Mourir* [When Memories Return, We Suffer and Die] (1986) by Jean-Michel Dagory; and *Roulette Russe* [Russian Roulette] (1985) by Daridjana (a pseudonyme of Vladimir V. Bodianski), all published by *Anticipation*; and Maurice Mourier's *Parcs de Mémoire* [Memory Park] (1985) at *Présence du Futur*.

Mainstream Authors

Perhaps the most surprising mainstream author to write genre fiction during the 1980s was famous writer, economist and politician Jacques Attali, a special advisor to French President François Mitterand, who penned a series of themed novels including *La Figure de Fraser* [Fraser's Figure] (1984) and, especially, *La Vie Éternelle* [Eternal Life] (1989), a novel in which space travelers stranded on an alien world replay mankind's history.

Professor Rémy Chauvin, a renowned popular psychologist, penned a number of genre novels on the cutting-edge of science and philosophy, such as *Voyage Outre-Terre* [Journey Beyond Earth] (1983), *Les Veilleurs du Temps* [The Time Watchers] (1984) and *Le Nouveau Golem* [The New Golem] (1993).

Other notable genre works published in mainstream imprints included:

André Audureau's *Feminapolis* (1979), a novel in which women rule the world.

Le Dernier de l'Empire - K'harmattour [The Last of the Empire] (1981) by Senegal author Smbeme Ousmane, a fascinating two-volume African political fiction.

Michel Braudeau's *Fantôme d'une Puce* [Ghost of a Chip] (1982), a cyberpunk tale ahead of its time.

Michel Arrivé's *L'Horloge sans Balancier* [The Clock Without Pendulum] (1983), the diary of a mutant.

René Dzagoyan's *Le Système Aristote* (1984).

And, finally, Alain Nadaud with *L'Envers du Temps* [The Other Side of Time] (1985), a wonderful novel in which a Roman legionary discovers that time was running backwards.

The YAs

The popularity of *Star Wars* and other media products ensured that genre concepts showed up with increasing regularity in YA and children's books published throughout the decade.

One of the best authors of the period was Thérèse Roche, who won the 1984 YA category of the French science fiction award for her series of humorous, creative novels about children and alien lifeforms, published by Magnard. Among her best titles were *Garlone et les Snils* [Garlone & The Snils] (1982), *Le Naviluk* (1983), *Les Extra-Chats* [The Extra-Cats] (1984), *Lily Moon et la Lucarne* [Lily Moon & The Small Window] (1988) and *Appoline et la Porte du Temps* [Appoline & The Gate of Time] (1989).

Joëlle Wintrebert made a notable entry in the genre with *Nunatak* (1983), published by Casterman. She then continued to produce a series of colorful YA novels characterized by their skillful handling of difficult or sophisticated themes. Her best works included *La Fille de Terre Deux* [The Girl from Earth-Two] (1987), *L'Océanide* (1992), the award-winning *Les Diables Blancs* [The White Devils] (1993), *Les Ouraniens de Brume* [The Ouranians of Mist] (1996) and *Les Gladiateurs de Thule* [The Gladiators of Thule] (1997).

Maurice Bitter wrote the time-traveling adventures of *Les Robinsons du Temps* [The Robinsons of Time], published by La Farandole, starting in 1982.

Emmanuel Baudry and Alain Royer's penned the adventures of *Les Invisibles* [The Invisibles], also starting in 1982.

Jean Chalopin & Nina Wolmark novelized the popular animated series transplanting the tale of Ulysses into the 31st century, *Ulysse 31* (1982).

Lucien-Guy Touati and Claude Rose penned *Guillou dans les Étoiles* [Guillou Among the Stars] (1979).

René Escudié wrote *L'Enfant qui avait accroché la Lune* [The Child Who Had Hooked the Moon] (1980) and *La Charrette à Traverser le Temps* [The Time-Traveling Cart] (1982).

Dominique Peko wrote *La Planète des Norchats* [Planet of the Norcats] (1981).

René Durand penned *Ludine de Terrève* (1981).

Georges Goetz wrote *L'Efface-Temps* [The Time Eraser] (1983).

Valérie Groussard wrote *Caravane Interstellaire* [Interstellar Caravan] (1984) and *Le Tour de Xrom* [The Tower of Xrom] (1986).

And, finally, Michel Lamart penned *Le Rire du Robot dans les Champs Magnétiques* [The Laughter of the Robot in the Magnetic Fields] (1984).

LAURENT GENEFORT
LA COMPAGNIE DES FOUS

SPACE
FLEUVE NOIR

The 1990s

The fourth and last chronological sub-division of this book runs from the late-1980s to about 2000. It was characterized by a new, more modest, upswing in authors and publishing, as well as a return to more traditional story-telling techniques—in other words, a decade of recovery for French science fiction.

Commercially, the genre regained some of the ground it had lost during the 1980s. By the late 1990s, with slightly over one hundred new novels per year, and numerous new authors and magazines, French science fiction was both quantitatively and qualitatively flourishing again.

Creatively, a new generation of writers generally returned to more conventional themes and narratives, ensuring greater readability. The influence of American science fiction, was pronounced, and yet more fully assimilated, leading to novels that could arguably compete with the best of American production.

The Publishers

In 1992, Fleuve Noir split its classic *Anticipation* imprint into five sub-imprints: *Legend*, devoted to fantasy; *Space*, for space operas; *Métal*, for cyberpunk, *Delirius*, for satire; and finally, *Panik*, for horror sf. In 1997, it finally discontinued its numbering and started from scratch with a new imprint simply called *SF*, comprised of five new sub-imprints: *Zone Rouge*, *Métal*, *Space*, *Polar* and *Mystère*, the latter two devoted to mystery-themed science fiction. Throughout this period, editors such as Daniel Riche, Nicole Hibert and Philippe Hupp managed to foster a slate of new talents, such as Ayerdhal,

Richard Canal, Serge Lehman, Roland C. Wagner, Jean-Claude Dunyach, Laurent Genefort, and Alain le Bussy.

At Denoël, Jacques Chambon continued to edit *Présence du Futur*, publishing new works by Joël Houssin, Serge Brussolo, Dominique Douay and André Ruellan. He also added two new imprints, *Présence du Fantastique* and the more literary-aimed *Présences*.

At J'ai Lu, Jacques Sadoul published Ayerdhal and Richard Canal.

Gérard Klein at *Ailleurs & Demain*, and Jacques Goimard at Presses-Pocket did not play significant roles in terms of new French authors.

The torch was instead picked up by new publishers, including:

L'Atalante, a small company based in Nantes in Western France, which introduced Pierre Bordage and Paul Borrelli, and also published translations of Terry Pratchett and Michael Moorcock.

Mnemos and Bragelonne published mostly fantasy novels, while Belgian Publisher Claude Lefrancq mostly reprinted classic works by Stéfan Wul, Francis Carsac, etc.

Some new magazines also made their first appearances in the late 1990s: *Bifrost, CyberDreams, Étoiles Vives, Galaxies* and *Ozone*.

Major Authors

One of the best new science fiction writers revealed by *Anticipation* during the 1990s was Ayerdhal. His books formed complex, richly textured, intricate multi-chaptered sagas, taking place in elaborate space empires *à la* Frank Herbert, who was an acknowledged influence. His first saga was *La Bohême et l'Ivraie* (4 volumes, 1990), in which a group of artists challenges the power of the galactic Homeocracy. It was followed by the intricate galactic epic, *Mytale* (3 volumes, 1991); then *Demain, une Oasis* [Tomorrow, an Oasis] (1991);

the two-volume *Le Chant du Drille* [The Drille's Song] (1992); *Cybione* (1992); and, finally, *Polytan* (1993). In 1993, the author moved to J'ai Lu, for which he created the *Dune*-like *Daym Universe* with two brilliant novels, *L'Histrion* (1993) and *Sexomorphoses* (1994). The Daym universe was a galaxy in turmoil, filled with conflicting powers such as the Empire, the Confed, the Nauts, the Scients, the Church and the mystic Taj Ramanes. At the center of the plots and counter-plots was Genesis, the planet-wide living computer, who sought to bring peace to it all. Genesis' tool was Aimlin(e), a two-brained sexomorph whose role was to act as a galactic jester, but whose origins remained shrouded in mystery. For J'ai Lu, the author also wrote *Balade Choreïale* [Choreial Ballad] (1994), a tale exploring the moral and political consequences of exposing a medieval planet to the advanced technology of the Human Federation. Ayerdhal also edited *Génèses* [Genesis] (1996), a remarkable original anthology of modern French science fiction *à la Dangerous Visions*.

Pierre Bordage was, without a doubt, the other major new author of the 1990s. In his trilogy *Les Guerriers du Silence* [The Warriors of Silence] (1993-95), comprised of three 500-page volumes published by L'Atalante, the author recaptured the strengths of Dan Simmons' *Hyperion*. *Les Guerriers du Silence* is a rich and strongly structured space opera, with numerous characters and subplots, telling the story of a Galactic Empire in chaos, threatened by the mysterious alien Scaythes of Hyponeros, the tools of a power which wishes to un-create the universe. Against them stand the eponymous Warriors, a band of reluctant heroes with unique abilities, selected by the forces of Life to save the cosmos. Bordage followed it with *Wang*, a two-volume series taking place in the year 2211 on a planet not unlike ours, divided into two worlds separated by a mysterious "curtain". Wealth and technological comfort exist on its Western side, savagery and poverty reign on its Eastern side. The hero, Wang, breaks the law of Assol, an Eastern clan leader, and is condemned to exile in the West. He crosses the Curtain at Most, a town located in Bohemia, unaware of what exists on the other side, for no one has ever before returned from the West. *Wang* won the 1997 Best Novel award for the Eiffel Tower Prize.

Richard Canal wrote exotic, poetic and intriguing novels influenced by African traditions. (He lived in Senegal for a time.) His earlier works included *La Malédiction de l'Éphémère* [The Curse of the Ephemereal] (1986), in which aliens interested in mankind's arts kept it prisoner within the solar system; the *Animamea* trilogy (1986-87); and *La Guerre en ce Jardin* [The War in This Garden] (1991), both published by *Anticipation*; and *Villes-Vertiges* [Vertigo-Cities] (1988) by Aurore. In 1990, he began producing a series of major novels for J'ai Lu, starting with the award-winning trilogy *Swap-Swap* (1990), *Ombres Blanches* [White Shadows] (1993), *Aube Noire* [Black Dawn] (1994), in which racial and economic conflicts tore up a near-future grain-producing Africa and industrially exhausted America. Other works included *Le Cimetière des Papillons* [The Graveyard of the Butterflies] (1995) and *Les Paradis Piégés* [The Trapped Paradises] (1997), also published by J'ai Lu.

Serge Lehman's first novel was *La Loi Majeure* [The Major Law] (1990), written under the pseudonym of "Don Herial" for *Anticipation*. It became the first volume of a trilogy entitled *La Guerre des Sept Minutes* [The Seven-Minute War] (1990) that remained uncompleted. The author's next novel, *Espion de l'Étrange* [Spy of the Weird] (1992), was signed "Karel Dekk", which was also the name of the book's protagonist. During the four years that followed, the author wrote mostly short stories. In 1995, he published his fourth novel, *Le Haut-Lieu* [The High Place], followed by a collection of short stories, *La Sidération* (1996). In 1996, Fleuve Noir launched Lehman's latest series, *F.A.U.S.T.* (3 volumes, 1996-97) in its own dedicated imprint. This series was set at the beginning of the 21st century, when two huge megacorps join forces to take over the world. The self-styled "Defenders" was a group of men and women dedicated to fight them. Other works, also published by Fleuve Noir, included a *F.A.U.S.T.*

spin-off, *Wonderland* (1997), the colorful tale of a near-future garbage dump, and *L'Ange des Profondeurs* [The Angel of the Depth] (1997), the first of a new series featuring *Martin Dirac*, a man haunted by the disappearance of his father, whose quest brings him face to face with the secrets behind modern myths such as lycanthropy, Hollow Earth, etc. In 1998, the author also edited *Escales sur l'Horizon* [Stopovers Over the Horizon] for Fleuve Noir, an original anthology devoted to modern French SF.

Roland C. Wagner discovered science fiction through *Anticipation* in the 1960s and grew up to become one of its most prolific and popular writers in the 1990s. The author's novels blended humor, action and rock music weirdness, in a fast-paced, easy to read narrative. His first novel was *Le Serpent d'Angoisse* [The Terror Snake] (1987), later incorporated into the series *Histoire du Futur Proche* [Tales of the Near Future] (see below). He wrote nineteen novels for Fleuve Noir, including the following series: *Le Faisceau Chromatique* [The Chromatic Cluster] (4 volumes, 1988-91). *Poupée aux Yeux Morts* [Dead-Eyed Doll] (3 volumes, 1988), the story of Kerl, an astronaut who returns to Earth after a fifty-year cosmic journey, only to be confronted by several mysteries, such as, why did he age fifty years and his girlfriend who stayed on Earth did not. Guided by a Fouinain, a cartoon-like alien, Kerl embarks on a complex journey of discovery that ends with a battle between two Gestalt entities, one embodying the forces of neo-puritanism, tyranny and repression, the other the future of mankind among the stars. The third volume of *Poupée aux Yeux Morts*, entitled *Les Futurs Mystères de Paris* [The Future Mysteries of Paris], gave its name to his most-popular series (1996-97), featuring the adventures of private detective Tem (short for "Temple Sacré de l'Aube Radieuse" [Sacred Temple of the Radiant Dawn]), a mutant who has the power of going unnoticed. Tem is not invisible, just "transparent" to other people. The series took place in 2063, fifty years after the mysterious "Great Terror" which shook up civilization.

Wagner's other series included *Histoire du Futur Proche* [Tales of the Near Future] (4 volumes, 1987-89); *La Sinsé Gravite au 21* [The Sinsey GravitatesaAt 21] (2 volumes, 1991), written under the pseudonym of "Red Deff"; *Les Psychopompes de Klash* [The Psychopumps of Klash] (1990), a space opera, (originally written as "Red Deff", but recently reprinted under Wagner's own name.) The author also used the pseudonym of "Richard Wolfram", to pen a parodic series of short stories making fun of French fandom, collected in *Quelqu'un Hurle Mon Nom* [Someone Howls My Name] (1993), and numerous novels published under Jimmy Guieu in hat imprint.

Jean-Claude Dunyach's first published book, *Autoportrait* [Self-Portrait], published by *Présence du Futur* in 1986, was a collection of poetic, sensitive stories. He made his mark at *Anticipation* with the award-winning trilogy *Étoiles Mortes* [Dead Stars] (1991-92). In it, giant alien creatures the size of a city enable mankind to reach the stars, but only wealthy people can use their services. Another notable work was *Roll Over, Amundsen* (1993).

Laurent Genefort is a prolific writer whose first novel for *Anticipation* was *Le Bagne des Ténèbres* [The Penitentiary of Darkness] (1988), the first volume in the *Vangke Universe*, a series taking place in the far future, when the eponymous, mysterious alien race has left behind strange artefacts. The series also featured another mysterious race, the godlike Yuweh, who had the power to build worlds. The title in the series included *Le Monde blanc* [The White World] (1992), *Les Peaux épaisses* [The Thick Skins] (1992), *Haute Enclave* [High Enclave] (1993), *La Troisième Lune* [The Third Moon] (1994) and *L'Homme qui n'existait plus* [The Man Who No Longer Existed] (10996). Another notable series connected to the *Vangke Universe* was *Interregnum* trilogy (1992-94), which included the award-winning *Arago* (1993). The author's masterpiece was the two-volume *L'Opéra de l'Espace* [The Space Opera] (1993) in which an opera singer, after losing his voice, embarks on a quest to find a Yuweh who might help him regain what he had lost. During his travels, he assembled a company of various other artists. Genefort's novels emphasized adventure and action and displayed his concern for ecology. He was particularly skilled at building colorful yet believable alien worlds and cultures. In total, he wrote twenty-one novels for *Anticipation*.

Belgian author Alain le Bussy was an active member of French fandom for years before finally publishing his first novel, the award-winning *Deltas*, in *Anticipation* in 1992. It was the first volume of the *Aqualia trilogy* (1992-93), the story of a one-legged space pilot. His other works included *Deraag* (1993), *Garmalia* (1994), *Quête Impériale* [Imperial Quest] (1994), *Soleil Fou* [Mad Sun] (1995) and *Équilibre* [Balance] (1997), the story of a water world which was the sole meeting point between mankind and an alien reptilian race.

After studying psychology and being a keyboard player for a free-jazz band in the 80s, Paul Borrelli decided to become a writer. His first novel, *L'Ombre du Chat* [The Shadow of the Cat], published by L'Atalante in 1994, was a detective story set in a future Marseille. The hero is an illegal weapon manufacturer who is suspected of being a serial killer and has to find the real murderer. *Désordres* [*Disorders*] (1997) was yet another serial killer story, featuring some of the same characters. The novels were remarkable for their numerous details.

Finally, Swiss writer Wildy Petoud wrote *La Route des Soleils* [The Road of the Suns] (1994) for *Anticipation*. It was a space opera filled with parodic elements, but offering a subtler and more complex read. *Tigre au Ralenti* [Tiger in Slow Motion], published by *Destination Crépuscule* in 1996, told a strange and unsettling story, fascinating in the way it was told and structured.

Other Notable Authors

Other notable writers who came out of the 1990s and were published at *Anticipation* included:

Alain Billy, with the series *Le Bateleur*, featuring a futuristic alien hunter (2 volumes, 1994); *L'Orchidée Rouge de Madame Shan* [Mrs. Shan's Red Orchid] (1988), *Maaga-la-Scythe* (1988) and *Les Fruits Sataniques* [Satan's Fruits] (1993).

Gilbert Gallerne (using the pseudonym of "Milan"), with *Le Clone Triste* [The Sad Clone] (1988) and *Le Rire du Klone* [The Klone's Laughter] (1988).

Thomas Bauduret (using the pseudonym of "Samuel Dharma"), with *Traqueur* [Tracker] (1988) and *Nécromancies* (1988).

Bertrand Passegué, with the *Bêta IV Hydri* series (5 volumes, 1988-89), the *Troglo Blues* series (2 volumes, 1991), and *Métacentre* (1992).

François Rahier, with *Le Crépuscule du Compagnon* [The Twilight of the Companion] (1988) and *L'Ouragan des Enfants Dieux* [The Storm of the God Children] (1991).

"Max Anthony" (a pseudonym of Maxime Philippon), with *L'Androïde Livide de l'Asteroïde Morbide* [The Livid Android of the Morbid Asteroid] (1989), *Le Huitième Crystal du Docteur Mygale* [The Eighth Crystal of Doctor Tarentula] (1993) and *Boulevard des Miroirs Fantômes* [Boulevard of the Phantom Mirrors] (1993).

Yves Carl, with *Jhedin Ovoghemma* (1989).

Patrick Lacheze, with *Fleur* [Flower] (1989).

Jean-Claude Lamart, with *Top Niveau* [Top Level] (1989).

Gérard Néry, with a series entitled *1999* (6 volumes, 1989-90) in which Jason Zède, a "trunk-man" who survived a terrible accident, fathers mutant children who plot to take over the planet. Belle, his only natural daughter, discovers his secret and decides to fight her family.

Philippe Guy, with *Dernière Tempête* [Last Tempest] (1989) and *Phalènes* (1996).

Manuel Essard, with a series entitled *Au Nom du Roi* [In the King's Name] (2 volumes, 1991).

Dominique Brotot, with *Penta* (1992), one of the first cyberpunk novels published in France, *Neurovision* (1993) and *Le Voleur d'Organes* [The Organ Thief] (1994).

Marc Lemosquet, with *Plug-In* (1992) and *Cobaye* [Guinea Pig] (1993).

Daniel Ichbiah & Yves Uzureau, with *Xyz* (1993), a purposefuly confusing, satirical, nonsensical novel about a man who is the last hope of humanity and who is sent down to a mysterious planet from which no one has ever returned.

Thierry Pastor, with *Les Yeux de la Terre Folle* [The Eyes of the Mad Earth] (1993).

Christophe Kauffman, with *Nickel le Petit* [Nickel the Small] (1994) and *Jalin Ka* (1994)

Franck Morrisset, with *Alice qui dormait* [Alice Who Slept] (1996) and *La Résolution Andromède* [The Andromeda Resolution] (1997)., in which a woman, Alice Douglas, returns to the world in 2148 after having been frozen for 150 years. She is then robbed of her fortune and has to hire two strange detectives, Campbell and Goren.

Philippe Renford, with *Plus Proche que vous ne Pensez* [Closer Than You Think] (1997), the story of an amnesiac mutant in search of his past and of the purple-eyed woman he loves, set in an apocalyptic background where every plant, animal and insect can be lethal.

Serge Séguret, with his *Zone Rouge* [*Red Zone*] trilogy (1997), about futuristic bikers in a *Damnation Alley*-type world.

The writing team of "G. Elton Ranne" (a pseudonym of Anne & Gérard Guéro, who also used "Ange" to pen some YA novels), with *Double Jeu* [Double Game] (1997) and *Chute Libre* [Free Fall] (1997).

Christian Vilà with *Ice Flyer* (1997).

Other notable authors who emerged during the period at other imprints included:

Gilles Dumay was, for many years, one of the major writers in French science fiction fandom, where he published a great number of short stories. In the late 1980s, he created *Destination Crépuscule*, a small press that grew quickly, first in association with publisher Encrage, an already established company, then by itself, changing its name to Orion in 1997. He also edited the magazine, *Étoiles Vives* [Living Stars]. As he became more involved in editing, his writing became more scarce. He is the author of one novel, *Strange Rock Anathema* (1993).

Other notable authors published by *Destination Crépuscule* included: Guillaume Thiberge with *L'Appel de l'Espace* [The Call from Space] (1996); Nicole Bouchard with *Terminus Fomalhaut* (1997) and Thierry Di Rollo with *Number Nine* (1997).

Another fan turned writer turned publisher was Francis Valéry, also a renowned essayist. His best novel was *Les Voyageurs sans Mémoires* [The Travelers Without Memories], published by *Destination Crépuscule* in 1997. Other notable works included *L'Arche des Rêveurs* [The Ark of the Dreamers] (1991) and *Altneuland* (1995). Valéry then created the imprint *Cyberdreams* at publisher DLM. One of the best authors published there was Sylvie Denis with *Jardins Virtuels* [Virtual Gardens] (1995).

Publisher Mnemos' leading authors were fantasy writer Mathieu Gaborit and Fabrice Colin with *Neuvième Cercle* [Ninth Circle] (1997) and *Les Cantiques de Mercure* [The Canticles of Mercury] (1997), about underground life in 1999 New York.

Another active member of French fandom, Raymond Milési, co-edited the renowned anthology *Mouvance* in the 1980s. His novels included *Chien Bleu Couronné* [Crowned Blue Dog] (1991) at *Anticipation* and *Salut Delcano!* [Hello Delcano!] (1996) and *Futur sans Étoiles* [Starless Future]

(1997), the first two installments in a space opera series, at new publisher SENO.

Another notable SENO author was Éric Cowez with *Island One: L'Arche des Outre-Ciel* [The Ark from Beyond the Sky] (1995) and *Geminga, La Civilisation Perdue* [Geminga, the Lost Civilization] (1996), a Martian space opera taking place in the year 3115.

Convention organizer, fanzine editor, reviewer, radio DJ and short-story writer Jean Millemann wrote *Fumeterre* [Smokey Earth] (1994), a collection of dark science-fantasy stories.

Alain Duret penned *Kronikes de la Fédérasion* [Kronikles of the Federasion] (1997) for Belgian publisher Lefrancq.

Finally, François Tessier, with *Les Foudres de l'Abîme – La Directive Exeter* [The Lightning from The Abyss - The Exeter Directive] (1997), penned the first in a series of futuristic thrillers entitled *Polaris*, published by new publisher Khom-Heidon.

Mainstream Authors

The most astounding success of the decade for a genre novel published in mainstream literature was Bernard Werber's *Les Fourmis* [The Ants] (1991). The author combined his knowledge of ants with a real talent of scientific vulgarization to offer a startling, if anthropomorphized, inside look at the world seen through the eyes of ants. The lack of conventional dramatic structure helped legitimize the novel as something other than science fiction. Two sequels were published, *Le Jour des Fourmis* [The Day of the Ants] (1992) and *La Révolution des Fourmis* [The Revolution of the Ants] (1996). Werber also applied his talents to *Les Thanatonautes* [The Thanatonauts] (1994), a novel dealing with the exploration of what lies beyond death.

Another major genre author was Maurice G. Dantec, whose notorious, best-selling thriller *Les Racines du Mal* [The

Roots of Evil] was published in the famous *Série Noire* crime imprint in 1995, even though it featured cyberpunk themes, such as the recording of the entire contents of a man's mind into a computer and the survival of his electronic personality after his physical death.

Other works in the same vein included René Belletto's *La Machine* (1990), a novel about mind transfer, adapted into an eponymous 1994 film; and some of Serge Brussolo's thrillers, such as the *Conan Lord* series (1995).

Other notable genre works published in mainstream literature included:

Amin Maalouf's *Le Premier Siècle Après Béatrice* [The First Century After Beatrice] (1992), in which a new drug enables women to give birth only to boys.

Jean-Pierre Berbier's *Le Soleil et la Mort en Face* [The Sun and Death in My Face] (1994), in which the hero receives the thoughts of a murderer from the future.

Hervé Bazin's *Le Neuvième Jour* [The Ninth Day] (1994).

Vladimir Makanine's *La Route est Longue* [The Road Is Long] (1994), which described a future world where animals were no longer butchered for food.

Loup Durand's *Le Grand Silence* [The Great Silence] (1994), a novel about telepathy.

And, finally, Tunisian author Alia Marbrouk's *Le Futur est déjà là* [The Future Is Already Here] (1997).

The YAs

The publishing of genre books for children and young adults exploded in the 1990s. New imprints were created such as *Livre de Poche Jeunesse*, *Pleine Lune* [*Full Moon*] and *Vertige*, edited by Denis Guiot, already mentioned.

Classic novels by Stefan Wul were reprinted for a new public; famous authors like Jean-Pierre Andrevon, Michel Honaker, Jean-Marc Ligny, Michel Jeury (in collaboration his daughter Dany), and François Sautereau, all contributed new works.

The most successful genre writers for young adults to have come out of the decade were the writing team of Alain Grousset and Danielle Martinigol (who also used the pseudonym "Kim Aldany") with novels like *Les Oubliés de Vulcain* [Forgotten on Vulcan] (1995), *L'Enfant-Mémoire* [The Memory Child] (1996), *Les Mondes Décalés* [The Out-Of-Line Worlds] (1997) and the popular series of *Kerri & Megane*.

François Appas created the series of *Les Quatre Voyageurs* [The Four Travelers], time-traveling children, for younger readers in 1992 with *Les Quatre Voyageurs à la Poursuite d'Aspirinus* [The Four Travelers Pursue Aspirinus].

Pascal Garnier penned *À rebrousse temps* [Time Backwards] (1993).

Robert Belfiore published *La Pieuvre de Xeltar* [The Octopus of Xeltar] (1995) (co-written with Philippe-Henri Turin) and *Le Maître de Juventa* [The Master of Juventa] (1996).

SERGE LEHMAN

F.A.U.S.T.

F.A.U.S.T.
Fleuve Noir

Afterword: 2022

Hundreds of writers. Thousands of novels. Most with a very distinctive voice. This is a considerable achievement for a country with a population one-fifth that of the United States, and a mainstream environment generally dismissive, if not downright hostile, to science fiction.

Despite the material obstacles thrown in its path, such as having to compete economically and creatively with American and English authors, and the difficulty of making a living from writing genre fiction, French science fiction has known both glorious and difficult times, but always, the flame stayed alive. Its authors, writers of unassailable talent—easily the equals of their English-speaking counterparts—have managed to leave a powerful mark on the history of French literature.

The previous pages were written as the 20th century came to an end. We weren't able to entirely update this book by devoting as much time and space to the last twenty years as we did with the earlier decades, which were written in the late 1990s. However, it is fair to ask what major changes, significant events and new names appeared in French fantasy and supernatural fiction since we brought the original project to a close in 2000.

Here is, then, a brief overview of what we consider to be important occurrences in the field during the last two decades.

First and foremost, book publishing in general took a hit after the economic downturn of 2009. Also, the massive advent of Twitter, Instagram, Facebook, Youtube, Tiktok and other social media, as well as streaming networks like Netflix, has cannibalized precious time that might otherwise have been used to read books, purchasing power that might otherwise have been used to buy them, and even the space necessary to discuss them. It is no exaggeration to say that the art of the book review is. if not totally dead, but on its last legs; besides, even excellent reviews no longer seem to impact sales, as readers are too busy or too distracted to follow up and buy the reviewed item. Yes, there are still best-sellers racking in the big bucks, but what used to be known as the midlist is now gone.

In terms of major influences during the last two decades on French science fiction, one must include the perennial film and television franchises of *Star Wars* and (to a much lesser degree than in the United States) *Star Trek* and *Doctor Who*), and the continuing influence of the *Dune* books published by the *Ailleurs & Demain* imprint (which otherwise became quasi-moribund).

Fantasy (as well as *noir* thrillers, but these are not our object here) were by far the most successful genres of the last two decades. Classic SF such as space opera or futuristic novels were steamrolled out of the marketplace by the growing popularity of other genres, especially fantasy, with the exception of steampunk, which managed to carve itself out a place in the publishing world. Paradoxically, science fiction continued to be co-opted by mainstream literature as had been the case with René Barjavel and Robert Merle previously, with the 2019 French Academy Grand Prize being bestowed upon Laurent Binet's *Civilizations* and the 2020 Goncourt Award going to Hervé Le Tellier *L'Anomalie* [The Anomaly].

The publishers ineluctably mirrored this evolution, concentrating on translations, novelizations and fantasy of various kinds, with the notable exception of L'Atalante, which continued to publish Pierre Bordage, Jean-Claude Dunyach and Roland C. Wagner. In science fiction, for example, Bragelonne published Arthur C. Clarke, Peter F. Hamilton, and Connie Willis; Mnemos, Frank Herbert and A. E. Van Vogt. At Denoël, *Présence du Futur* was cancelled in 2000, reprints being farmed out to Folio SF. *Ailleurs & Demain*, as mentioned above, no longer played a significant role, except to feature the return of Michel Jeury (who passed away in 2015) in 2010 with the remarkable *May le Monde* [May the World]. In 2013, the name "Fleuve Noir" disappeared entirely, the company being folded into its parent, Univers Poche, rebranding itself as *Outrefleuve*, but also no longer playing a major role in the genre. The publishers still laboring in the field included J'ai Lu, Pocket and Pocket Junior/Jeunesse (YAs), Albin Michel's *Imaginaire* (started in 2018), plus a number of smaller presses, the most notable being Argyll, Critic, Les Moutons Électriques, La Volte, and Le Chat Noir.

One notable exception was *Rivière Blanche*, the French-language imprint of Black Coat Press, founded by Jean-Marc Lofficier in 2004 and edited by Philippe Ward until 2019. Rivière Blanche published books harking back to the style of the old Fleuve Noir's *Anticipation* imprint, mixing "old" authors with "new" ones. The former included Jean-Pierre Andrevon; André Caroff (who passed away in 2009), Hugues Douriaux (who passed away in 2018); Paul-Jean Hérault (who passed away in 2020), who made a very successful return in 2004 with *La Fédération de l'Amas* [The Cluster Federation]; Jacques Hoven (who passed away in 2018); Gabriel Jan; Alain le Bussy; Piet Legay, Gilles Morris (who passed away in 2016); Daniel Piret (who passed away in 2020); Max-André Rayjean, Louis Thirion (who passed away in 2011); and Daniel Walther (who passed away in 2018); and the latter, Jean-Michel Archaimbault, with *Seentha* (2009); Alain Blondelon, with *Onde de Choc* [Shockwave] (2009); André Borie, with the *Masas Hirzingue* series (2016-22); X. M. Fleury, with *Oublier les Étoiles* [Forget the Stars] (2021); Jean Christophe Gapdy, with the *SysSol* series (2018-22); Thomas Geha, with the *Alone* series (2005-08); Arnauld Pontier, with the *F.E.L.I.N.E.* series (2017-20); popular stand-up comedian Sellig with the *Koumlak* series (2010-13); Hervé Thiellement (who passed away in 2018), with *Le Dieu était dans la Lune* [The God Was In The Moon] (2011); and Laurent Whale, with *Les Etoiles s'en balancent* [The Stars Don't Care] (2011). As of mid-2022, Riviere Blanche had published 211 science fiction volumes

Some of the major authors of the 1990s who blossomed during the last two decades, reaching an even greater audience, often beyond the limits of the genre, were Ayerdhal (who passed away in 2015), with *Transparences* (2004)and *Rainbow Warriors* (2013); Pierre Bordage, with *InKARMAtions* (2019) and *Metro Paris 2033* (2020-22); and Laurent Genefort, with *Étoiles sans issue* [Stars Without Exits] (2017), *L'Espace entre les guerres* [Space Between Wars] (2020) and *Les Temps ultramodernes* [Ultramodern Times] (2022). Others included Francis Berthelot, with *Carnaval sans Roi* [Kingless Carnival] (2011) and *Abîme du rêve* [Abyss of Dreams] (2015); Maurice G. Dantec (who passed away in 2016), with *Cosmos Incorporated* (2005) and *Satellite Sisters* (2012), a sequel to his controversial *Babylon Babies* (1999); Jean-Claude Dunyach, with the *Troll* trilogy (2015-21); Christian Léourier, with *Helstrid* (2019); Jean-Marc Ligny, with *Les Guerriers du Réel* [The Warriors of Reality] (2007) and *Des Yeux dans le Ciel* [Eyes in the Sky] (2012); Henri Lœvenbruck, with Les Enfants de la Veuve [The Children of the Widow] (2006) and the *Ari MacKenzie* series (2008-13); and Roland C. Wagner (who passed away in 2012), with *La Saison de la Sorcière* [Season of the Witch] (2003) and *Rêves de Gloire* (2011).

The most important new author of the period was Alain Damasio, with *La Zone du Dehors* [The Outside Zone] (2001; rev. 2007), a futuristic technothriller that imagines a new form of democracy; *La Horde du Contrevent* [Windwalkers] (2004), a quest on a world plagued by stormy winds; and *Les Furtifs* [The Furtives] (2019), the story of a father looking for his daughter, taken by invisible beings. All three were major commercial successes beyond the usual genre readership.

Other new authors included Sabrina Calvo, with *Wonderful* (2001) and *Toxoplasma* (2017); Nadia Coste, with the YA series *SpeaceLeague* (2013-14) and *Ascenseur pour le Futur* [Elevator to the Future] (2014); Jeanne-A Debats, with *La Vieille Anglaise et le Continent* [The Old Englishwoman and the Continent](2008) and *Plaguers* (2010); Victor Dixen, with several notable YA series such as *Le Cas Jack Spark* (2009-12), *Animale* (2013-15), *Phobos* (2015-17), and *Vampyria* (2020-22); Catherine Dufour, with *Le Goût de l'Immortalité* [The Taste of Immortality] (2005) and *Entends la Nuit* [Hear the Night] (2019); Victor Fleury, with *La Croisade Eternelle* [The Eternal Crusade] (2019-21); Anthelme Hauchecorne, with *Journal d'un Marchand de Rêves* [Diary of a Dream Merchant] (2018); Johan Héliot, with *La Quête d'Espérance* [Quest for Hope] (2009-10) and *Grand Siècle* [Grand Century] (2017-19); Léo Henry, with *Thecel* (2020); Jean-Philippe Jaworski, avec *Même Pas Mort* [Not Even Dead] (2014); Christophe Lambert, with the YA series *Les Chroniques d'Arkhadie* [The Chronicles of Arkhadia] (2001-03); Romain Lucazeau, with *Latium* (2016); and Émilie Querbalec, with *Les Oubliés d'Ushtâr* [The Forgotten Ones of Ushtar] (2018) and *Quitter les monts d'automne* [To Leave the Autumn Mountains] (2020).

Across the centuries, the children of Cyrano de Bergerac and Jules Verne are still embarking on imaginary journeys and extraordinary voyages, adding new vistas to ancient maps, and continuing the exploration of the infinite mindscapes of imagination.

Index

Abellio, Raymond, 184, 225
About, Edmond, 107
Adam, Paul, 97, 109
Adam, Pierre, 62, 118, 133, 134
Agapit, Marc, 219
Agraives, Jean d', 118, 135
Alain, Jean-Claude, 233
Albérès, René, 226
Alberny, Luc, 137
Aldany, Kim, 309
Aldiss, Brian W., 190
Alexandre, Robert, 274
Alhaiza, Adolphe, 80
Alkine, Serge, 219
Allais, Alphonse, 98, 107, 110, 160
Allorge, Henri, 118, 129, 147, 151, 171
Alpérine, Paul, 177
Amfreville, Henri d', 184
Amfreville, Henri d', 224
Amila, John, 218
Anderson, Poul, 189, 192, 210
Andrau, Marianne, 190, 198
André, Dominique, 224
André, Phuilippe d', 269
Andrevon, Jean-Pierre, 239, 240, 243, 244, 259, 278, 308, 313
Anet, Claude, 140
Annemary, Francis, 136
Anthony, Max, 304
Anton, Emil, 233
Appas, François, 309
Arcadius, 217
Archaimbault, Jean-Michel, 313
Armandy, André, 118, 135, 153
Armen, Guy d', 62, 136
Arnaud, G.-J., 229, 240, 253, 281
Arnoux, Alexandre, 161
Arnyvelde, André, 155, 156
Aron, Robert, 172
Arrivé, Michel, 293
Arthez, Danielle d', 92
Artus, Louis, 151
Asimov, Isaac, 9, 120, 175, 189
Aslan, 153
Asso, Raymond, 224
Attali, Jacques, 293
Audiberti, Jacques, 223
Audigier, Camille, 139
Audois, A., 94

Audry, Bernard, 151
Audureau, André, 293
Aujay, Édouard, 178
Austruy, Henri, 92
Auzias-Turenne, Raymond, 83
Avril, Marc, 289
Ayerdhal, 297, 298, 299, 314
Bacon, Roger, 20
Bailly, Albert, 62, 131
Ballard, J. G., 169, 190
Balnec, André H., 184
Bameul, Pierre, 267
Banville d'Hostel, Lucien, 151
Baranger, Léon, 145
Barbéri, Jacques, 284, 292
Barbet, Pierre, 189, 209, 210, 241
Barbier-Daumont, J.-A., 141
Barbusse, Henri, 156
Bardanne, Jean, 181
Barillet-Lagargousse, 103
Barjavel, René, 165, 171, 172, 187, 190, 221, 267, 312
Baronian, Jean-Baptiste, 192, 241
Barrault, Jean-Michel, 269
Barsac, Luc, 228
Baruc, André, 232
Baudry, Emmanuel, 294
Bauduret, Thomas, 304
Bax, Bruno, 229
Bayard, Georges, 234

Bayle, Louis, 267
Bazin, Hervé, 308
Beau de Loménie, Gilbert, 268
Beauvais, Robert, 229
Begouën, Max, 139
Belfiore, Robert, 309
Béliard, Octave, 62, 100, 116, 148
Belletto, René, 308
Benâtre, Michel, 191, 219
Beno, Jean-Luc, 235
Benoît, Pierre, 140
Benoit-Jeannin, Maxime, 240, 258, 259
Béra, Paul, 178, 191, 216, 217, 260, 292
Berbier, Jean-Pierre, 308
Berger, Eugène, 20, 100, 129
Berger, Jean-Philippe, 264
Berger, Yves, 227
Bergier, Jacques, 165, 188, 190, 191, 234, 241
Bergman, Jean-Christian, 264
Berna, Paul, 233
Bernanose, George-Marie, 228
Bernard, Gabriel, 146
Bernay, Henri, 118, 147, 151
Bernède, Arthur, 105
Béroalde de Verville, 16
Berthelot, Francis, 278, 284, 314
Berthet, Elie, 82

Berthoud, Samuel-Henry, 46, 82
Besse, Dominique, 243
Bessière, Henri Richard, 189, 202, 203, 229
Besson, Jean-Pierre, 177
Bessot de Lamothe, Alexandre, 79
Bester, Alfred, 190
Béthune (Chevalier de), 23
Bigot, Raoul, 62, 145, 152
Billy, Alain, 304
Binet, Laurent, 312
Bitard, Adolphe, 62
Bitter, Maurice, 294
Blanc, Aimé, 182
Blanc, Bernard, 240, 242, 258
Blanche, Francis, 229
Blanqui, Auguste, 108
Bleunard, Albert, 91
Blish, James, 190, 210
Blond, Georges, 226
Blondel, Roger, 200
Blondelon, Alain, 313
Bodin, Félix, 44
Bogdanoff, Igor & Grichka, 291
Boireau, Jacques, 259
Boitard, Pierre, 37
Bommart, Jean, 220
Bonaventure des Périers, 16
Bonneau, Albert, 62, 88, 118, 135
Bonnéry, Jean, 143
Bonzon, Paul-Jacques, 235
Boo-Silhen, Henri, 147
Bopp, Léon, 182
Bordage, Pierre, 298, 299, 312, 314
Borie, André, 313
Bornert, Lucien, 219
Borrelli, Paul, 298, 303
Bouchard, Nicole, 306
Boucher de Crèvecoeur, Jacques, 37
Boué, Maurice, 178
Boulle, Pierre, 174, 222
Bourbon, Louis de, 46, 126
Bourgeois, Marc, 291
Boussenard, Louis, 61, 62, 66, 118
Bouyxou, Jean-Pierre, 242
Brackett, Leigh, 190
Bradbury, Ray, 9, 190, 222
Brainin, Grégoire, 191, 218
Brat (Colonel), 181
Braudeau, Michel, 293
Bréhal, Marc, 264
Brémond, Raoul, 132
Brooker, Edward, 220
Brotot, Dominique, 305
Brouillaud, Pierre-Jean, 266
Brown, Alphonse, 87
Brown, Fredric, 190
Bruce, Jean, 228
Bruller, Jean, 225

Brunner, John, 193
Bruno-Ruby, J., 145
Bruss, B.-R., 165, 172, 174, 178, 189, 200
Brussolo, Serge, 240, 249, 278, 279, 280, 281, 292, 298, 308
Brutsche, Alphonse, 240, 244
Bucline, Jean, 180
Bulwer-Lytton, Edward, 69
Burger, Chris, 265
Burguet, Frantz-André, 269
Burroughs, Edgar Rice, 29, 69, 72, 139, 159, 173, 242
Butor, Michel, 221, 268
Buzzati, Dino, 254
Byron (Lord), 55
Cabarel, 130
Cabet, Etienne, 41
Caen, Raymond, 225
Cahu, Jules, 80
Calixte, Hervé, 191
Calonne, Michel, 291
Calvet, Émile, 95
Calvo, Sabrina, 314
Cambon, René, 220
Campanella, Tommaso, 20, 21
Campbell, John W., 121
Camus, William, 272, 274
Canal, Richard, 43, 44, 298, 300
Cap, Jean, 219
Capek, Karel, 93, 94, 176
Capoulet-Junac, Edward de, 221
Carey, Mary, 234
Carl, Yves, 304
Caro, Marc de, 189
Caroff, André, 215, 229, 262, 313
Carrère, Jean, 141
Carrière, Huguette, 274
Carsac, Francis, 189, 190, 191, 194, 195, 298
Cartier, Éric, 228
Cassagnac, Paul-Adolphe de, 142
Casteret, Norbert, 233
Cazal (Commandant), 181
Cazotte, Jacques, 32
Celier, François, 275
Celval, Félix, 174, 178
Cénac, Claude, 235
Cernaut, Jean, 275
Chabar, Jacques, 234
Chable, Jacques, 180
Chalopin, Jean, 294
Chambon, Jacques, 278, 298
Champagne, Maurice, 62, 88, 118, 135
Champsaur, Félicien, 158, 159
Chanbert, Jean-Yves, 264
Chancel, Hules, 144
Chantepie, Yves, 264
Chanut, Roger, 154
Chapel, Félix, 285
Charmasson, Guy, 291

Chauvin, Rémy, 293
Chenevière, Jacques, 161
Chevalier, Omar, 127
Chillicothe, Zeb, 292
Choisy-Clouzet, Maryse, 225
Chomet, Richard, 192
Chousy, Didier de, 94
Christin, Pierre, 266
Clancy, Tom, 102
Clar, Fanny, 233
Claretie, Jules, 90, 96
Claretie, Léo, 96
Clarke, Arthur C., 120, 126, 189, 190, 312
Clauzel, Robert, 240, 260, 292
Clérisse, Henry, 228
Clifden, Michael, 292
Clouet, A., 183
Cobb, William, 69
Cocteau, Jean, 208, 221
Coeurderoy, Ernest, 47
Cogan, Paul, 234
Colin, Fabrice, 306
Collard, Robert, 226
Conrad, Joseph, 254
Considerant, Victor, 37
Constant, Jacques, 112
Conty, Jean-Pierre, 229
Cooper, Edmund, 157
Corbière, Stéphane, 148
Corday, Michel, 77, 93, 116
Corman, Terence, 292
Coste, Nadia, 314
Cotard, Jean, 177

Coué, Jean, 274
Courcel, Pierre, 263
Cousin de Grainville, Jean-Baptiste, 43, 106
Cousin Jacques, 25
Cousin, Philippe, 258, 259
Couteaud, P., 141
Couture, Émile, 180
Couvreur, André, 76, 77, 116, 118, 119
Cowez, Éric, 307
Crémieux, Albert & Jean, 219
Creux, Léon, 138
Creuzé de Lesser, Auguste-François, 43
Cronenberg, David, 227
Cros, Charles, 107, 108, 110
Cryde, Th., 290
Curtis, Jean-Louis, 190, 221
Curval, Philippe, 189, 190, 191, 195, 240, 241, 242, 248, 249, 279, 282
Cyrano de Bergerac, Savinien de, 15, 20, 21, 22, 32, 36, 63, 315
Cyril, Victor, 100, 129, 146
Cyril-Berger, 100, 129, 146
d'Argyre, Gilles, 189, 193
Dac, Pierre, 229
Dagory, Jean-Michel, 292
Dalrune, Arnaud, 209
Damasio, Alain, 314

Daniel, Gabriel, 26
Daninos, Pierre, 269
Danio, D.A.C., 220
Danrit (Capitaine), 62, 102, 103, 181
Dantec, Maurice G., 307, 314
Danville, Gaston, 85, 146
Darblin, Henri, 148
Darcy, Gil, 253
Darcy, Paul, 131
Daridjana, 292
Darrau, Jean, 233
Darry, Michel, 179
Dartal, Frank, 265
Dartevelle, aLAIN, 284
Dastier, Dan, 264
Daudet, Alphonse, 108, 163
Daudet, Léon, 163
Dazergues, Max-André, 118, 138
Debans, Camille, 97, 103
Debats, Jeanne-A, 314
Deff, Red, 302
Defontenay, Charles-Ischir, 38, 39, 57, 172
Déglantine, Sylvain, 82
Déjacque, Joseph, 45, 97
Dekk, Karel, 300
Del Duca, Cino, 62
Del Rey, Lester, 192
Delhoste, Georges, 178
Delisle de Sales, Jean-Baptiste-Claude, 31
Delly, 145
Delteil, Gérard, 290

Demolder, Eugène, 103
Demousson, Pierre, 144
Demuth, Michel, 191, 206, 241, 242, 243
Denis, Sylvie, 306
Derennes, Charles, 89
Dermèze, Yves, 165, 178, 191, 216, 217, 241, 260, 292
Descartes, René, 19, 21, 26
Desclaux, Pierre, 146
Deshusses, Jérôme, 268
Desmarest, Henri, 112
Desnoyers, Louis, 37, 44
Desorties, Raymond, 183
Devaux, Pierre, 229, 230
Devigne, Roger, 141
Dharma, Samuel, 304
Di Rollo, Thierry, 306
Diamant, Jacques, 136
Dick, Philip K., 64, 222, 245
Diderot, Denis, 19
Dimt, Elga, 182
Disch, Thomas, 169
Dixen, Victor, 314
Dodeman, Charles, 105
Domange, Daniel, 190
Dominique, Pierre, 153
Doom, Kitty, 198, 281
Dorémieux, Alain, 191, 240, 242, 243, 254
Douay, Dominique, 240, 241, 255, 256, 298
Douriaux, Hugues, 289, 313

Doyle, Arthur Conan, 74, 85, 89
Driou, Alfred, 38
Drode, Daniel, 195
Du Roure, Henry, 145
Dubois, Pierre, 223, 264, 292
Duchesne, René, 179
Duesberg, Raymond, 227
Dufour, Catherine, 315
Duguet, Roger, 104
Duhamel, Georges, 182, 233
Duhemme, Charles, 154
Dulac, Odette, 163
Dumas, Alexandre, 40, 51, 55
Dumas, Alexandre (fils), 91
Dumay, Gilles, 306
Dunan, Renée, 157
Dunyach, Jean-Claude, 298, 302, 312, 314
Durand, Loup, 308
Durand, René, 295
Duras. Marguerite, 195
Duret, Alain, 307
Durtain, Luc, 184
Duval, Jean, 138, 148
Duvernois, Henri, 173
Duvic, Patrice, 240, 291
Dzagoyan, René, 293
Eaubonne, Françoise d', 196, 234
Ébly, Philippe, 273
Ecken, Claude, 290
Eekhoud, Georges, 91
Ellison, Harlan, 239, 254
Epuy, Michel, 127
Erasmus, 13, 14
Erboy, Franck, 228
Erland, Jean, 233
Errer, Emmanuel, 263
Escarpit, Robert, 227
Escudié, René, 295
Esme, Jean d', 141
Espiard de Colonge, Alfred d', 41
Espitallier, Georges, 91
Eyraud, Achille, 40
Falcoz, André, 62, 118, 136
Falk, Henri, 144, 152
Fardet, Jean, 142
Farney, Roger, 132
Farrère, Claude, 119, 155
Fast, Jan de, 261
Fayard, Arthème, 61, 118, 119
Fearn, John Russell, 190
Ferenczi, Joseph, 118, 123, 187
Fernez, André, 230
Ferreol, Pierre, 103
Ferrer, Jean-Michel, 206
Ferry, Alfred de, 96
Féval, Fils, Paul, 123, 141, 147
Féval, Paul, 123
Figuier, Louis, 62
Flammarion, Camille, 39, 62, 63, 66, 105, 106
Flammarion, Ernest, 61
Fleuret, Fernand, 176

Fleury, Victor, 315
Fleury, X. M., 313
Foigny, Gabriel de, 25, 32
Fontana, Jean-Pierre, 192, 241, 257, 286
Fonteneau, Jean-Marie, 268
Fontugne, Christian, 234
Forbin, Victor, 140
Forest, Jean-Claude, 189
Forest, Louis, 92
Fort, Charles, 79
Fouquet, J., 148
Fournel, Victor, 96
Fournier, Christiane, 175
Frachet, Léopold, 180
France, Anatole, 111
Franklin, Alfred, 96
Franklin, Alfred-Louis, 46
Frémion, Yves, 240, 241, 258
Fribourg, Roger, 147
Froelich, Jean-Claude, 232
Fronval, George, 179
Furne, Charles, 67
Gaborit, Mathieu, 306
Gadeyne, Roger, 226
Gagne, Élise, 43
Gagne, Paulin, 43
Gail, Otto Willi, 127
Gailhard, Gustave, 178
Gain, Raoul, 146
Gallaix, Vincent, 265
Gallart, Rémy, 209
Gallerne, Gilbert, 304
Gallet, Georges H., 165, 188, 189, 241

Galopin, Arnould, 72, 81, 102, 137, 147
Galopin, Auguste, 137
Galouye, Daniel F., 190
Gance, Abel, 106
Gandon, Yves, 184, 224
Gapdy, Jean Christophe, 313
Garen, Jean-Pierre, 261
Garnier, Charles-Georges-Thomas, 32
Garnier, Pascal, 309
Gary, Romain, 184, 223
Gastine, Louis-Jules, 153
Gatti, Armand, 226
Gauckler, 255
Gauthier, Nicolas, 209
Gautier, Théophile, 47, 96
Gayar, Henri, 72, 81
Geha, Thomas, 313
Genefort, Laurent, 209, 298, 302, 303, 314
Geoffroy, Louis, 47, 101
Géraud, V., 178
Géris, R.F., 101
Gernsback, Hugo, 8, 57, 79, 117
Gheusi, Pierre-Barthélemy, 154
Ghilini, Hector, 228
Gide, André, 109
Giffard, Pierre, 93, 104
Gilkin, Iwan, 47
Gille, Elizabeth, 240
Gillet, Henri, 227
Gineste, Raoul, 91
Giraudeau, Fernand, 46

Giuliani, Pierre, 266
Glénat, Jacques, 242
Gloria, Mona, 179
Godwin, Francis, 20
Goemaere, Pierre, 140
Goethe, Johann Wolfgang von, 19
Goetz, Georges, 295
Goffart, Vincent, 266
Goimard, Jacques, 242, 279, 298
Goissert, Michel, 233
Golding, William, 169
Goncourt, Edmond de, 73, 111, 155, 161, 223
Goriellof, Michel, 151
Goult, Dominique, 283
Gourmont, Rémy de, 110
Gouvieux, Marc, 104
Goy, Philip, 240, 257
Graffigny, Henry de, 66, 67, 115, 118, 129
Grandjean, Georges, 141
Grandville, Isidore, 42, 63
Grave, Charles-Joseph de, 41
Grave, Jean, 98
Grenier, Christian, 271, 272, 274
Gril, Étienne, 148, 153, 182
Grimaud, Michel, 273
Gripari, Pierre, 7
Grivel, Louis, 175
Groc, Léon, 118, 141, 166
Gros, Jules, 86
Groussard, Valérie, 295
Grousset, Alain, 309
Gsell, Paul, 162
Guadalcazar, 292
Guibert, Marius-Pierre, 269
Guichard, Marcel, 228
Guieu, Jimmy, 189, 206, 207, 208, 209, 226, 230, 292, 302
Guignard, Denis Gabriel, 219
Guillot, René, 235
Guiot, Denis, 273, 308
Guitton, Gustave, 71, 72, 99
Guttin, Jacques, 30
Guy, Philippe, 305
Guyon, Charles, 79
Hachette, Louis, 62, 188
Haggard, H. Rider, 85, 87, 158
Halévy, Daniel, 111
Hamilton, Edmond, 189
Hamilton, Peter F., 312
Hanost, Paul, 266
Haraucourt, Edmond, 83, 84
Hauchecorne, Anthelme, 315
Hautem, Stéphane, 182
Hecht, Yvon, 218
Heinlein, Robert A., 57, 175, 189, 206, 230, 272
Held, Claude & Jacqueline, 274
Held, Serge, 152
Héliot, Johan, 315

Henneberg, Nathalie C., 189, 191, 197, 241
Hennebert, Eugène, 87
Henry, Léo, 315
Hérault, Paul-Jean, 262, 313
Herbert, Frank, 15, 133, 240, 298, 312
Hergé, 89
Herial, Don, 300
Hervilly, Ernest d', 83
Hetzel, Pierre-Jules, 51, 52, 53, 55, 61, 64, 94
Hibert, Nicole, 297
Higon, Albert, 189, 195, 245, 246, 248
Hoche, Jules, 142
Hoebke, Lionel, 242
Holberg, Ludvig, 27
Homer, 15
Honaker, Michel, 278, 289, 308
Hougron, Jean, 190, 221
Hourey, P.-A., 220
Houssaye, Arsène, 96
Houssin, Joël, 240, 254, 255, 278, 292, 298
Houville, Gérard d', 150
Hoven, Jacques, 261, 313
Howard, Robert E., 242
Hubbard, L. Ron, 190
Hubert, Jean-Pierre, 154, 192, 240, 256, 258, 278
Hubert-Jacques, 154
Hugo, Victor, 47, 51, 53
Hupp, Philippe, 297
Huxley, Aldous, 45

Huysmans, Joris-Karl, 111
Ichbiah, Daniel, 305
Ikor, Roger, 225
Ilan, Red, 264, 292
Ivoi, Paul d', 61, 62, 67, 68, 73, 103, 118, 132
Jacolliot, Louis, 86
Jacquart, Roger-Henri, 180
Jan, Gabriel, 262, 313
Jansen, Michel, 233
Jarry, Alfred, 110
Jaworski, Jean-Philippe, 315
Jean, Albert, 119
Jean-Boulan, Robert, 175, 179
Jean-Charles, L., 234
Jeanjean, Marcel, 132
Jeanne, René, 154
Jessua, Alain, 200
Jeury, Dany, 248, 309
Jeury, Michel, 189, 195, 240, 241, 242, 245, 246, 247, 248, 249, 258, 259, 270, 278, 279, 308, 312
Jonchère, Ernest, 46
Jonquel, Octave, 128
Jouanne, Emmanuel, 240, 277, 278, 279, 283
Jouly, André, 233
Juillet, Jacques-Henri, 219
Juin, Hubert, 192
Jullien, Jean, 99
Kanters, Robert, 190, 221, 240
Kast, Pierre, 222

Kaszuk, Cyrille, 267
Kauffman, Christophe, 305
Keller, Dominique, 204
Keller, Henri, 191, 218
Kemmel, 220
Kenny, Paul, 189, 205, 229
Kerlecq, Jean de, 140
Kery, Jean, 180
Kesselring, Rolf, 240, 258, 278
Kijé (Lieutenant), 218
Kistemaekers, Henry, 112
Klein, Gérard, 189, 190, 191, 192, 193, 194, 239, 240, 242, 246, 258, 279, 298
Kock, Henry de, 42
Kolney, Fernand, 98
Korb, Laurence, 269
Kulavik, R., 219
L'Andelyn, Charles de, 140, 153, 182
La Batut, Pierre de, 138
La Follie, Louis-Guillaume de, 24, 31
La Hire, Jean de, 61, 70, 71, 73, 116, 118, 130, 133, 145, 173, 181
La Marche, Marc, 153
La Ville de Mirmont, Alexandre-Jean-Joseph, 44
Lacheze, Patrick, 304
Lafferty, R. A., 92
Laffont, Robert, 193, 239

Lafitte, Pierre, 62
Laloux, René, 199
Lamart, Jean-Claude, 304
Lamart, Michel, 295
Lambert, Christophe, 315
Lambry, Léon, 140
Landay, Maurice, 149
Lang, Fritz, 176, 180
Langelaan, George, 192, 227
Langlais, Xavier de, 180
Lanos, Henri, 89, 130, 145
Larigaudie, Guy de, 140
Larousse, Pierre, 118
Lassalle, Thierry, 290
Lattès, Jean-Claude, 242, 266
Laumann, E.-M., 145, 155
Laurian, Marcel, 127
Laurie, André, 61, 63, 64, 65
Lautrec, Gabriel de, 160
Lavaur, Pierre, 131
Le Bovier de Fontenelle, Bernard, 22
le Bussy, Alain, 298, 303, 313
Le Clerc de la Herverie, Jean, 266
Le Drimeur, Alain, 96
Le Faure, Georges, 61, 66, 67, 103, 115
Le Jeune, Raoul, 178
Le May, Jean-Louis & Doris, 189, 210, 211

Le Rouge, Gustave, 61, 70, 71, 72, 73, 116, 118, 128, 129, 132, 173, 175
Le Tellier, Hervé, 312
Le Wailly, Gaston, 62
Lebas, Georges, 153
Lebey, André, 150
Leblanc, Maurice, 124, 125
Lec, Jean, 219
Leconte, Marianne, 242
Lecornu, Joseph-Louis, 127, 150
Lefrancq, Claude, 298, 307
Legay, Piet, 287, 313
Legendre, Pierre, 141
Legrand, Anxdré, 139
Legray, Jacques, 231
Lehman, Serge, 298, 300
Leiber, Fritz, 189
Leinster, Murray, 190
Lemercier, Népomucène-Louis, 41
Lemosquet, Marc, 305
Léonard, François, 100, 104
Léonnec, Félix, 179
Léourier, Christian, 270, 271, 314
Leprince, X. B., 234
Lermina, Jules, 68, 69
Leroux, Gaston, 62, 133
Levis, Pierre-Marc-Gaston de, 43
Lewis, C. S., 72

Lhostis, Christian-Yves, 266
Libert, Jean, 205
Lichtenberger, André, 84, 139
Ligny, Jean-Marc, 249, 278, 282, 283, 308, 314
Limat, Maurice, 118, 165, 174, 177, 178, 189, 191, 211, 212, 292
Listonai, 23, 31
Lœvenbruck, Henri, 314
Lofficier, Jean-Marc, 313
Loisy, Jean, 174
Long, Y.F.J., 219
Loria, Jacques, 174
Lorrain, Jean, 110
Lorraine, René, 100
Lortac, Raoul, 177
Louit, Robert, 241
Lourbet, François, 220
Lovecraft, H. P., 158, 190
Lucazeau, Romain, 315
Luguet, Pierre, 88
Maalouf, Amin, 308
MacDonald, George, 29
Magog, H.-J., 118, 122, 123, 141, 167
Magué, Charles, 141
Maillet, Benoit de, 30
Maillot (Abbott), 26
Maine, David, 210, 241
Makanine, Vladimir, 308
Malato, Charles, 89, 90
Mallarmé, Stéphane, 110
Manceau, Marcelle, 234

Manchette, Jean-Patrick, 242
Mantey, Christian, 264, 292
Marabini, Jean, 269
Marbrouk, Alia, 308
Marcy, Gérard, 263
Margueritte, Victor, 161
Marlson, Pierre, 258, 259
Martel, Adrien, 275
Martel, Serge, 196
Martini, Rodolphe, 104
Martinigol, Danielle, 309
Marx, Karl, 35
Mas, André, 82, 129
Massacrier, Jacques, 269
Massepain, André, 234
Massiéra, Léopold, 218
Matheson, Richard, 75, 120, 173, 190
Matieson, Budy, 264
Mauclair, Camille, 110
Maupassant, Guy de, 109
Maurois, André, 163, 165, 183, 221
Max, Paul, 83
Mazarin, Jean, 263
McKenna, Richard, 254
Méliès, Georges, 55
Menez, Yann, 253
Merault, Maurice, 292
Mercier, Louis-Sébastien, 30, 31, 32
Méric, Victor, 154
Méricant, Albert, 61
Merillac, Landry, 241, 265
Merle, Robert, 267, 312
Merritt, Abraham, 74
Méry, Joseph, 48
Messac, Régis, 169, 170
Mettais, Hippolyte, 45
Mettra, 149
Meurville, Louis de, 100
Meynier, Yvonne, 275
Mézière, J.-J., 230
Michel, André, 179
Michel, Louise, 108
Milan, 304
Milési, Raymond, 306
Millanvoy, Louis, 101
Mille, Pierre, 150
Millemann, Jean, 307
Miral-Viger, 127
Moilin, Tony, 46
Mondoloni, Jacques, 278, 286
Monjardin, Alin, 142, 173
Monsigny, Jacqueline de, 275
Montaigne, Michel de, 15
Montesquieu, 27, 32
Montfort, Elie, 62, 136
Moorcock, Michael, 109, 254, 298
Moore, Catherine L., 189
More, Thomas, 14
Morelly, 30
Moreux, Théophile (Abbott), 82
Morris, Gilles, 270, 287, 313
Morris, William, 29
Morrisset, Franck, 305
Morrisson, Roy, 292

Morvers, L., 136
Moselli, José, 62, 118, 120, 122, 124, 125, 133, 165, 175, 187
Motus (Professor), 154
Mouhy (Chevalier de), 29, 32
Mourier, Maurice, 293
Mouton, Eugène, 106
Mundy, Talbot, 69
Murail, Lorris, 266
Murcie, Georges, 263
Murey, Georges, 253
Mysor, Fernand, 140
Nadaud, Alain, 293
Nagrien, X., 94
Nathan, Fernand, 118, 187
Nau, John-Antoine, 111
Nécrorian, Charles, 263
Ner, Henri, 97
Néry, Gérard, 304
Nettesheim, Agrippa de, 21
Newton, Isaac, 19
Niven, Larry, 75, 77
Nizerolles, René-Marcel de, 89, 174, 202
Nodier, Charles, 44
Nolane, Richard D., 292
Nolant de Fatouville, 22
Nolhac, Pierre de, 182
Normand, Jean, 179
Norwood, Sam P., 220
Nothomb, Pierre, 129
Nubé, 149
Nyst, Ray, 83
Oberth, Herman, 54, 127
Offenstadt (Brothers), 62, 118
Olasso, Pierre, 180
Ollier, Claude, 269
Osterrath, Jacqueline H., 192
Ottange, Jules d', 142
Ousmane, Smbeme, 293
Pagel, Michel, 278, 285
Paré, Ambroise, 13, 16
Paris, Alain, 257, 278, 286
Parville, Henri de, 40
Pasquier, Alex, 101
Passegué, Bertrand, 304
Passover, Geoffrey X., 275
Pastor, Thierry, 305
Pastre, Gaston, 143, 181
Patmos, Jean de, 226
Paulhac, Jean, 221
Paulin, Christophe, 182
Pawlowski, Gaston de, 113
Peko, Dominique, 295
Pellerin, Georges, 94
Pelot, Pierre, 240, 241, 242, 249, 250, 252, 258, 274, 278, 279
Pénard, Eugène, 101
Pérochon, Ernest, 161, 162
Pérot, Maurice, 175, 179
Perrier, E.-G., 181
Perrin, Jules, 89
Peslouan, Hervé de, 150
Petithuguenin, Jean, 118, 130, 137, 154

Petoud, Wildy, 303
Picard, Gilbert, 290
Pierroux, Jacques, 230
Pilotin, Michel, 188, 189, 190
Pineau, Christian, 234
Piret, Daniel, 264, 292, 313
Planchat, Henry-Luc, 241
Poe, Edgar Allan, 36, 48, 51, 68, 160, 224
Polac, Michel, 270
Pontier, Arnauld, 313
Pouvourville, Albert de, 181
Pratchett, Terry, 298
Pratt, Fletcher, 149, 152, 177
Prioly, Lucien, 232
Probst, Pierre, 275
Proudhon, Pierre, 35
Proumen, H.-J., 140, 167, 172
Pujol, René, 131, 147
Pulicani, Suzanne, 235
Quatremarre, Jean, 182
Quéneau, Raymond, 221
Querbalec, Émilie, 315
Quirielle, Jean de, 93, 116, 145
Rabelais, François, 14, 15, 20, 28, 63
Rahier, François, 304
Rameau, Jean, 96
Ramonet, Yves, 284
Randa, Peter, 189, 213
Randa, Philippe, 209, 214
Ranne, G. Elton, 305
Raspail, Jean, 269
Ravignant, Patrick, 266
Ray, Jean, 167, 233
Rayjean, Max-André, 189, 214, 313
Rémy, Yves & Ada, 258
Renard, Christine, 198
Renard, Maurice, 8, 62, 77, 78, 79, 116, 119, 120, 122, 124, 160, 165, 166, 168, 175, 187, 189
Renaud, Janine, 292
Renault, Maurice, 190, 191
Renford, Philippe, 305
Renouvier, Charles, 101
Réouven, René, 190, 221
Restif de la Bretonne, Nicolas-Edmé, 27, 28, 31, 32, 42
Rex, Lionel, 292
Rey-Dussueil, Antoine-François, 43
Ribes, F.-H., 229
Richard, François, 189, 202
Richard-Bessière, 189
Riche, Daniel, 243, 297
Riche, Étienne de, 132
Richepin, Jean, 112
Richter, Charles de, 177
Rienzi, Raymond de, 140
Rigaut, Jacques, 155
Rignac, Jean, 227
Rimbaud, Arthur, 107
Rivages, Philippe V., 275

Rivet, Charles, 151
Robida, Albert, 62, 63, 64, 69, 104, 110, 116
Robitaillie, Henriette, 234
Roc, Gil, 218
Roche, Thérèse, 294
Roger, Noelle, 141, 146, 153, 157
Roisel, Godefroy de, 41
Roland, Marcel, 99
Rolland, Romain, 224
Romains, Jules, 225
Rondard, Patrice, 192
Rose, Claude, 294
Rosel, Michel, 228
Rosny Aîné, J.-H., 8, 36, 62, 73, 74, 75, 76, 79, 82, 83, 85, 115, 119, 127, 139, 158, 165, 172, 176, 189, 197, 224
Rosny Jeune, J.-H., 176
Rostand, Edmond, 21
Rouff, Jules, 118, 134
Rouff, Marcel, 134
Roumier-Robert, Marie-Anne de, 24
Rouquette, Louis-Frédéric, 119, 144
Rousseau, Jean-Jacques, 171
Rouzade, Léonie, 112
Royer, Alain, 294
Royet (Colonel), 68, 103, 152, 154
Ruellan, André, 190, 199, 200, 240, 298
Ryner, Han, 97, 104, 153

Sadoul, Jacques, 190, 191, 241, 279, 298
Sagan, Françoise, 195
Saint-Gilles, 253
Saint-Moore, Adam, 229, 289
Saint-Yves, Claude, 142, 225
Sand, George, 42
Sarcus, Pierre de, 234
Sautereau, François, 309
Schlockoff, Alain, 243
Schmidt, Valérie, 190
Schwob, Marcel, 110
Scovel, Guy, 241
Seabury, Don A., 292
Sébillot, Paul-Yves, 144
Séguret, Serge, 305
Sélènes, Pierre de, 80
Sellig, 313
Sériel, Jérôme, 190, 196
Seuhl, Antonin, 134, 153
Séverac, Guy, 232
Sevestre, Norbert, 148
Shaw, Bob, 120
Sheckley, Robert, 92
Simak, Clifford D., 190
Simenon, Georges, 143
Simmons, Dan, 299
Siry, Patrick, 240, 278
Smith, Thorne, 152
Sobra, Adrien, 219
Solari, Émile, 99
Sorel, Charles, 20
Soria, Georges, 266
Soulier, Jacky, 274
Souvestre, Émile, 44

Spens, Willy de, 269
Spifame, Raoul, 16
Spinoza, Baruch, 19
Spinrad, Norman, 192, 239
Spitz, Jacques, 165, 168, 169, 175, 187
Spitzmuller, Georges, 141, 150
Spronck, Maurice, 96
SR 27 (Ex-Agent), 228
Stapledon, Olaf, 15, 30, 32, 73, 100, 113, 123, 167
Steeman, Stanislas-André, 184
Steiner, Kurt, 189, 190, 191, 199, 200
Sternberg, Jacques, 7, 190, 221
Stevenson, Robert L., 90
Stolze, Pierre, 286
Stork, Christopher, 288
Sturgeon, Theodore, 189
Suquet, Henri, 175
Suragne, Pierre, 240, 250
Sussan, René, 190, 221
Swift, Jonathan, 15, 21, 163
Talabot, Jean, 184
Tallandier, Jules, 61, 117, 187
Tarde, Gabriel, 97
Tavera, M. & T., 220
Teissier, François, 86
Teldy-Naïm, Robert, 219
Téramond, Guy de, 98, 134
Tessier, François, 307
Thébault, Eugène, 118, 142, 149
Thévenin, René, 62, 88, 118, 119, 125, 126, 140, 172, 175
Thiberge, Guillaume, 306
Thibon, Gustave, 224
Thiellement, Hervé, 313
Thierry, Georges, 104
Thilliez, Henry, 236
Thirion, Louis, 240, 252, 313
Thiry, Marcel, 172
Thomas, Gilles, 240, 253
Tilman, Adelin, 226
Tilms, Ege, 182
Tiphaigne de la Roche, Charles-François, 23, 27
Toepffer, Rodolphe, 41
Touati, Lucien-Guy, 294
Toudouze, Georges G., 133
Trotet de Bargis, René, 130, 140
Trubert, Roger, 232
Tubb, E. C., 190, 292
Turin, Philippe-Henri, 309
Twain, Mark, 150, 160
Tyssot de Patot, Simon, 26
Uzureau, Yves, 305
Valérie, André, 126
Valéry, Francis, 306
Valetti, Oscar, 284

Valiant, Daniel, 275
Vallée, Jacques, 88, 157, 179, 190, 196
Vallène, Paul, 230
Vallerey, Tancrède, 119, 175
Van Herp, Jacques, 116, 166, 233, 241
Van Vogt, A. E., 9, 175, 189, 190, 192, 217, 222, 312
Vance, Jack, 15, 109
Vandel, Jean-Gaston, 189, 205, 206
Vandenpanhuyse, Gaston, 205
Varende, Yves, 266
Varlet, Théo, 128, 129, 150
Vattel, Emmerich de, 23
Vaulx, Henri de la, 148
Vaury, Louis, 127
Vautel, Clément, 146
Vauthier, Maurice, 236
Vauzière, Claude, 230
Veber, Pierre, 139
Veillot, Claude, 257
Veiras, Denis, 25, 26, 32
Velle, Louis, 226
Vercors, 225
Verdun (Commandant), 181
Verlaine, Paul, 107
Verlanger, Julia, 240, 253
Verlomme, Hugo, 270
Vernay, Jean-Pierre, 283, 291

Verne, Jules, 8, 15, 25, 27, 35, 36, 38, 40, 42, 51, 52, 53, 54, 55, 56, 57, 58, 61, 62, 63, 64, 66, 67, 68, 71, 72, 73, 76, 79, 80, 85, 87, 89, 94, 96, 106, 115, 117, 125, 127, 131, 133, 139, 143, 146, 148, 150, 176, 188, 189, 195, 196, 258, 315
Vernes, Henri, 230
Verniculus, 95
Versins, Pierre, 27, 32, 166, 190, 191, 217, 242
Vert, Marie-Louise, 235
Veuzit, Max du, 145
Vian, Boris, 190, 221, 222
Vidal, Florence, 270
Vignaud, Jean, 145
Vilà, Christian, 254, 306
Vilgensofer, A., 97
Villaret, Bernard, 241, 265
Ville d'Avray, A. de, 79
Villiers de l'Isle-Adam, Jean-Marie-Matthias, 109
Vimereu, Paul, 139
Viot, Henri-Georges, 230
Volkoff, Vladimir, 196, 232, 242, 279
Volodine, Antoine, 277, 278, 285
Volta, H. de, 142
Voltaire, 19, 21, 22, 27, 31, 32, 162
von Helders (Major), 181

Vonnegut, Kurt, 171, 172, 190
Wagner, Roland C., 209, 278, 298, 301, 302, 312, 314
Wailly, Gaston de, 88, 118
Wallace, Edgar, 159
Walther, Daniel, 240, 241, 254, 278, 313
Ward, Henry, 227
Ward, Philippe, 313
Weinbaum, Stanley, 76
Wells, H. G., 8, 36, 38, 53, 62, 70, 73, 76, 78, 81, 97, 99, 120, 128, 143, 145, 150, 160, 171, 188, 233
Werber, Bernard, 307
Wersinger, Marc, 173
Whale, Laurent, 313
Williamson, Jack, 189
Willis, Connie, 312
Wintrebert, Joelle, 243, 258, 283, 294
Wolfram, Richard, 209, 302
Wollheim, Donald A., 192
Wolmark, Nina, 294
Wul, Stéfan, 189, 198, 200, 298, 308
Wylie, Philip, 171
Wyndham, John, 157, 190
Yanne, Jean, 229
Yaouanc, Alain, 218
Yelnick, Claude, 219
Zola, Émile, 110
Zorn, Jacqueline, 167

LES MYSTÈRES DE DEMAIN
LES FIANCÉES DE L'AN 2000

PAR
PAUL FÉVAL FILS
ET
H.-J. MAGOG

1.45 LE VOLUME COMPLET

www.ingramcontent.com/pod-product-compliance
Lightning Source LLC
Chambersburg PA
CBHW022103150426
43195CB00008B/243